NATIONAL GEOGRAPHIC LEARNING | CENGAGE Learning

MW00666970

Life

5

Paul Dummett
John Hughes
Helen Stephenson

NATIONAL GEOGRAPHIC LEARNING | CENGAGE Learning

Life Level 5 Student Book

Paul Dummett

John Hughes

Helen Stephenson

Publisher: Sherrise Roehr

Executive Editor: Sarah T. Kenney

Editorial Assistant: Patricia Giunta

Director of Global Marketing: Ian Martin

Senior Product Marketing Manager: Caitlin Thomas

Director of Content and Media Production: Michael Burggren

Production Manager: Daisy Sosa

Senior Print Buyer: Mary Beth Hennebury

Cover Designers: Scott Baker and Alex Dull

Cover Image: © Steve Bloom Images / Alamy

Compositor: MPS Limited

Cover Image

A male panther chameleon stalking prey in beach-side vegetation, Bay of Antongil, Masoala Peninsula National Park, Madagascar.

Student Book
ISBN-13: 978-1-305-25630-9

Student Book + CD-ROM
ISBN-13: 978-1-305-25634-7

Student Book + Online Workbook
ISBN-13: 978-1-305-26039-9

National Geographic Learning/Cengage Learning
20 Channel Center Street
Boston, MA 02210
USA

Cengage Learning is a leading provider of customized learning solutions with office locations around the globe, including Singapore, the United Kingdom, Australia, Mexico, Brazil, and Japan. Locate our local office at **international.cengage.com/region**

Cengage Learning products are represented in Canada by Nelson Education, Ltd.

Visit National Geographic Learning online at **NGL.cengage.com**
Visit our corporate website at **www.cengage.com**

Printed in the United States of America
4 5 6 7 8 19 18 17 16 15

UNIT 1
RELATIONSHIPS

UNIT 2
STORYTELLING

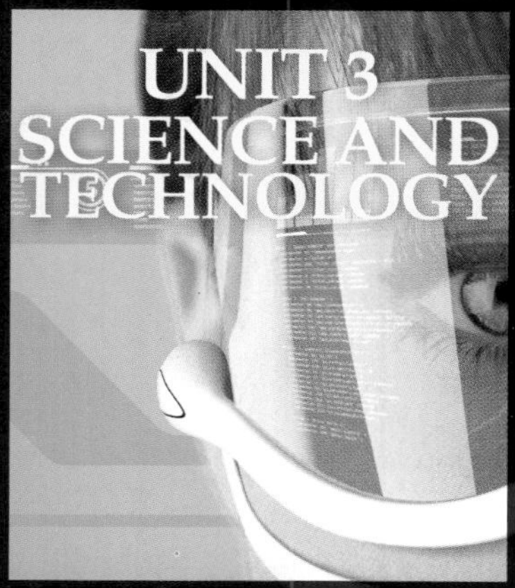
UNIT 3
SCIENCE AND TECHNOLOGY

UNIT 4
ART AND CREATIVITY

UNIT 5
DEVELOPMENT

UNIT 6
ALTERNATIVE TRAVEL

UNIT 7
NATURAL RESOURCES

UNIT 8
THE NEWS

UNIT 9
TALENTED PEOPLE

UNIT 10
CUSTOMS AND BEHAVIOR

UNIT 11
KNOWLEDGE AND LEARNING

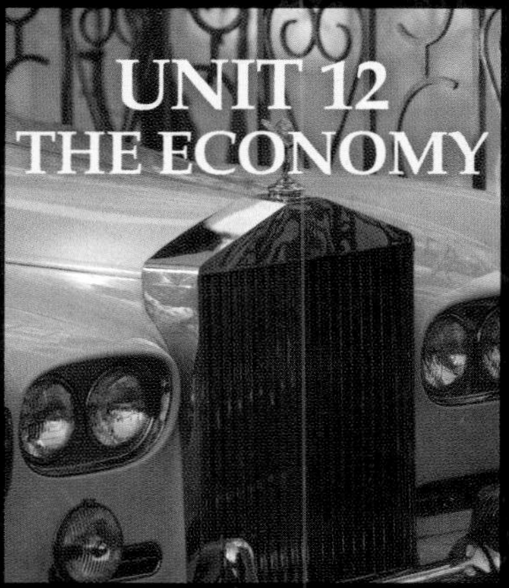
UNIT 12
THE ECONOMY

Contents

LISTENING	READING	CRITICAL THINKING	SPEAKING	WRITING
part of a radio show about animal friendships	an article about changing attitudes in China an article about immigrant families in New York	identifying the main theme	your friends the generation gap family influences	text type: an informal email (1) writing skill: greetings and endings
an interview with a film critic	a true story about dangerous animals an article about the brothers Grimm	close reading	the movie of the book a famous writer or filmmaker narrow escapes storytelling	text type: a story writing skill: using descriptive words
a presentation about overpopulation	an article about augmented reality an article about appropriate technology	balancing arguments	global problems overpopulation information age predictions technological solutions	text type: short email requests writing skill: being polite
part of a radio show about what's on in Melbourne an artist's opinion about what art is	an article about unusual street art an article about the origins of rap	analyzing contrasts	participation in the arts an art competition music and values	text type: an online review writing skill: personalizing your writing
an interview with a reporter about social development in southern India	an article about urban development in Dubai an article about a hydroelectric dam in Laos	fact or opinion	changes in your town a happy society sensitive development evaluating a development project	text type: an opinion essay writing skill: linking words
an interview about volunteer vacations	a blog about vacations at home part of a travel magazine article on unusual hotels	claims and justifications	local knowledge planning a staycation opinions about travel ideas for an unusual hotel	text type: a letter of complaint writing skill: formal language

LISTENING	READING	CRITICAL THINKING	SPEAKING	WRITING
four people talking about saving water	an article about Ecuador's plan to protect resources an article about Madagascar's unique ecology	emotive language	how we use water conservation wishes	text type: a letter to the editor writing skill: giving vivid examples
four feel-good news stories	an article about an iconic image an article about the power of the press	different perspectives	the ethics of taking photographs feel-good news stories reputations	text type: minutes from a meeting writing skill: impersonal language
an interview about Emerging Explorers	an article about an extraordinary career an article about a woman who was king	weighing the evidence	a career path personal qualities women at work	text type: an online profile writing skill: writing in note form
part of a radio show about a tribe with an unusual diet	an article about the "tiger mother" approach to parenting an article about body language	sources	typical behavior food and eating habits customs in your country wedding traditions	text type: an informal email (2) writing skill: elision in informal writing
a talk by a psychologist on memory	an article about an ethnobotanist an article about a parrot	reinforcing ideas	acquiring knowledge memory tests why you forgot types of learners	text type: an email about a misunderstanding writing skill: linking contrasting ideas
an interview with the author of *The Servant Economy*	an article about Norway's riches an article about an alternative economic model	signposts to key information	the economy in your country getting things done gift giving and exchange	text type: a report writing skill: subheadings and bullet points

Life around the world

Unit 10 Eating insects

Discover why eating insects could be good for you, and why one man is on a mission to change our tastes.

Unit 1 Immigration

The history of immigration in the United States.

Unit 2 History of film

A history of film, from its early beginnings in the 19th century to the Hollywood blockbusters of today.

Unit 4 Urban art

Discover the world of graffiti and innovative music.

Unit 5 Aquarium on Wheels

A special aquarium that gives its student teachers lessons in life.

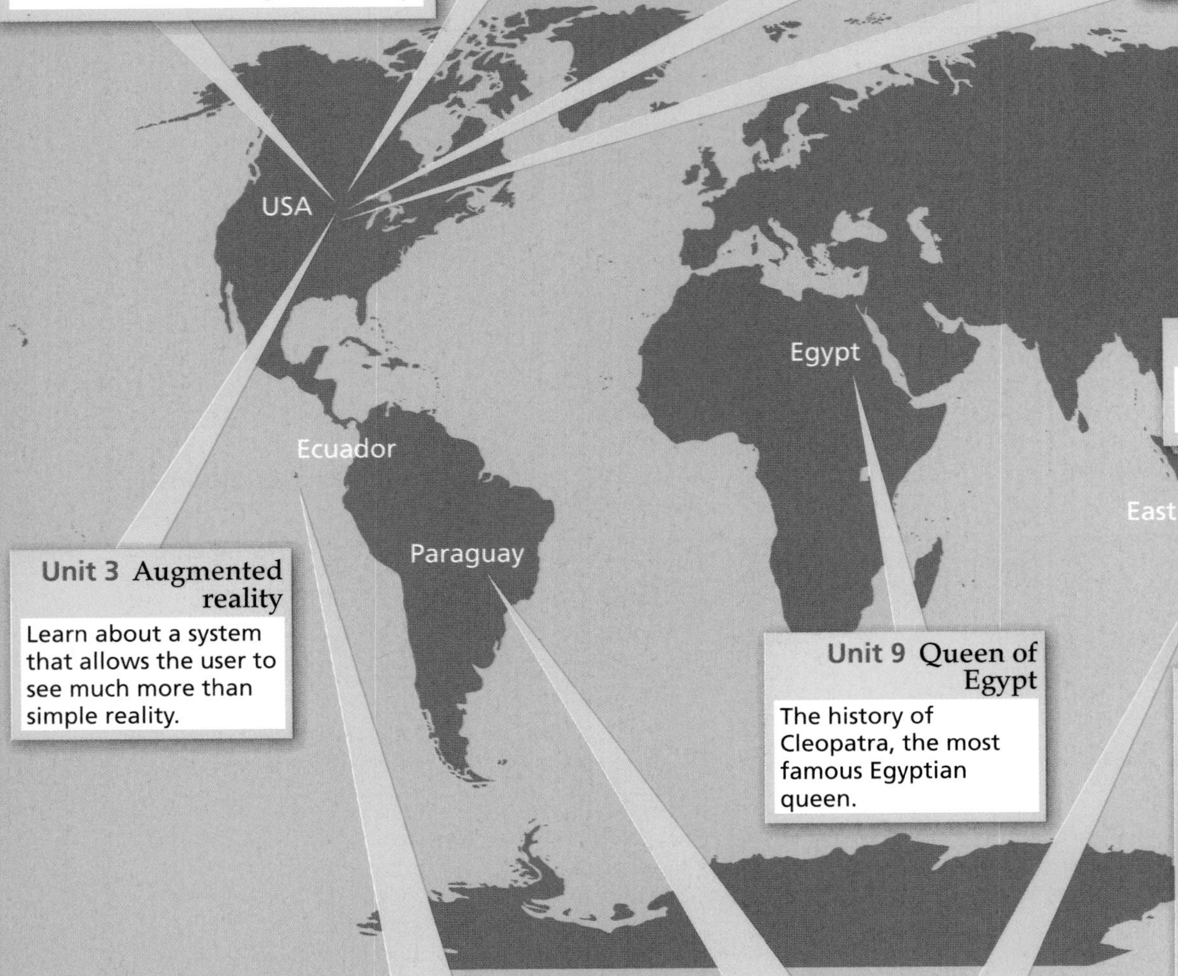

Unit 12 Japan

Learn more about the history and traditions of Japan.

Unit 3 Augmented reality

Learn about a system that allows the user to see much more than simple reality.

Unit 9 Queen of Egypt

The history of Cleopatra, the most famous Egyptian queen.

Unit 8 Mount Fuji

Find out what Mount Fuji means to the Japanese.

Unit 7 Galapagos energy

Find out about the impact of humans and tourism on the Galapagos Islands.

Unit 11 Paraguay shaman

Find out why it's essential to record plants from the rain forests of Paraguay before they disappear.

Unit 6 East Timor

The slow process of creating a new tourist destination.

Unit 1 Relationships

A baby camel gets a hug in Jordan.

FEATURES

1 Work in pairs. Look at the photo and the caption. Choose the phrase you think best describes the photo.

a faithful companion	blood relatives
an old friend	a passing acquaintance
mutual respect	a strong bond
true friends	an odd couple

2 Look at these English sayings about relationships. What do they mean? Do you have a similar saying in your language?

1 Blood is thicker than water.
2 A friend in need is a friend indeed.
3 Like father, like son.
4 No man is an island.

3 Think of a person (a) you have been meaning to contact for a long time and (b) you have shared a travel experience with. Tell your partner about these people.

1a Unlikely friends

Image by Stevi Calandra for the National Geographic Channel

Listening

1 Work in pairs. Look at the photo. Discuss the questions.

1 What are the two animals in the photo?
2 Are they normally pets, wild animals, or something else?
3 What does the photo suggest about these animals' characters?

2 **1** Now listen to part of a radio show about an unlikely friendship between these two animals. What things do they do together to enjoy each other's company?

3 **1** Listen again and choose the right word to complete each statement.

1 Cooperation between different species is not ______ .
a natural b easy c usual
2 Dogs are usually ______ apes.
a friendly toward b afraid of c aggressive towards
3 This particular dog and orangutan behave like ______ .
a old friends b children c people
4 Their behavior has attracted the interest of a lot of ______ .
a TV viewers b scientists c psychologists
5 Orangutans are very ______ creatures.
a physical b naughty c kind
6 Their relationship is based on their need to ______ .
a share new experiences b hunt together c be social

4 Do you believe animals can have friendships? Or do they form relationships only for practical reasons? Do you know other examples of sociable animals? Discuss.

Grammar present tenses review

▶ PRESENT TENSES REVIEW

Simple present
Suriya lives with his keepers.

Present continuous
The two animals are fulfilling a basic social need in each other.

Present perfect
Suriya has understood that the dog is very hungry.

Present perfect continuous
They have been doing this every day.

For more information and practice, see page 156.

5 Look at the grammar box. Match the tenses (1–4) with their uses (a–d).

1 simple present
2 present continuous
3 present perfect
4 present perfect continuous

a highlights a recent activity
b describes a situation in progress or happening around now
c describes a permanent / usual situation
d highlights the present result of a recent action

6 Choose the correct tense to complete this paragraph about animal friendships.

A number of recent videos on YouTube showing unlikely animal friends [1] *have started / have been starting* a debate about animal friendships. Lately many people [2] *have discussed / have been discussing* a particularly moving film which shows a dog making friends with an elephant. Elephants often [3] *show / are showing* concern for their social group, but there is one extraordinary scene where the elephant becomes distressed when the dog gets injured. The dog [4] *has recovered / has been recovering* now and the two animals have been inseparable. The question scientists [5] *ask / are asking* is: is such behavior normal, or do we just want it to be? Some say it happens when animals [6] *have lived / have been living* close to humans. No one [7] *has provided / has been providing* a definite answer, but it seems some animals are just naturally sociable. Others, like giant pandas, [8] *live / are living* more independent and solitary lives.

7 Work in pairs. Explain to each other the use of the verb forms in bold in sentences 1–10 using a–d from Exercise 5.

1 We're not close friends—we**'re** just **studying** French at the same evening class.
This sentence describes a situation in progress.
2 I **live** with Sarah, but each of us **has** our own group of friends that we hang out with.
3 Olivia and I went on a trip to Peru together ten years ago and we**'ve kept in touch** with each other ever since.
4 I wouldn't say we were friends really. We**'ve met** a couple of times at parties.
5 Oh, **do you know** Arun? He's a good friend of mine too. We should all meet up some time.
6 Jacob **always hangs around** when he's bored, but he **never comes over** when he has something better to do.
7 Kate **has always stood by** me in hard times. If ever I'm in trouble, I **know** I can rely on her for help.
8 Cho and I **have been teaching** at the same school for years. We get along well, even though we **never really see** each other socially. I think I've been over to his house once.
9 Kuma and I **have known** each other since we were in school. It doesn't matter if we **haven't seen** each other for a while; we just seem to pick up where we left off.
10 Jessica and I want a medieval-style wedding. Themed weddings **are becoming** very fashionable.

Vocabulary **friends: nouns and phrasal verbs**

8 Work in pairs. What type of friend or person is each person talking about in Exercise 7? Match each sentence with a person from the box.

acquaintance	fair-weather friend
fellow student	roommate
girlfriend	mutual friend
old friend	travel companion
true friend	colleague

9 Find the following phrasal verbs in the sentences in Exercise 7. Which ones contain two prepositions instead of one? Discuss what each verb means.

- 1 verb with *get*
- 1 verb with *stand*
- 2 verbs with *hang*
- 2 verbs with *over*
- 2 verbs with *up*

10 Choose the correct phrasal verbs to complete these sentences.

1 We come from different backgrounds but we .... really well.
2 We don't have to do anything special, like going to a show. It would just be nice to .... together.
3 Why don't you .... to my house for supper tonight?
4 Some friends are great just to have a good time with, but real friends are the ones who .... you when you're in trouble.
5 I'm busy at 6:00 but we could .... later, if you like. Say, 8:30?

Speaking

11 Work in pairs. Think about three of your friends. What kind of friends are they? Choose from the types in Exercise 8. Think also about how often you see these people and what things you do together. Discuss if your friendships are similar in any way.

1b A confused generation

Reading

1 Work in pairs. Look at the photo accompanying the article below. Discuss the questions.

1 What does it show?
2 What do you think is the matter?
3 Is this situation familiar to you?

2 Discuss what effects you think China's recent economic boom has had on the attitudes of the younger and older generations.

3 Read the article and compare your answers.

4 Find examples of the following to show how attitudes are changing in China.

- language use
- caring for the old
- the relationship between parents and children
- shopping
- knowledge of the world

5 Do Bella's parents seem to accept the changes that are happening in China or not? Do you think the changes are difficult for Bella too? Why? / Why not?

Grammar the passive voice

6 Work in pairs. Look at the examples of passive verbs (1–6). Then look at uses of the passive (a–d). Which are true and which are false?

1 Bella is the name that she **has been given** by her English teacher.
2 But at the same time, these new values **are** also **being questioned**.
3 **Have** our lives **been made** richer?
4 **Is** Chinese culture **being supplanted**?
5 When they go shopping Bella makes sure that the "right" Western brands **are selected**.
6 "Our advice **is not listened to** and **not wanted**," her mother says.

a The person doing the action—the agent—is not the main focus of the sentence.
b We use *from* to introduce the agent.
c The agent is often unimportant or unknown—it is the action that interests us.
d The passive is often used because we want to start a sentence with something that has already been mentioned.

Change brings problems. Bella lives with her parents in a brand new apartment in Shanghai. Her real name is Zhou Jiaying; Bella is the name that she has been given by her English teacher. Her parents are representative of a confused generation in a confused time. In modern Chinese society, different ideologies are fighting against each other. Enormous material benefits have been brought by China's economic boom, but the debate is not about these; it's about family life and values. Old values—the respect of family and the older generations—are being replaced by new ones which place money as the critical measurement of one's position in society. But at the same time, these new values are also being questioned. Have our lives been made richer by all our new possessions? Is Chinese culture being replaced? As in all changing societies, people are trying to find the right balance between the new and the old.

Recently, Bella's family put their grandfather into a nursing home. It was a painful decision. In traditional China, caring for aged parents has always been an unavoidable duty, but times are changing. Bella's ambition? "I want one day to put my parents in the best nursing home"—the best that money can buy, she means.

"When she told us that," Bella's father says, "I thought, Is it selfish to think she will be a dutiful and caring daughter and look after us? We don't want to be a burden to her when we get old. This is something my daughter has taught us. Once it was parents who taught children, but now we learn from them." The family can buy many more things these days, and when they go shopping, Bella makes sure that the "right" Western brands are selected. (Pizza Hut is her favorite restaurant.) She also teaches her parents the latest slang.

Her parents want to be supportive, but they no longer help with Bella's homework; in spoken English, she has surpassed them. She has already learned much more about the outside world than they have. "Our advice is not listened to and not wanted," her mother says. "When she was little, she agreed with all my opinions. Now she sits there without saying anything, but I know she doesn't agree with me." Bella glares, but says nothing. "I suppose our child-raising has been a failure." In China there is no concept of the rebellious teenager.

▶ THE PASSIVE VOICE

Simple present passive
I am given, you/we/they are given, he/she/it is given

Present continuous passive
I am being given, you/we/they are being given, he/she/it is being given

Present perfect passive
I/you/we/they have been given, he/she/it has been given

For more information and practice, see page 157.

7 Look at the grammar box. Transform the sentences from active to passive where appropriate. Check your answers with your teacher.

There are many children like Bella in China. They [1] **admire** Western brands. Their parents [2] **have spoiled** them a little, perhaps. Often these children [3] **receive** a better education than their parents. Their parents [4] **send** them to private schools and they [5] **encourage** them to go to college. In China, the new economy [6] **is raising** everyone's hopes.

▶ WORDBUILDING forming adjectives from nouns

There are various endings in English: *-ful*, *-ish*, *-ent*, *-ious*, *-ive*, used to form adjectives from nouns.
support → supportive, rebel → rebellious

8 Complete the sentences with the correct passive form.

1 A lot of changes .... (introduce) in China.
2 As a result, the average Chinese person .... (give) a better standard of living.
3 Couples .... (allow) to have only one child.
4 A lot of money .... (invest) in each child's future.
5 But changes in this policy .... (discuss).
6 The government .... (become) concerned by the growing number of people over 60.

9 Complete the sentences by putting the verb in the correct tense and the active or passive voice. More than one answer may be possible.

1 Children .... (grow) up much too quickly today. Girls of twelve *dress* (dress) as if they are eighteen.
2 We .... (leave) behind by all the new technology they use.
3 They .... (probably / work) harder than us, but they .... (not / have) so much fun.
4 They .... (live) longer and longer and we .... (expect) to look after them. It's not fair.
5 Our parents aren't so different from us: they .... (listen) to the same music, for example.
6 In recent years respect, old values like respect for wisdom and knowledge .... (replace) by respect for money.
7 I rebelled against my parents. My children feel that they .... (expect) to rebel, but in fact they have nothing to complain about or rebel against.
8 We .... (often / criticize) for being selfish and having no moral values, but that's our parents' fault: we .... (spoil) by them.

Speaking

10 Work in groups. Discuss whether it was a young person or an older person that said each of the items in Exercise 9. Which of the statements do you agree with?

11 Do you think the gap between your generation and your parents' generation is greater than the one between your generation and the next generation?

1c Bloodlines

Reading

1 Work in pairs. Why do people emigrate? What difficulties do people face in a new country? Compare your ideas with another pair.

2 Read the article about immigrants in New York. Answer the questions. Then compare your answers with your partner.

1 What is special about the area of Queens?
2 What do Richard and Tanja's families have in common?
3 How are their stories different?

3 Are the sentences true (T) or false (F) according to the article?

1 Immigrants in Queens feel attached to their new country.
2 People are much more interested in learning about distant ancestors than recent generations.
3 Years after immigrating to America, Tomas met his brother in New York by accident.
4 Richard's grandmother has kept the family history alive.
5 Tanja's mother wasn't able to balance work with looking after her children's education.
6 Tanja and her sister have chosen similar careers to their parents'.

4 Look at the article and choose the correct explanation for each phrase.

1 *a melting pot* (paragraph 1)
   a a place of conflict
   b a place where all mix together
   c a place which attracts
2 *their ancestral roots* (para 2)
   a where their family came from originally
   b how they got to America
   c their parents' character
3 *one recurring theme* (para 3)
   a a sad fact
   b a common story
   c an unusual quality
4 *seeking his fortune* (para 4)
   a hoping to get lucky
   b looking for the right job
   c looking for a way to get rich
5 *a must* (para 5)
   a a good thing
   b a right
   c a necessity

Critical thinking identifying the main idea

5 Work in pairs. This article deals with different aspects of emigration. Identify the themes in each of the first three paragraphs. Compare your answers with another pair to check you have identified the same themes.

6 Which themes do the personal accounts of the immigrants pick up on? Which are not really mentioned again?

7 What is the main idea, or message, of the article? Did other pairs reach the same conclusion?

Speaking

8 Look at these phrases describing family characteristics or traits and discuss what they mean.

"He was clearly something of a free spirit."
"My parents have a strong work ethic."
"We've both inherited that desire to get ahead."

9 Look at the questions below and write down your answers. Then ask your partner about their answers. Does family have a similarly strong influence in your lives?

HOW DOES FAMILY SHAPE YOU?

Are you a close family? How much time do you spend with family:
- out of a sense of duty?
- because you choose to?

Is family a consideration for you in choosing where to live?

How conscious are you of your family's history?

Is there a strong family trait? Have you inherited it?

Is there a head of the family? How important is it to have this person's approval?

Is there someone in the family you particularly admire? Why?

Has your family influenced the career path that you have chosen?

When seeking advice, are you more likely to turn to friends or family?

How important is it to you that your family approves of your partner?

Would you say your family members have the same attitude toward:
- money?
- bringing up children?

BLOOD LINES

America is well-known for being a melting pot of different ethnic groups and cultures, but nowhere is this diversity more pronounced than in Queens, New York. Here, second-generation Puerto Ricans live alongside third-generation Greeks and first-generation Koreans, all united by a common feeling of pride in their American identity.

However, they are also proud and curious about their ancestral roots. National Geographic's Genographic Project, also known as the Human Family Tree, set out to trace the origins and common ancestry of the community's immigrants by examining their genetic makeup using a simple DNA test. The study was well supported by local residents, but often what interested them more was something which intrigues us all: the history of our *recent* ancestry. In other words, how their ancestors arrived in America, and what brought them here in the first place.

One recurring theme among immigrants seems to be the hard work and sacrifices that went into building a new life, and how their descendants now feel a duty to honor that effort by working hard too. Here are two Queens residents' stories.

Richard, 38

My great-grandfather Tomas came to America from Poland when he was fifteen. His mother had died, and his father remarried so he could care for his seven children. Tomas didn't like his stepmother, so he ran away to Belgium, where he boarded a ship to America—without a ticket. He was clearly something of a free spirit. Arriving in America with nothing, he got a job on the railroads in California. Then one day he saw an announcement in a newspaper that was read by immigrants. It was from his brother in New York who was also seeking his fortune in America and was looking for him. Tomas got in touch and they had an emotional reunion in New York, where Tomas subsequently settled. This is the story that my grandmother has passed down to us, to my parents, and all my aunts and uncles. She is an amazing woman and the head of the family, I suppose; the one who holds us all together. She's actually quite forgetful now, but she never forgets family details. What that has meant is that all of us have a strong family bond and a strong sense of belonging to a group that has struggled and fought together to succeed here.

Tanja, 29

I'm a first-generation American. Both my parents came here from Jamaica, where getting a good education is a must. My mother always says that people may take everything away from you, but they can never take away your education. My father was a nurse in Jamaica, but he had an ambition to be a doctor in the US; when he first came here, he studied during the day and worked at night. My parents have a strong work ethic. My mom has always worked as a nurse, but at the same time has always been very involved in our lives, helping with our studies and following our careers with interest. Both my sister and I have followed them into the medical profession, and now I'm working as a doctor at Mount Sinai hospital in Queens. I don't know if that kind of dedication is genetic or just something that you learn from your parents, but that desire to get ahead… we've certainly both inherited it. The great thing about America is that it gives you the opportunity to live those dreams too.

1d A face from the past

Real life meeting people you know

1 Work in pairs. Discuss the questions.

1 When was the last time you bumped into someone that you hadn't seen for a while?
2 What did you talk about?
3 Had he / she changed a lot?

2 2 Listen to the conversation between two people who meet by accident in the street. Answer the questions.

1 What have they been doing since they last met?
2 What future arrangement do they make?

3 2 Look at the box, listen again, and mark the expressions the speakers use.

4 Match each situation (1–6) with an expression.

1 Greta expresses surprise at meeting Tan
2 Greta asks Tan for his news
3 what Tan says about Greta's appearance
4 how Greta describes her business
5 what Greta says about Amanda, their other friend
6 how Greta says she can't carry on the conversation

5 Pronunciation expressive intonation

a 3 Emotion (surprise, excitement) is often conveyed by expressive or exaggerated intonation. Flat intonation often suggests a lack of emotion or interest. Listen for these phrases and mark if the intonation is expressive (E) or flat (F).

		E	F
1	Imagine bumping into you here.	☐	☐
2	I had a contract with the consulate.	☐	☐
3	Is it going OK?	☐	☐
4	Do you see much of her?	☐	☐
5	We still get together now and then.	☐	☐
6	I'm only back for a week.	☐	☐

b Work in groups. Choose a phrase from the box and say it either with expressive intonation or with flat intonation. Ask the others in the group to say which intonation you used.

6 Imagine you are in a large mall during your lunch break. Walk around and "bump into" people you know. Find out what each person has been doing and make a future plan. Then move on until you bump into someone else. Use the box to help you.

▶ MEETING PEOPLE YOU KNOW

Imagine meeting / bumping into / seeing you here!
What a (nice) surprise!

How are things?
What have you been up to?
How's everything going?

Busy as ever.
I've been completely swamped.
It has its ups and downs.

You're looking well.
It obviously suits you.

Do you see much of Amanda?
How's Amanda doing?
She was asking about you the other day.

Give her my regards.
Say hello to her from me.

Well, I should probably go and...
Sorry, I've got to run. / I'm in a bit of a hurry.
I don't mean to be rude, but I need to...
It was really nice seeing you. / Great to see you.
Good luck with...

1e News from home

Writing an informal email (1)

1 How often do you send news to friends and family? Do you communicate by letter, email, or text message?

2 Read the email below from Ben to his friend. Where is Ben and what is he doing there? How would you summarize each paragraph?

> Hey Mark,
>
> How's it going? I've been meaning to write for a while, but my work takes up a lot of my time. Please don't think it's because I haven't been thinking about you all—I have, and I'm getting pretty homesick. But I have to remind myself why I am here: to get established as a freelance journalist and photographer.
>
> I'm now in Sri Lanka visiting some tea plantations and talking to people about how their lives have changed in the last 20 years or so. The countryside here is amazing, so lush and green, you wouldn't believe it. I'm trying to get an interview with one of the plantation owners so I can make it into a magazine feature. Fingers crossed!
>
> My plan is to stay here until the end of September and then get a plane back home and see if I can find someone to publish this stuff. It would be great to get together with you then. How is everyone? Is Mei still working for that horrible real estate agent? Say hi to everyone for me. I'll write again soon.
>
> Talk to you soon!
>
> Ben

3 What features of the language in this letter tell you that it is in an informal style?

4 **Writing skill greetings and endings**

Which of these phrases for greeting and ending would be appropriate in an informal email?

All my love	Best	Dear Mr. Franks
Dear Sir or Madam	Hello	Hi John
Kind regards	Hey	Regards
Thanks	Love	Warm regards
Sincerely	Yours	Yours faithfully

5 **Word focus *get***

a The verb *get* is often used in spoken or informal written English. Find five phrases or sentences in the letter where it is used. What does it mean in each case? Think of a synonym for *get* in each case.

b Read the sentences. Match the uses of *get* to a word with a similar meaning in the box.

be (in passive sentences) catch persuade reach receive

1 Did you get my last letter?
2 I got a virus which kept me in bed for weeks.
3 We got delayed for four hours at the border.
4 I'm going to try to get him to come with me.
5 I'll call you when I get to Buenos Aires.

c Write three sentences of your own with *get* giving recent news about yourself. Work in small groups and read them to each other.

6 Imagine you have been away from home for some time. Write an email (200 words) to a friend or family member asking them for news from home and giving them your news. Try to use *get* at least twice.

7 Work in pairs. Exchange letters. Check for the following:

- Is the use of tenses correct?
- Is the style not too formal?
- Did they use the correct greeting and ending?

1f Immigration

Video

Fleeing economic and political hardships, many millions left their homelands in Europe and Asia in search of a better life.

Before you watch

1 In groups, discuss the questions.

1 Where are the people in the photo?
2 What do you think they are doing?
3 What does the caption tell us about the people?

2 Work in pairs. Write down five images you think you will see in the video.

An immigration officer checking the documents of a person arriving in the US by boat.

While you watch

3 Watch the video and check your ideas from Exercise 2.

4 Watch the first part of the video (to 02:30). Find and underline eleven errors and correct them below.

Immigrants have come to the United States since the early 17th century. Europeans settled mainly in the western half of the country, immigrants from Asia and Mexico in the east and northwest. Between 1892 and 1954, Ellis Island in Los Angeles Harbor admitted 17 million immigrants. In 1907, as many as 11,000 people a week were processed. Today, four out of every five Americans can trace part of their family history directly back to Ellis Island. Many of these immigrants settled on the Upper East Side of Manhattan. Large families often lived in just two rooms. On the West Coast, families arrived at Devil Island, where conditions were more relaxed for Asians.

1 ....   7 ....
2 ....   8 ....
3 ....   9 ....
4 ....   10 ....
5 ....   11 ....
6 ....

5 Watch the second part of the video (02:31 to the end). Answer these questions.

1 How many legal immigrants arrive in the US each year?

....

2 What particular challenge is there along the US–Mexico border?

....

3 What have immigrants brought to the US?

....

4 How is the US economy affected by immigration?

....

5 What do immigrants usually share with people already living in the US?

....

6 How does this help the immigrants?

....

After you watch

6 Roleplay arriving at Ellis Island

Work in pairs.

Student A: You are an immigrant arriving at Ellis Island. Prepare the information below.

Student B: You are an immigration officer at Ellis Island. Read the information below and prepare questions to ask Student A.

- where you come from
- your journey
- why you want to come to the US

Act out the interview, then change roles and act out the interview again.

7 Lavinia Limon says, "We're in a much better position because we have maintained our immigration flows." What do you think she means? Do you agree with her?

8 Work in groups and discuss these questions.

1 What kind of problems do you think immigrants faced when they arrived in the United States in the 1920s?
2 Do you think immigrants face similar problems today?
3 Do you think immigrants should try to keep the customs and values of their home countries, or adopt those of their new country?

contend with (v) /kən'tend wɪð/ deal with a difficult situation
discrimination (n) /dɪsˌkrɪmə'neɪʃən/ treating a group of people in an unfair way
diverse (adj) /dɪ'vɜrs/ varied
flee (v) /fli/ escape from
hardship (n) /'hɑrdʃɪp/ something that makes life difficult
harsh (adj) /hɑrʃ/ extremely difficult to live in
leap (n) /lip/ jump
partition (v) /pɑr'tɪʃən/ divide
shore (n) /ʃɔr/ coast
tenement (n) /'tenəmənt/ a large building divided into apartments in a poor area of a city

UNIT 1 REVIEW

Grammar

1 Read the article below about families. Answer the questions.

1 What is the difference between a nuclear and an extended family?
2 What are the benefits of an extended family?

2 Underline the best option to complete the text. Then check your answers with your partner.

3 Work in pairs. Make a list of other advantages and disadvantages of living in an extended family. Then compare your answers with another pair.

When talking about family, a distinction [1] *is making / is made* between extended and nuclear families. The nuclear family includes only parents and children. The extended family is everyone who [2] *is related / has been related* by blood and by marriage: aunts, uncles, grandparents, nieces, nephews, in-laws, etc. In the West, the importance of extended family [3] *has decreased / has been decreased* greatly in the last 50 years. But the extended family has many economic benefits. Grandparents [4] *help / are helped* with childcare, and in turn they [5] *are looked after / have been looked after* when they are old. Also, when domestic chores [6] *are sharing / are shared* by many, living costs decrease. But in recent years, young people [7] *are choosing / have been choosing* to live in nuclear families so the economics [8] *have changed / have been changing*. The older generation say that traditional family values [9] *are losing / are being lost*; but the more serious economic issue is that everyone's support network [10] *has been taking / has been taken* away.

I CAN	
use present tenses	☐
talk about events in present time using active and passive forms	☐

Vocabulary

4 Read each definition and then put in the correct word.

1 Someone who is also studying, like you = a ______ student
2 Someone you go on a trip with = a ______ companion
3 Someone who you can really depend on = a ______ friend
4 Someone you and another friend both know = a ______ friend
5 Someone you share an apartment with = a ______
6 Someone you know who is not really a friend = an ______
7 Someone you are related to by birth = a ______ relative

5 Work in pairs. Give details about one of the people in Exercise 4:

- who you hang out with regularly
- who you haven't kept in touch with
- whose house you go over to regularly

I CAN	
describe different types of friends and acquaintances	☐
use phrasal verbs that describe relationships	☐

Real life

6 Put the sentences below in the right order to complete the conversation between Katia (K) and Julio (J).

K: Hello Julio. Imagine bumping into you here. *1*
K: Great. Well, I should probably go. I need to get to the bank.
K: Of course I will. We should get together some time.
K: You know—busy as ever.
K: You too. Good luck with the work in New York.
K: Not bad, thanks. What have you been up to?
K: Really? That's sounds exciting. You're looking well.
J: Thanks. You too. How's David doing these days?
J: Well, tell him I say hi.
J: Yes, that would be nice. I'll get in touch when I'm back next month.
J: Well, it was great seeing you.
J: I've been working in New York for the past month.
J: Oh hello, Katia. What a nice surprise! How are things?

7 Work in pairs. Imagine you meet each other in the street by accident. Act out a similar conversation.

I CAN	
have a conversation with someone I haven't seen for some time	☐

Speaking

8 Work in pairs. Tell each other about a relationship with a family member or friend that is important in your life.

Unit 2 Storytelling

Race car driver Ayrton Senna at his last race, Imola, Italy, 1994
Photograph by Dario Mitidieri

FEATURES

1 Work in pairs. Look at the photo and the caption. What do you know about race car drivers? Answer the questions.

1 What facts about a race car driver's life do you think would make a good movie?
2 Which would interest you more, a biography of Senna or a movie about his life? Why?

2 Match these adjective to their opposites.

accurate	unfair
fair	impartial
objective	biased
partial	misleading
sympathetic	subjective
truthful	critical

3 Match the adjectives (1–5) with the genres (a–e).

1 sentimental, touching	a thriller
2 creepy, scary	b historical drama
3 fast-moving, gripping	c science fiction
4 original, thought-provoking	d romantic comedy
5 powerful, authentic	e horror

4 Describe to your partner a book you have enjoyed recently. Would you like to see the movie or read the book your partner has described?

2a From page to screen

Vocabulary books and movies

1 Work in pairs. Look at the photo below. What kind of movie do you think this was a location for?

2 Do the words in the box relate to books, movies, or both? Put them into three categories.

audience	author	best seller
blockbuster	box office	cast
chapter	characters	director
location	plot	portrayal
producer	publisher	readers
scene	screenwriter	script
setting	storyline	theme
trilogy		

3 Match words from the books list and the movies list to make pairs of words that are related. What is the difference between the words in each pair? Compare your list with others.

Example:

author and screenwriter—the author is the writer of a book, a screenwriter writes the script of a movie

▶ WORDBUILDING synonyms

Synonyms are words which are close in meaning but not exactly the same, or the same in meaning but different in use: *storyline* and *plot*

Speaking and listening

4 Work in pairs. Ask each other the questions.

1 Do you like to see movie adaptations of books you have read?
2 Do you sometimes read a book because you saw the movie?

5 **4** What do you think is the secret of making a good movie adaptation of a book? Tell your partner if you agree with a, b, or c. Then listen to an interview with a film critic and say which answer he gives.

a to remain completely faithful to the details of the story and the characters in the book
b to remain faithful to the spirit and main themes of the book
c to create a story that works on film, even if it is not faithful to the book

6 4 Answer the questions. Then listen again and check.

1 What do people generally think are the ingredients for a box office success?
2 What does the critic say about the success of movie adaptations of books?
3 What are *Sense and Sensibility* and *The Shining* examples of, according to the critic?
4 To what does the critic compare making a good movie from a book?
5 What is the central theme of *The Lord of the Rings*?
6 Why was it difficult to reproduce the world J.R.R. Tolkien created?
7 How did director Peter Jackson compensate for leaving out elements of Tolkien's story?

7 Work in groups. Discuss the questions.

1 Have you seen any good movie adaptations of books? And any bad ones?
2 What made them good or bad?
3 Were the reasons similar to the ones described by the critic?

Grammar simple past and present perfect

8 Work in pairs. Match each sentence (1–5) to one of the uses of the simple past and present perfect (a–e).

1 Some film adaptations **have worked**, others **have flopped**.
2 "What is the secret?" That **was** the question I **put** to him earlier.
3 He **has followed** the progress of many book-to-film adaptations in his time.
4 The author, Tolkien, **created** a magical world.
5 It **has become** one of the most successful movies of all time.

a When the action is clearly linked to a specific time in the past, we use the simple past.
b When the experience is more important than the time, and the time is not stated, we use the present perfect.
c We use the present perfect to talk about people's life experiences.
d If the person is dead, we use the simple past to talk about their lives.
e When we talk about a period of time that is not finished (over the past few weeks, this year), we use the present perfect even if the action itself is finished.

▶ SIMPLE PAST and PRESENT PERFECT

Simple past
I visited / He visited...
I didn't visit...
Did you visit... ?

Present perfect
I have visited / She has visited...
I have not visited...
Have you visited... ?

For more information and practice, see page 158.

9 Look at the grammar box. Then choose the best option to complete the sentences.

1 I first .... (read) *The Hobbit* when I was twelve years old. What about you?
No, I .... (never / read) *The Hobbit*, but I know a guy who .... (read) it 24 times. He never gets tired of it.
2 There .... (be) a lot of movie adaptations of Stephen King's books over the years.
Yes, I know. There .... (be) a great adaptation of *The Green Mile* a few years ago.
3 .... you ever .... (write) a play or a screenplay?
No, but my great grandfather .... (write) a play for radio.
4 .... you .... (see) *2001: A Space Odyssey* on TV last night?
No, but I .... (see) it before.

Writing and speaking

10 Think about a living writer or filmmaker. Make notes about their life and work. Use the chart to help you. Then describe this person's work to your partner. Ask questions about the person your partner chose.

What is the person's name?	
Where is he/she from?	
Is he/she an author, screenwriter, or other?	
What are three famous works from this person?	
What style of movie or book does he/she make?	
What is your favorite example of this person's work?	
Why?	

2b A close shave

Reading

1 Work in pairs. Discuss how you would react if faced with the following dangerous situations. What do you think would be the right thing to do?

- a snake hissing at you
- a shark swimming near you
- a bear approaching when you are having a picnic

2 Have you had any "close shaves" with dangerous animals? What happened? Tell the class.

3 Read the story below about three encounters two National Geographic reporters had with rhinos on the same day. What did the rhinos do in each case and how did the people react?

4 Look at the eight highlighted verbs in the article and guess their meaning from the context. Check your answers in a dictionary.

5 What effect does the use of these verbs have on the story?

KAZIRANGA NATIONAL PARK in India is home to two of the world's most endangered species: the tiger and the single-horned rhino. Photographer Steve Winter and writer Douglas Chadwick had only been working there a few days when they had a very close shave with some rhinos.

They were driving into the park to start filming when their guide stopped the jeep to move a turtle from the middle of the road just ahead of them. Winter, Chadwick, and their guard got out to stretch their legs and watch. But when Chadwick turned to look up the road, he saw something terrible: a rhino charging at them!

Rhinos can sprint more than 25 miles an hour, so there was no time to leap back in the car. Instinctively, the guard fired a shot into the ground just in front of the rhino. The crack of the rifle and the dirt that the bullet kicked up was enough to distract their attacker and it veered off into the grass seconds before reaching them.

Shaken, but relieved the incident had not been worse, they drove on. As they were entering the forest area, three young rhinos entered the road in front of them. The jeep stopped hurriedly, but this time the animals seemed uninterested and disappeared into the forest. Just then, however, the mother of the three, who had been keeping an eye on her young, came crashing through the trees. No time to shoot this time. The female rhino slammed into the side of the jeep and started to wrestle it off the road. Indian rhinos don't use their horns in a fight; instead they bite and this female's teeth were gouging deep into the side of the jeep.

The guide had laid down a rule for his guests at Kaziranga: no one was allowed to be scared. But his guests were breaking the rule, praying the driver could get them out of there. With the engine screaming, at last the vehicle skidded free. Even then the rhino came after them and it was only 500 feet later that she gave up the chase.

Grammar **past tenses review**

6 Look at the grammar box. Match the tenses (1–4) with their uses (a–d). Then find other examples of the tenses in the article.

1 past continuous
2 simple past
3 past perfect
4 past perfect continuous

a to describe the main events in sequence
b to refer to an action that happened earlier but not in the main sequence of events
c to describe a (background) event in progress around the time of the main event
d to describe an action in progress before or up to the main event(s) in the past

> **PAST TENSES REVIEW**
>
> **Past continuous**
> *They were driving into the park to start filming when their guide stopped the jeep.*
>
> **Simple past**
> *Winter, Chadwick, and their guard got out to stretch their legs and watch.*
>
> **Past perfect**
> *Shaken, but relieved the incident had not been worse, they drove on.*
>
> **Past perfect continuous**
> *Winter and Chadwick had only been working there a few days when they had a very close shave.*
>
> For more information and practice, see page 158.

7 Complete the summary of Winter and Chadwick's story using the past tense of the verbs given. Use contracted forms where possible.

Steve Winter and Douglas Chadwick, who [1] .... (work) in Kaziranga National Park, [2] .... (have) three close encounters with rhinos all on the same day. Before entering the park, their guide [3] .... (tell) them not to be afraid, so they [4] .... (be / not) especially worried, but clearly the incidents [5] .... (shock) them. They [6] .... (know) that filming in the park was dangerous work, but they [7] .... (not / expect) to meet danger so soon or so frequently. But it [8] .... (not / keep) them from carrying on!

8 Pronunciation **contracted negative forms**

5 Listen and repeat these sentences after the speaker. Pay attention to the negative contractions.

1 I *haven't* been to India.
2 It *isn't* far.
3 You *aren't* allowed.
4 It *doesn't* matter.
5 I *hadn't* noticed.
6 They *weren't* late.
7 She *hasn't* called.
8 We *didn't* care.

9 Complete these reports of lucky escapes by putting each verb in the most appropriate past tense. Use contracted forms where possible. Check your answers with your teacher.

THE NEAR MISS

I [1] .... (mountain bike) with a friend in Wales and we [2] .... (just / finish) a long off-road climb out of the Dysynni Valley. It [3] .... (rain) earlier but now the sun [4] .... (shine) and we [5] .... (feel) pretty warm. Since the rest of the route was downhill on paved roads, I [6] .... (take) off my bike helmet and [7] .... (set) off. Suddenly the road [8] .... (become) very steep and the bike [9] .... (pick) up speed quickly. There was a turn ahead in the road and I knew I was going to crash. The bike [10] .... (go) straight into a wall, but luckily I...

THE UNEXPECTED

Mr. Charles Everson and his wife Linda [11] .... (drive) home from a friend's house one Sunday when a cow [12] .... (fall) from the sky and [13] .... (land) on the hood of their van. The cow, which [14] .... (escape) from a breeding farm, [15] .... (graze) too close to the edge of a cliff next to the road and [16] .... (slip) and plunged 200 feet. When the emergency crew [17] .... (arrive) at the scene they...

10 In pairs, complete the last sentence of each story. Then get together with another pair and share your endings.

When the emergency crew arrived at the scene, they had to call a vet to take care of the cow!

Speaking

11 Prepare a description of a time that you had a near miss or lucky escape. Choose one of the following themes and use each tense at least once. Then tell your story to your partner. When you come near the end, stop and ask your partner what they think happened next.

- escaping injury or physical accident
- a scary incident when something unexpected happened
- getting away with something you did wrong
- seeing something dangerous happen and trying to help

2c Once upon a time...

Reading

1 Work in pairs. What were your favorite stories as a child? Tell your partner what they were about and why you still remember them.

2 Look at these titles of fairy tales by the brothers Grimm. Discuss the questions.

Cinderella	The Elves and the Shoemaker
Snow White	Little Red Riding Hood
Sleeping Beauty	The Frog Prince

1 Which of these fairy tales is depicted in the photo on page 27?
2 Which are well known in your country?
3 What is the name for them in your language? Is the name similar or very different?

3 Where did the stories in Exercise 2 come from originally and what did the brothers Grimm do to them? Read the article and find out.

4 Look back at the article and find significant (or surprising) facts about the following:

1 the popularity of the Grimms' fairy tales now
2 how popular they were at the time
3 Germany at the time the brothers were writing
4 *Little Red Riding Hood* and *Snow White*
5 the attitude of parents to the stories

5 The writer uses various words and expressions associated with fairy tales. Find and match them with the definitions below.

1 a long time ago (para 1)
2 the opposite of *a hero* (para 1)
3 clever and knowledgeable (para 1)
4 distant countries (para 1)
5 the lesson to be learned (para 5)
6 a woman (often bad) who does magic (para 6)
7 the opposite of *kind* (para 6)
8 for the rest of time (para 7)

Critical thinking **close reading**

6 What conclusions can you draw about the brothers Grimm from reading this article? According to the text, are these statements true (T) or false (F)? Or is there not enough information (N) to say?

1 They were very motivated young men.
2 They had an academic interest in the stories.
3 Their aim was to write down stories that had previously been told orally.
4 They were interested in the stories themselves, not the social message behind them.
5 Wilhelm disliked their cruelty and violence.
6 In the end, the stories reached the mass audience that the brothers had wished them to.

7 Work in pairs. Summarize the brothers Grimms' achievement, according to the writer.

Word focus ***keep***

8 Work in pairs. In the article, find three phrases with the word *keep*. Discuss what each one means. Then do the same with the phrases below.

1 Please **keep an eye on** the time. We shouldn't leave any later than ten thirty.
2 Try to **keep your chin up**. I'm sure things will get better.
3 I wouldn't tell him your news just yet, if I were you. He's not very good at **keeping a secret**.
4 Technology is moving so fast these days. It's difficult to **keep track** of all the changes.
5 Sorry, I don't want to **keep** you. I just need to ask you a quick question.
6 I always think it's a good idea to **keep a diary** that you can look back on later.

Writing and speaking

9 Think of a traditional story or fairy tale you know well. Make notes on the main elements of the story. Use a dictionary if necessary.

10 Work in pairs. Tell each other your story as you remember it, or tell the same story but in a modern setting. When you have heard each other's stories, change partners and tell your new partner the story you were told.

Once upon a time…

Once upon a time there lived in Germany two brothers who loved a good story—one with magic and danger, royalty and villains. At school they met a wise man who led them to a treasure—a library of old books with tales more enchanting than any they had ever heard. Inspired, the brothers began collecting their own stories, listening to the folktales people told them. Soon they produced their own treasure—a book of fairy tales that would charm millions in faraway lands for generations to come.

The brothers Grimm, Jacob and Wilhelm, named their story collection *Children's and Household Tales* and published it in Germany in 1812. The collection, which has been translated into more than 160 languages, from Inupiat in the Arctic to Swahili in Africa, is a publishing phenomenon that competes with the Bible. The stories and their characters have appeared in theater, opera, comic books, movies, paintings, rock music, advertising, and even fashion. The Japanese have built two theme parks devoted to the tales, and in the United States, the Grimms' collection helped launch Disney as an entertainment giant.

Such fame would have shocked the humble Grimms. During their lifetimes, the book sold few copies in Germany. The early editions were not even aimed at children. They had no illustrations, and scholarly footnotes took up almost as much space as the tales themselves. Jacob and Wilhelm Grimm viewed themselves as patriotic students of folklore. They began their work at a time when Germany had been occupied by the French under Napoleon. The new rulers suppressed local culture. As young scholars, the brothers Grimm began work on the fairy tale collection in order to save the endangered oral storytelling tradition of Germany.

Long before the Grimms' time, storytelling thrived in inns, barns, and peasant homes. During winter nights, as they sat spinning wool, women kept each other company and entertained each other with tales of adventure, romance, and magic. Altogether, 40 such storytellers delivered tales to the Grimms, many of them coming to their house in Kassel. One of them, "Marie," was credited with narrating many of the most famous tales: *Little Red Riding Hood, Snow White,* and *Sleeping Beauty*. But these were not from the German oral tradition. Marie had had French nannies who retold stories that they themselves had read in a collection written by Charles Perrault in 1697, *Tales of My Mother Goose*.

Although the brothers implied that they were just recording the tales, Wilhelm polished and reshaped them up to the final edition of 1857. In an effort to make them more acceptable to children and their parents, he stressed the moral of each tale, and emphasized gender roles. According to the Grimms, the collection served as "a manual of manners." To this day, parents read them to their children because they approve of the lessons in the stories: keep your promises, don't talk to strangers, work hard, obey your parents.

Yet despite Wilhelm's polish, the coarse medieval core of the stories remained untouched. The cruel treatment of children (like Hansel and Gretel, who are put in a cage and fattened for eating), the violent punishments handed out to the villains (like Snow White's evil stepmother, who in the original story is forced to dance in red-hot iron shoes until she falls down dead), are too much for some parents.

So what accounts for their popularity? Some have suggested it is because the characters are always striving for happiness. But the truth probably lies in their origin. The Grimms' tales were born out of a storytelling tradition without boundaries of age or culture. The brothers' skill was to translate these into a universal style of writing that seems to mirror whatever moods or interests we bring to our reading of them. And so it was that the Grimms' fairy tales lived happily ever after.

coarseness (n) /ˈkɔrsnɪs/ being rough and down-to-earth; a lack of sophistication or refinement
folklore (n) /ˈfoʊkˌlɔr/ the traditional songs, stories, proverbs, legends of a society
nanny (n) /ˈnæni/ a woman paid to look after young children
spin (v) /spɪn/ to make natural fiber (like wool) into thread

2d What a disaster!

Real life reacting to stories

1 Work in pairs. What kind of things do you find often go wrong day-to-day: computers, transport, things in the house, forgetting things?

2 **6** Look at these extracts from six personal accounts of things that went wrong. Discuss what you think happened next. Then listen and check.

1 The bus broke down on the highway so we were all left stranded until help could arrive.
2 My pants got caught on the door handle and as I walked away they tore.
3 I bent the key trying to force it into the lock and when I tried to straighten it, it snapped.
4 The elevator got stuck between floors twenty-five stories up.
5 The tires on my bicycle were badly worn and when I hit a bump in the road one of them burst.
6 My computer froze while I was working.

3 **6** Look at the responses below. Tell your partner which ones were used in each of the conversations in Exercise 2. Then listen again and check your answers.

REACTING TO STORIES

Sympathizing when something bad has happened
Oh, that's awful.
How embarrassing!
What a disaster!
Oh, that's really awkward.
Poor you!
What a nightmare!
Really? That's odd.
Really? How strange!

Commenting on a good outcome to a bad situation
Phew!
That must have been a relief.
That was clever.
That was good thinking.
That was lucky.
That was a stroke of luck.

Talking about similar experiences
I can sympathize with that.
Yeah, I think I would have done the same thing.
Yeah, something like that happened to me once.
Yeah, I once had the same experience…

4 Pronunciation **linking and assimilation**

a **7** Listen to these short responses. Notice how the underlined sounds are either linked (as in *been a*) or assimilated (as in *what did*, where the *t* of *what* disappears and is replaced by the *d* of *did*). Repeat each phrase.

That must have been‿a relief.

So what‿did you do?

b **8** Work in pairs. Underline the sounds in these sentences that you think are linked or assimilated. Then listen and check. Practice saying the sentences.

Linked
1 What a nightmare!
2 Oh, that's awful.
3 How embarrassing!
4 Really? That's odd.

Assimilated
5 That was good thinking.
6 Something like that happened to me.

5 Work in groups. Choose two of the following topics each and prepare to tell a short story about something that happened to you. Those listening to the story should react.

- a time you were lost or stranded
- something embarrassing that happened to you
- a minor accident you had
- a computer problem
- a situation when someone you were with panicked
- a situation where something broke or got stuck

2e A real-life drama

Writing a story

1 Read the opening paragraph from a story about two men walking in the Amazon rain forest in Peru. Answer the questions.

1 What happened to Rowan?
2 How are the two characters feeling?

2 Work in pairs. Identify the events in the story. Put them in chronological order.

> "I can't move," cried Rowan, "my foot's caught in something – it's really painful!" Chris knew that Rowan was struggling. He had been moaning all day about his sore feet and they had only covered a mile in the last half hour. Chris was tired too from trudging through the thick jungle, but was eager to get back to the camp before it got dark. They weren't carrying many supplies with them and neither had eaten anything for at least three hours. "It's probably just a thorn bush or something," he said encouragingly, walking back slowly to see what the problem was. "Reach down and try to free your foot." But as he got nearer, he could see that it wasn't a bush that had caught Rowan but a metal animal trap which had clamped itself firmly to his right ankle.

3 Why does the writer choose to start the story at the point when Rowan cries out?

4 Writing skill **using descriptive words**

a Look at the highlighted expressions in the story. Which describe movement and which a way of speaking? Discuss the exact meaning of each expression.

b Look at the words in bold in these sentences. Try to work out their meaning from the context. Then check in a dictionary to see if you were right.

Speaking

1 "Help," she **screamed**, "that man took my wallet!"
2 Jin could tell Ping was unhappy because she kept **muttering** under her breath.
3 He **mumbled** something about it being unfair, but I couldn't catch his exact words.
4 "OK, let's try your way then," she **said wearily**. She had lost the energy to argue anymore.
5 "I'll go first," he **said bravely**, but he was scared.

Moving

6 We **edged** our way along the narrow path, conscious of the steep drop to our left.
7 When he heard the car arrive, he **leapt** to his feet and ran to the door.
8 She **stumbled** on a rock and almost fell, but then regained her balance.
9 We **walked briskly** for the next hour but then slowed to our usual pace.
10 She **turned apprehensively** towards the door, as heavy footsteps approached.

c Do you know any other verbs that describe a particular way of speaking or moving? Tell the class.

5 Write the ending of the story (at least five sentences). Try to use some descriptive verbs and adverbs, but don't overuse them!

6 Exchange your ending with your partner. Did he or she:

- use the different past tenses correctly?
- include some descriptive verbs and adverbs?

7 Now read other students' stories. Decide which ending you like best.

2f History of film

Inventors realized they could create the illusion of motion by presenting a quick succession of pictures.

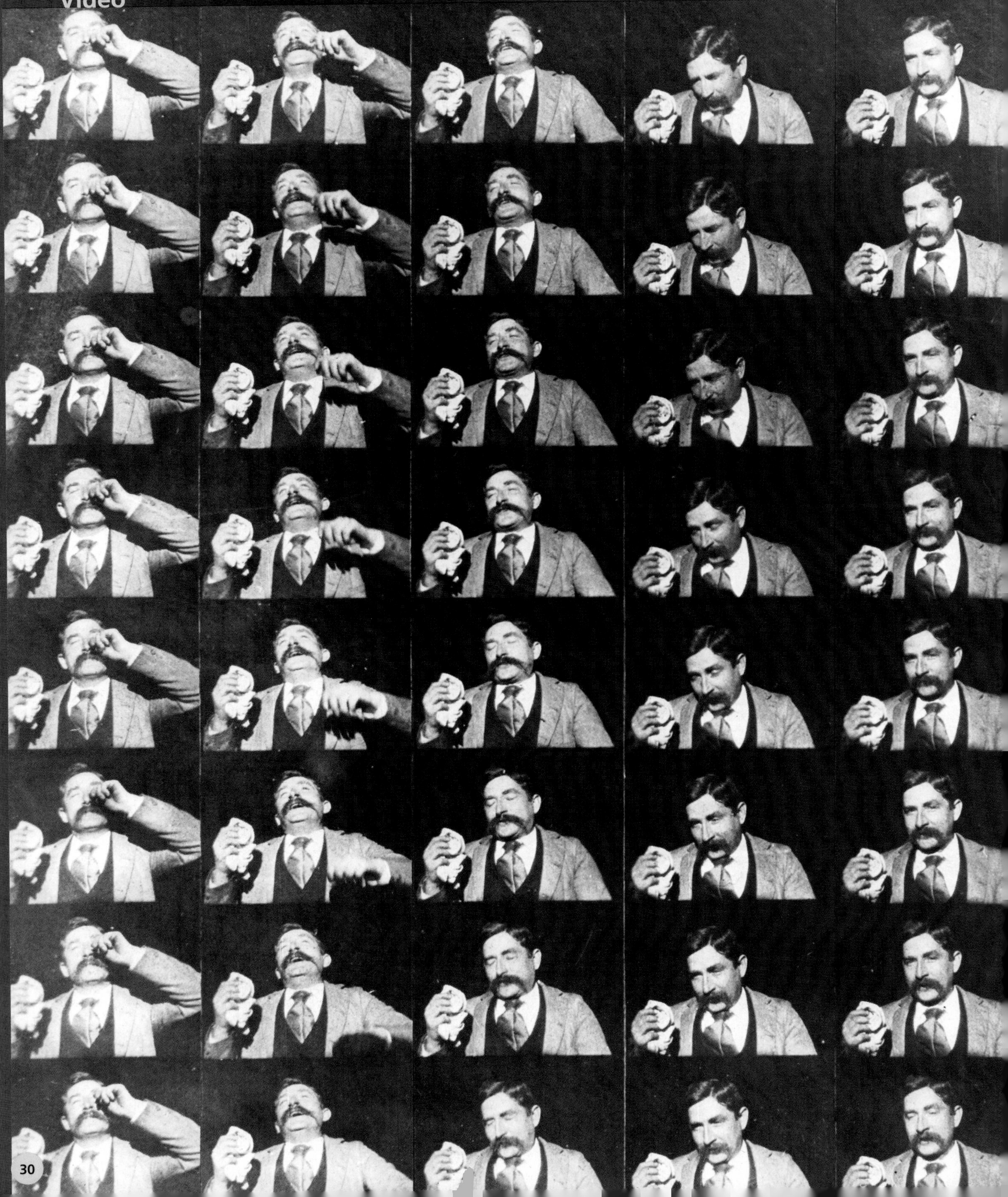

Before you watch

1 Work in groups. Look at the photo and discuss the questions.

1 What do you think the man in the photo is doing?
2 When do you think the photo was taken?
3 Why do you think the photo is made up of several images?

2 You are going to watch a video about the history of film. Mark the things and people you think you will see in the video.

an old film projector	an Oscar statue
a documentary filmmaker	an earthquake
a scene from a melodrama	Charlie Chaplin
a scene from an animated movie	the Arctic
actors arriving at an awards ceremony	

While you watch

3 Watch the video and check your answers from Exercise 2. Which other early actor is mentioned in the video?

4 Watch the first part of the video (to 01:36). Number the events in the order they happened.

a The projector was developed.
b People watched movies in arcades.
c Hollywood became the center of the studio system.
d Melodramas became popular.
e Actors became part of a new American aristocracy.
f Edison and Dickson invented the kinetoscope.

5 Watch the second part of the video (01:37 to the end). Answer the questions.

1 What have movies allowed us to do outside of Hollywood?

....

2 Name three events that the video shows being covered by early newsmen.

....
....
....

3 Name two unusual activities you see as examples of how documentary filmmakers have used the camera in new ways.

....
....

4 How have studio blockbusters influenced documentaries?

....
....
....

6 Watch the video again. Complete the phrases with the missing time expressions.

1 ...., movies have captured the imagination of audiences all over the world.
2 ...., inventors realized they could create the illusion of motion.
3 ...., projection allowed large audiences to view the spectacle at the theater.
4 ...., the emerging movie studio system was centered in Hollywood, California.
5 ...., newsmen carried cameras looking for history in the making.
6 .... documentary filmmakers have learned to borrow from the studio blockbusters.

After you watch

7 Roleplay an interview with an actor or actress

Work in pairs.

Student A: Imagine you are a famous Hollywood actor or actress. Choose who you want to be. Read the information below and make notes.

Student B: You are going to interview a famous Hollywood actor or actress. Read the information below and prepare questions.

- background
- career to date (movies and other work)
- how Hollywood has changed over the years

Act out the interview, then change roles. Student B should choose a different actor or actress.

8 Work in groups and discuss these questions.

1 What kind of movies do you prefer watching?
2 Do you enjoy watching documentaries? Why?
3 How important is the movie industry in your country?

arcade (n) /ɑr'keɪd/ a passage with a roof and stores on both sides
entrancing (adj) /en'trænsɪŋ/ fascinating
flickering (adj) /'flɪkərɪŋ/ quick-moving and not very clear
landmark (n) /'lændˌmɑrk/ an important historical moment
loop (n) /lup/ a circle
melodrama (n) /'meləˌdrɑmə/ an old style of drama that has exaggerated emotion and action
nickelodeon (n) /ˌnɪkə'loʊdiən/ an old type of movie theater
peep (v) /pip/ look at something through narrowed eyes
projection (n) /prə'dʒekʃən/ putting an image on a screen
Tinseltown (n) /'tɪnsəlˌtaʊn/ another name for Hollywood
train (v) /treɪn/ point a camera lens at something
vaudeville (n) /'vɔdˌvɪl/ a type of variety show

UNIT 2 REVIEW

Grammar

1 Complete the story below about a narrow escape. Put each verb into the correct tense: present perfect, simple past, past continuous, past perfect, or past perfect continuous.

I [1] _____ (film) lions a lot—ever since I was 25 years old—and I [2] _____ (never / have) serious problems with them. Strangely, I [3] _____ (feel) most at danger when lions [4] _____ (want) to play. I remember an expedition a few years ago in Tanzania. I [5] _____ (sit) in my tent reading just after sunset. One of our guides [6] _____ (call) out "Lion!" That [7] _____ (not / be) particularly unusual, so I [8] _____ (not / take) much notice. But when the guide [9] _____ (call) out again, I looked out and saw that two lions [10] _____ (slowly / approach) our camp. We [11] _____ (park) our car some distance away and it was too far to reach. So I [12] _____ (run) back to the tent and quickly [13] _____ (zip) it up. I could hear a lot of noise coming from the kitchen, so I [14] _____ (assume) the guides [15] _____ (go) back there to make noise to scare the lions off. I [16] _____ (wait), and when the noise [17] _____ (die) down, I [18] _____ (look) out again. The two guides [19] _____ (lock) themselves in the car. The lions were gone, but where they [20] _____ (play) in the kitchen, there was an incredible mess.

2 Work in pairs. Answer these questions.

1 Where did the filmmaker hide from the lions?
2 What did he think the guides had done to save the situation?
3 What had actually happened?

I CAN	
talk about past experience	☐
use narrative tenses to tell a story	☐

Vocabulary

3 Choose the correct words.

1 A documentary should be *biased* / *impartial* and factually *accurate* / *authentic*.
2 The *author* / *publisher* of a book must make sure the *characters* / *cast* are believable.
3 I'm reading a thriller. The *script* / *plot* is very *gripping* / *touching*.
4 The movie gives the *audience* / *cast* a very realistic *scene* / *portrayal* of life in the nineteenth century.
5 The movie was a *bestseller* / *blockbuster* based on a science fiction book with some very *thought-provoking* / *sympathetic* ideas.

4 Work in pairs. Describe a movie based on a book you have read. Was it a successful adaptation? How faithful was it to the book?

I CAN	
describe movies and books	☐
talk about the different elements of a movie or book	☐

Real life

5 Match the piece of news (1–6) with a response (a–f).

1 My pen leaked and ink got all over my jacket and my shirt, but it came out in the wash.
2 The garden was OK because we had asked a neighbor to water it while we were away.
3 When I got home at midnight all the lights in the house were on, but no one was there.
4 I went all the way downtown to get my new passport, only to find the office is closed on Mondays.
5 He asked me for my honest opinion, so I gave it.
6 The car I had hit was my boss's!

a Poor you!
b Yes, I think I would have done the same thing.
c Really? That's odd.
d That must have been a relief.
e How embarrassing!
f That was good thinking.

6 Work in pairs. Tell each other about something bad (embarrassing, annoying, a narrow escape) that happened to you recently.

I CAN	
react to stories in a natural way	☐

Speaking

7 Work in small groups. Use the first and last lines below to make your own fairy tale. When you are ready, each person should tell the story to a member of another group.

"There were once two neighbors, one very lazy and the other very hard-working…

…And so it was that these two, who had been enemies for so long, became the greatest of friends."

Unit 3 Science and technology

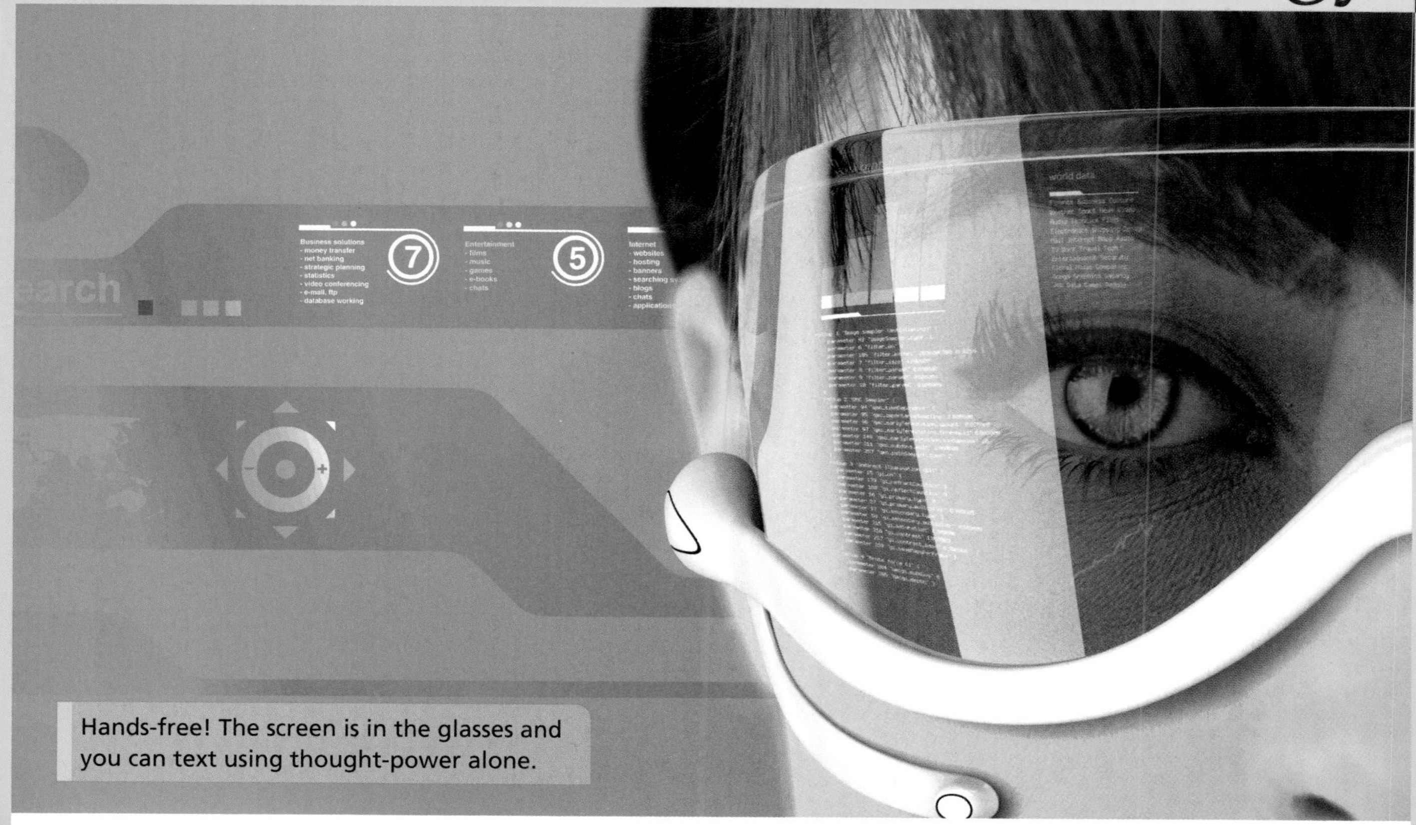

Hands-free! The screen is in the glasses and you can text using thought-power alone.

FEATURES

1 How much do you depend on technology in your day-to-day life and work? What happens if you lose your phone or your computer crashes?

2 Work in pairs. Look at the photo and read the caption. Now look at the words below. In which area(s) is the technological breakthrough in the photo? Which area will give rise to the main breakthrough of the next 50 years?

artificial intelligence	communications	energy use
medicine	space exploration	transportation

3 In pairs, discuss these predictions about the future. Do you think they are justified? Why? Which do you think will come true?

1 I expect that most of my generation will live to be around 100 years old.
2 I think in the future people will interact with intelligent machines even more than they do now.
3 I don't think global warming is going to be the problem that everyone says it is.

3a Is technology the answer?

Kolkata's streets crammed with vendors, pedestrians, and taxis

Speaking

1 Work in groups. Look at the photo. Which problems does the photo illustrate?

congestion	epidemic
overpopulation	pollution
poverty	starvation

2 Which of these problems could have a technological solution?

Listening

3 9 Read the opinions (1–3). Then listen to the presentation about overpopulation. Match the opinion with the people (a–c).

1 Whenever the population is too big, a disaster reduces it.
2 Many people will die because there will not be enough food.
3 Science and technology will find a solution.

a the speaker
b Thomas Malthus
c Paul Ehrlich

4 9 Listen again. Are the sentences true (T) or false (F)?

1 The speaker has some ideas for action which can immediately solve the problem of overpopulation.
2 Paul Ehrlich thought that we should control the number of babies being born.
3 There will be 7 billion people in the world by the middle of the century.
4 Nanotechnology has saved the world from mass starvation.
5 Earth does not have space for 9 billion people.
6 The growth in the "global middle class" will put big pressure on resources.
7 According to the speaker, people are basically lazy.

5 What is the meaning of each underlined prefix in these words from the speech? Match the prefix (1–6) to the meaning (a–f).

1 <u>bio</u>fuels	a very small
2 <u>nano</u>technology	b very big
3 <u>mega</u>cities	c extremely
4 <u>micro</u>phone	d of life or living things
5 <u>semi</u>-retired	e half
6 <u>ultra</u>cautious	f $\times 10^{-9}$

▶ WORDBUILDING prefixes

There are many prefixes in English taken from Latin and Greek, each of which have a particular meaning: *<u>micro</u>phone*, *<u>mega</u>city*

6 Do you share the speaker's faith in science and technology? Why?

Grammar future forms review

> **FUTURE FORMS REVIEW**
>
> ***will***
> *One moment, I'll just adjust my microphone.*
> *It will be a bad thing for the planet if all those people start eating meat and driving big cars.*
> *The population will probably peak at around 9 billion by the middle of the century.*
> ***going to***
> *I'm not going to speak for too long.*
> *Those of you who have come here looking for answers are going to be disappointed.*
> ***about to***
> *Science is about to step in again with nanotechnology solutions.*
> **Present continuous**
> *I'm speaking to a government committee tomorrow.*
> **Simple present**
> *France is the world's favorite vacation destination.*
>
> For more information and practice, see page 159.

7 Look at the grammar box. Match the verb forms (1–5) with their uses (a–i). Some verb forms have more than one use.

1 *will*
2 *going to*
3 *about to*
4 present continuous
5 simple present

a a scheduled event
b a future event in an *if* or *when* clause
c a prediction
d a confident prediction based on present information
e a decision made at the time of speaking
f an intention or previously made decision
g a formal arrangement
h a simple statement of fact
i an event in the immediate future

8 Underline the correct future forms in this presentation. Sometimes there is more than one possibility.

"I think [1] *we wait / we'll wait* a few moments until everyone [2] *arrives / will arrive*… OK, [3] *I am beginning / I'll begin* now. Hello everyone and thank you for coming to hear my presentation about appropriate technology. I am [4] *about to / going to* speak for about 30 minutes and then I [5] *will take / am taking* your questions. If there [6] *is / is going to be* anything that you don't understand, please ask me then, rather than during the presentation. My colleague, Liesel Babel, [7] *talks / is talking* this afternoon in the green seminar room, if people would like to learn more about appropriate technology. I think her session [8] *starts / is starting* at two o'clock. She [9] *is speaking / will speak* about her experiences in the field, working on various development projects in Africa. OK, [10] *I am going to show / I'll show* you a short video now…"

9 Complete the news headlines using an appropriate future form. Check your answers with your teacher.

1 World leaders .... (meet) in Geneva tomorrow to discuss the issue of overpopulation.
2 In the next few weeks, the government .... (introduce) a fee for each child that couples have after their first two children.
3 Scientists say that space colonies .... (be) the only solution for overpopulation in the near future.
4 Doctors have said that in the future they .... (not / spend) so much effort keeping the old alive.
5 The government .... (launch) a new education program later today to encourage women to have fewer children.
6 People .... (have to) change their lifestyles if they .... (want) the world's resources to support the growing population in the coming years.

10 Work in pairs. Underline all the time expressions in the sentences in Exercise 9. Then put them in order of the nearest to the most distant future. Compare your answers with another pair.

1 *later today*
2 ....
3 ....
4 ....
5 ....
6 ....

Speaking

11 Work in groups. Decide which of the ideas in Exercise 9, or one of your own, are the best course of action for dealing with overpopulation. Then explain your plan and the reasons for it to the class.

3b Revealed world

Speaking

1 Work in pairs. What information (news, travel advice, maps) do you get through printed media and what through digital media?

> **WORDBUILDING compound nouns (noun + noun)**
>
> We can use two nouns together to mean one thing.
> *information overload, computer graphics*

Reading

2 Work in pairs. Look at the picture and the labels. Which information would you find useful or interesting if you were a visitor in Washington, DC? What other information might you want?

3 Read the article about augmented reality and complete the table.

Other terms for augmented reality:	1 *AR* 2 ....
Examples of augmented reality already in use:	3 *restaurant menus and prices* 4 ....
Devices we will use to see the augmented reality world:	5 .... 6 ....
Future applications for augmented reality technology:	7 *3-D repair instructions* 8 ....

REVEALED WORLD

By Tim Folger

The regular world presented to us by our five senses—you could call it reality 1.0—is not always the most user-friendly of places. We get lost in unfamiliar cities; we meet people whose language we don't understand. So why not try the improved version: augmented reality (AR) or reality 2.0? AR technology superimposes computer-generated information on the real world, via a cell phone camera or special video glasses.

Early forms of AR are already here. With the right downloads, smart phones can deliver information about nearby ATMs and restaurants and other points of interest. Not only can you see that there's a Chinese restaurant on the next block, you can read the menu and prices, read reviews, and even find out how busy it is at the time.

This is where the next revolution in computing will take place: not in ever-more-sophisticated virtual-reality games, but rather in the interface between the real world and the information brought to us via the Internet. Imagine bubbles floating before your eyes, filled with cool information about anything and everything that you see in front of you. Information overload? Maybe not.

Let's jump ahead ten years. People trying to fix their cars won't be looking at online repair manuals or books; they will be wearing a device that projects animated 3-D computer graphics onto the equipment under repair, labeling parts and giving step-by-step guidance. Such technology is already being used by the US Marines.

Today's window into the AR world can be a smart phone or special video glasses that look like wraparound sunglasses. But in ten years' time, cell phones and video glasses will have been replaced by contact lenses etched with tiny LEDs which display text and images at a readable distance in front of the eye. A deaf person wearing these inconspicuous lenses will be able to see a real-time transcript of what people are saying as they speak.

The question is: while we are all absorbed in our new AR worlds, how will we be interacting with each other?

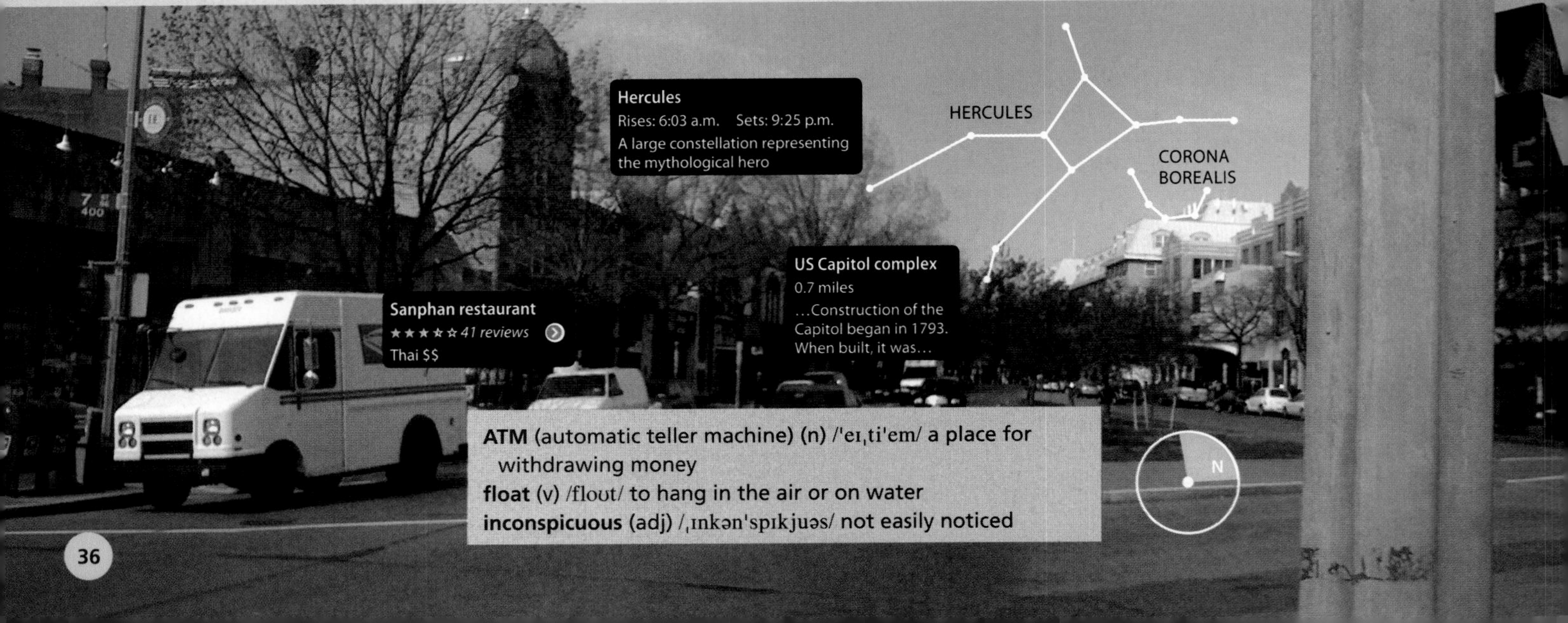

ATM (automatic teller machine) (n) /ˈeɪˌtiˈem/ a place for withdrawing money
float (v) /flout/ to hang in the air or on water
inconspicuous (adj) /ˌɪnkənˈspɪkjuəs/ not easily noticed

4 As a class, discuss the questions.

1 Which of the AR applications described in the article do you think will be really useful?
2 Can you think of any other applications?
3 What do you think is the answer to the author's final question?

Grammar **future continuous and future perfect**

5 Look at the sentences (a–e) and the verbs in bold. Which sentences describe:

1 an action in progress some time in the future?
2 an action completed before a certain point of time in the future?

a A few years from now, the quantity of information available **will have increased** enormously.
b Ten years from now, people trying to fix their cars **won't be looking** at repair manuals.
c They **will be wearing** a device that projects animated 3-D computer graphics onto the equipment under repair.
d In ten years' time this device **will have been replaced** by contact lenses etched with LEDs.
e But in our new AR worlds, how **will we be interacting** with each other?

> **▶ FUTURE CONTINUOUS and FUTURE PERFECT**
>
> **Future continuous**
> *We will be using...*
> *We won't (will not) be using...*
> *Will we be using...?*
> **Future perfect**
> *We will have used...*
> *We won't (will not) have used...*
> *Will we have used...?*
>
> For more information and practice, see page 160.

6 Look at the grammar box. Complete the predictions (1–10) by putting the verb in the future continuous or future perfect.
Ten years from now:

1 very few people in the developed world .... (use) credit cards because cell phone payment .... (replace) them.
2 people .... (sit) in front of traditional computers much less than they do now.
3 data security .... (become) a huge issue because mobile devices will store so much personal information.
4 advertisers .... (put) their ads on mobile devices instead of in traditional media like TV, magazines, etc.
5 we .... (get) used to ads which target us directly with personalized messages.
6 body sensors connected to our mobile devices .... (provide) us with real-time information about our health.
7 the problem of short battery life .... (disappear) because phones and mobile devices .... (use) more sophisticated power sources, like kinetic energy.
8 cell phones .... (become) very sophisticated, so that in addition to using them as a calendar, address book, and music player, you .... (also / use) them as your secretary, accountant, and lawyer.
9 everyone .... (use) universal translators in their cell phones, which will make language learning less necessary.
10 it is unlikely that we .... (find) a way to use technology to know exactly where people are, because legally it is so difficult.

Speaking

7 Work in groups. Discuss the predictions for mobile technology in Exercise 6 and decide which ones you think will come true and which not. Then make two more predictions of your own.

3c One size doesn't fit all

Reading

1 What does the term "one size fits all" mean about a product? What products could it be applied to?

2 Read the article once quickly. Are the facts about appropriate technology true (T) or false (F)?

1 It's simple technology.
2 It's used in developing countries.
3 It improves people's lives.

3 Find a phrase in the article that defines what "appropriate technology" means these days. What does the author say about this?

4 Work in pairs. Discuss what each of these devices is and what it's an example of according to the author.

a central heating system	a solar-powered lamp
a device for shelling corn	a water purifier
a sewing machine	an efficient stove

5 Look at these phrases in bold from the article. Then choose the correct definition of the sentence.

1 in a way that **empowered** them (para 1)
gave them more *energy* / *control*
2 **intermediate** technology solutions (para 2)
temporary / *not too complicated* solutions
3 **has its place** in the developed world (para 3)
can also *be useful* / *be found* in
4 a way to **harness** the energy (para 4)
a way to *convert* / *make use* of the energy
5 they **valued** the time (para 5)
they *appreciated* / *calculated* the time
6 **gas-guzzling** cars (para 6)
cars that consume *a lot of gas* / *little gas*

Critical thinking balancing arguments

6 What are the potential risks and benefits associated with appropriate technology? Find the arguments in the article and make notes.

7 Work in pairs. Compare your answers. Is the author in favor of appropriate technology or not?

Vocabulary useful devices

8 Complete the definitions with these adjectives.

appropriate	easy	efficient	long-term
renewable	useful	old	

1 It's a very **neat** solution: both clever and *appropriate* .
2 It's a **time-consuming process**. We need to find a solution that's more ________ .
3 We don't just want a **quick fix**; we want a ________ solution.
4 It's a **handy gadget**, much more ________ than an average penknife.
5 It's not **cutting-edge technology**, but often the ________ ways are the best.
6 It's essentially a **labor-saving device**; it makes cutting up wood very ________ .
7 It's an **environmentally-friendly product** because it's made from ________ materials.

9 Work in pairs. Tell your partner about your favorite device or gadget using one of the expressions in Exercise 8.

Speaking

10 Work in pairs. Complete the sentences (1–8) using these phrases. What is each product?

6 hours	about 4 pounds
6 people	light and a little heat
only $3.10	put up in a few minutes
solar power	strong nylon

Product 1
1 It can hold up to…
2 It's made of…
3 It can be…
4 It weighs…

Product 2
5 It runs on…
6 It lasts up to…
7 It costs…
8 It provides…

11 Work in groups. You are going to take part in a competition: "Best appropriate technology product of the year." Your group will have to present one of the products shown below. Look at the instructions on page 153.

one size doesn't fit all

Even if the term "appropriate technology" is a relatively new one, the concept certainly isn't. In the 1930s, Mahatma Gandhi claimed that the advanced technology used by Western industrialized nations did not represent the right route to progress for his homeland, India. His favorite machines were the sewing machine, a device invented "out of love," he said, and the bicycle, which he rode all his life. He wanted the poor villagers of India to use technology that empowered them and helped them to become self-reliant.

This was also the philosophy promoted by E. F. Schumacher in his famous 1970s book *Small Is Beautiful*, which called for "intermediate technology" solutions. Do not start with technology and see what it can do for people, he argued. Instead, "find out what people are doing and then help them to do it better." According to Schumacher, it did not matter whether the technological answers to people's needs were simple or sophisticated. What was important was that solutions were long-term, practical, and, above all, firmly in the hands of the users.

More recently, the term "appropriate technology" has come to mean not just technology which is suited to the needs and capabilities of the user, but technology that takes particular account of environmental, ethical, and cultural considerations. That is clearly a much more difficult thing to achieve. Often it is found in rural communities in developing or less industrialized countries. For example, solar-powered lamps that bring light to areas with no electricity and water purifiers that work simply by the action of sucking through a straw. But the principle of appropriate technology does not only apply to developing countries. It also has its place in the developed world.

For example, a Swedish state-owned company has found a way to harness the energy produced by the 250,000 bodies rushing through Stockholm's central train station each day. The body heat is absorbed by the building's ventilation system, then used to warm up water that is pumped through pipes over to the new office building nearby. It's old technology, a system of pipes, water, and pumps, but used in a new way. It is expected to bring down central heating costs in the building by up to 20 percent.

Wherever it is deployed, there is no guarantee, however, that appropriate technology will in fact be appropriate. After some visiting engineers observed how labor-intensive and slow it was for the women of a Guatemalan village to shell corn by hand, they designed a simple mechanical device to do the job more quickly. The new device certainly saved time, but after a few weeks the women returned to the old manual method. Why? Because they valued the time that hand-shelling gave them to chat and exchange news.

In another case, in Malawi, a local entrepreneur was encouraged to manufacture super-efficient wood-burning stoves to sell to local villagers. Burning wood in an open fire, which is traditional in the developing world, is responsible for 10–20 percent of all global CO_2 emissions, so this seemed to be an excellent scheme. However, the entrepreneur was so successful that he bought himself a whole fleet of gas-guzzling cars. "We haven't worked out the CO_2 implications of that yet," said a spokesman for the organization that promoted the scheme.

3d Computer problems

Real life asking for and offering technical help

1 Work in pairs. Ask and answer the questions.

1 How are your computer skills?
2 Can you use the following applications proficiently?

- a search engine (like Google)
- spreadsheets (like Microsoft Excel)
- a presentation slide show (like PowerPoint)
- photo editing (like Photoshop)
- word processing (like Microsoft Word)

2 Where do you turn for computer help? Do people turn to you?

3 **10** Listen to a conversation about a computer problem. What is Ben trying to do? What two possible solutions does Sophie propose?

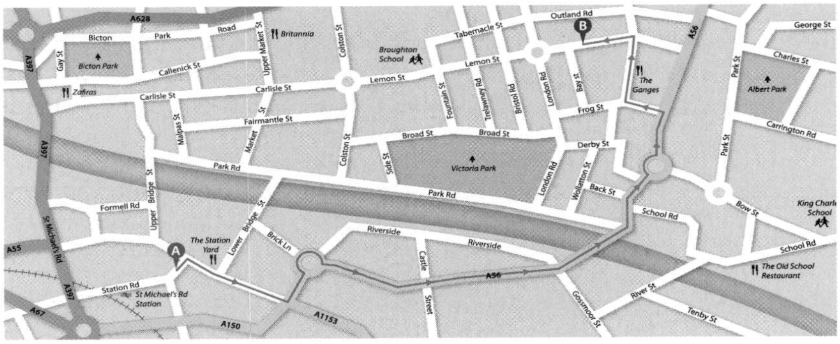

4 **10** Listen again and complete sentences 1–10.

ASKING FOR AND OFFERING TECHNICAL HELP

Person in need of help	Helper
Can you give me a hand? I'm having trouble 1 ______ .	OK. What do you want to do exactly?
I'm trying to 2 ______ .	You could just 3 ______ .
The trouble is 4 ______ .	Let me take a look.
What should I do then?	There are two possibilities. You can either 5 ______ or…
What does that involve?	I'll show you. Just 6 ______ . That should do the trick.
I see, but 7 ______ . What else do you suggest?	Have you tried 8 ______ ? If you do a search, you might 9 ______ .
OK I'll give that a try.	Feel free to 10 ______ .

5 **Pronunciation stress in two-syllable verbs**

a **11** Work in pairs. Listen for these phrases and note how the stress in the two-syllable verbs falls on the second syllable. Then practice saying them.

What do you suggest?
What does that involve?
It won't allow me to copy it.
First select the picture,…
What are you trying to achieve?
What solution do you propose?
Did you attach the document?

b Think of two more two-syllable verbs. Put them into a phrase or sentence. Then tell another pair your words.

6 Choose one of the tasks below or think of a technical problem that you have had. Then roleplay a conversation similar to the one in Exercise 4. Use the box to help you. Begin like this:

Can you help me? I'm trying to edit this photo.

I'll try. What do you want to do exactly?

- editing a photo of a person (to leave only the head and shoulders)
- sorting a list of names (members of a club you are the secretary of) alphabetically from A–Z
- adding your comments to someone else's document (a report written by a colleague)
- making your presentation slides more interesting (they are just plain text for now)
- searching the Internet to get the right information (such as up-to-date news about smart technology)

3e A technical problem

Writing short email requests

1 Match the emails (1–4) with the correct reply (A–D) below. Answer the questions.

1 What is the relationship between the correspondents in each case?
2 What help is offered in response to each request?

2 Writing skill being polite

a How polite you are depends on your relationship to your correspondent and on what you are asking for. Underline the phrases used to make polite requests in emails 1–4 and the polite forms used to apologize in emails A–D.

b Now answer the questions.

1 What word is used for more formal requests?
2 What is the difference between *can you* and *could you*?
3 Is *would you mind* more or less direct than *could you please*?
4 What is a more formal way of saying *I'm sorry*?

3 Word focus *out of*

a Work in pairs. Circle the expressions with *out of* in the emails and discuss what you think they mean. Then compare your answers with another pair.

b Complete these other expressions with *out of* using the words given.

blue   date   hands   luck   order   time

1 I've done all I can to get them to change their decision. It's out of my ________ now.
2 She is still in shock after losing her job; the news came out of the ________.
3 I'm afraid that printer is out of ________. You'll have to use the one in the next office.
4 This information is out of ________. It has last year's numbers on it, not this year's.
5 I'm sorry we are out of ________. Let's continue the discussion tomorrow.
6 You're out of ________, I'm afraid. We sold the last one an hour ago.

4 Look at the following situation and write a short email requesting help.

You buy two cartridges for your printer online, but when they arrive you notice that the expiration date on them has already passed. Write and ask for replacements to be sent.

5 Exchange emails with your partner. Use these questions to check your partner's email. Then write a reply.

- Are the situation and the action demanded clear?
- Is the email in the right tone (formal or informal) and polite in its request?

1 Three months ago I bought one of your X3000 digital cameras from a store that has since gone out of business. The camera is fine but I cannot find the user manual. Could you please tell me where I can find one? I've looked on the Internet, but without success. Thank you.

2 I bought a printer at your store only five weeks ago and the pages are coming out very light. I am very disappointed and would like to return it and get a new one. Can you please tell me how?

3 Thanks a lot for the advice with the car, Jim. I changed the air filter and it's running much better now. Just out of curiosity, do you happen to know anything else I could do to improve its performance? Let me know!

4 Would you mind stopping by and having a look at my bike sometime? It's making a strange noise. I'd be really grateful. Please don't go out of your way, though. Anytime in the next week is fine.

A Sorry, I'd love to help, but I'm going on vacation tomorrow for three weeks. Why not take it to Cycle Surgery on Main Street? They know their stuff.

B I am sorry, but an exchange is out of the question. It is too long after the original purchase date. However, from what you say, it may be that it is just out of ink. Please check the ink cartridges. If that does not work, contact our technical team for further advice.

C I'm afraid I'm out of my depth there. Try looking at the discussion boards on the Internet for your particular model. I'm sure someone'll know.

D I regret to say that we only supply user manuals with the equipment at the time of purchase. However, you can download one using the link below.

3f Augmented reality

Video

It's a relationship all built on numbers and hard work.

Before you watch

1 Work in groups. Look at the picture and discuss the questions.

1 What do you know about augmented reality?
2 Where do you think the man in the picture is?
3 What is he wearing? Why?
4 What do you think the caption means?

2 How do you think a headset like this could be used? Work in pairs and write down three things you think you could use it for.

While you watch

3 Watch the video and check your ideas from Exercise 2. Which three groups of people does the video say could benefit from this technology?

4 Watch the video again and correct these sentences.

1 Professor Feiner is working with a group of biology students.

……………………………………

2 The team wants to develop a virtual world that is separate from the physical world.

……………………………………

3 The virtual world can provide extra information about what you feel.

……………………………………

4 A global positioning system allows the team to use the equipment in the laboratory.

……………………………………

5 The system wouldn't be very useful for people to find their way around places they don't know well.

……………………………………

6 Professor Feiner developed the technology because he has a bad sense of smell.

……………………………………

5 Watch the video again and answer the questions.

1 What is the Columbia University program trying to do?

……………………………………

2 How could these people use this technology?
a firefighters ……………………
b pilots ……………………
c tourists ……………………

3 What do you think a "situated documentary" is?

……………………………………

4 What would visitors to the campus "see" in addition to the library?

……………………………………

After you watch

6 Roleplay an interview with Professor Feiner

Work in pairs. Use the information in the list.

Student A: Imagine you are a reporter for the Columbia University newspaper. Prepare a list of questions to ask Professor Feiner.

Student B: Imagine you are Professor Feiner. You are going to be interviewed for the Columbia University newspaper. Think about what you are going to say to the reporter.

- when you started the project
- how many students work with you
- what the technology could be used for
- what you have to do in the laboratory
- why you decided to do research on augmented reality
- how you think the technology could be advanced in the future

Act out the interview. Then change roles and act out the interview again.

7 Work in pairs and discuss these questions.

1 Have you ever seen or used any of the following devices?

- simulators for learning to drive
- night vision glasses for seeing in the dark
- billboard ads that speak to pedestrians
- Wii™ games
- T-shirts with moving images

2 How useful do you think they are?
3 What are the advantages and disadvantages of augmented reality technology?

asylum (n) /əˈsaɪləm/ a hospital for mentally ill patients
blueprints (n) /ˈbluˌprɪnts/ building plans
cockpit (n) /ˈkɑkˌpɪt/ place in an airplane where the pilot sits
handheld (adj) /ˈhændˌheld/ carried in the hand
obscure (v) /əbˈskjʊr/ hide
overlay (v) /ˌoʊvərˈleɪ/ show on top of
prototype (n) /ˈproʊtəˌtaɪp/ an experimental working model
superimpose (v) /ˌsupərɪmˈpoʊz/ put one image on top of another
surroundings (n) /səˈraʊndɪŋz/ the area around something or someone

UNIT 3 REVIEW

Grammar

1 Work in pairs. Name at least three of the global problems mentioned in the unit.

2 Look at the photo. What global problems could these windmills be the answer to?

3 Read the text and answer the questions.

1. What is the problem the author mentions?
2. What should be our target if we want to solve the problem?
3. How can we achieve this target?
4. Why are windmills not a solution?

4 Choose the correct option.

Reducing CO_2 emissions is perhaps the world's biggest problem. If we [1] *won't reduce / don't reduce* our emissions to almost zero, global temperatures [2] *will continue / are continuing* to rise. At the current rate, temperatures [3] *will be increasing / will have increased* by three or four degrees by 2050.

CO_2 emissions [4] *will come / are about to come* down if one of three things [5] *happens / will happen*. First, if we change our lifestyles and stop using electricity; second, if the gadgets we use don't need energy; or third, if we find a way to generate electricity without producing CO_2.

Well, people [6] *are not stopping / are not going to stop* using electricity. If anything, in 30 years' time, they [7] *will be using / will have used* more. Perhaps in the future, gadgets [8] *will consume / will be consuming* less energy, but certainly not zero energy.

That leaves only one possibility. Scientists [9] *are having / will have* to find a way to generate CO_2-free electricity. Wind and solar power are only intermittent energy sources. What miracle invention [10] *will be generating / will have generated* our electricity in 2050? No one knows, but the miracle will need to happen soon.

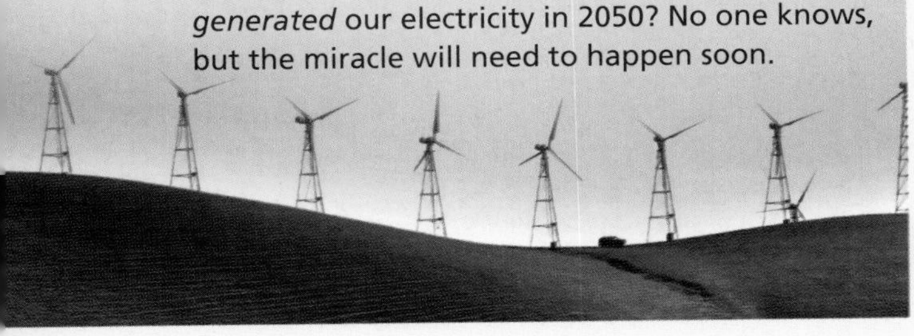

I CAN	
talk about future events, intentions, and arrangements using a variety of future forms	☐
make predictions using the future continuous and future perfect	☐

Vocabulary

5 Read the definitions. Complete the words. The first letter has been given for you.

1. too much information = information o__________
2. a big advance in science = a technological b__________
3. technology suited to its context = a__________ technology
4. a clever answer to a problem = a n__________ solution
5. a useful device = a h__________ gadget
6. a fast, easy solution to a problem = a quick f__________

6 Work in small groups and answer these questions.

1. Which of these problems do you think technology will solve? Why?

epidemics	overpopulation	pollution	starvation

2. In what area will new technology most change people's lives in the next 50 years?

I CAN	
talk about global problems and solutions	☐
talk about new technology: devices and gadgets	☐

Real life

7 Match each statement or question (1–5) with the correct response (a–e).

1. Can you give me a hand?
2. What do you want to do exactly?
3. If you restart the computer, that should do the trick.
4. What else do you suggest?
5. The trouble is the computer won't allow me to copy it.

a. Have you tried looking for another type of map?
b. Thanks. I'll give that a try.
c. Sure. I'll be with you in a second.
d. Let me have a look.
e. I'm trying to paste this map into a document.

8 Work in pairs. Act out a conversation asking for help with a computer problem.

I CAN	
ask for and give technical help	☐
talk about computing tasks	☐

Speaking

9 Work in pairs. Tell each other your predictions for your life (education, job, where you will live, travel, relationships, etc.). Use the future continuous and future perfect to talk about:

- a year from now
- three years from now
- ten years from now

10 Change partners and tell each other your original partner's predictions.

Unit 4 Art and creativity

A juggler in Scotland performs at dusk.
Photograph by Emanuele Picchirallo

FEATURES

1 Work in pairs. Match the performers with what and where they perform. How many combinations can you make?

Example:

a dance company + a performance + a theater

Who: a band, a comedian, a dance company, a circus act, a drama company, an orchestra, an artist

What: a gig, a show, an exhibition, a classical concert, a play, a musical, a performance

Where: a concert hall, a live music venue, a theater, a gallery, a club, the street

2 Look at the photo and caption. Which words from Exercise 1 can describe what is happening? Have you seen anything like this in your country?

3 What's your favorite type of performance? What performance do you dislike? Tell a partner.

4a All about Melbourne

Listening

1 Work in pairs. Ask and answer the questions.

1. What art forms are popular in your city or country: theater, dance, music, movies, art (like painting and sculpture)?
2. Which of the arts have you practiced yourself?
3. Which of the arts do you follow?
4. Can you describe an exhibition or a performance that you've enjoyed recently?

2 Discuss what type of activities and opportunities Australia offers visitors and tourists.

3 **12** Listen to part of *The Travel Show*, a weekly radio program, about Melbourne, and answer the questions.

1. What is the essential difference between Melbourne and Sydney?
2. What does Melbourne offer visitors?
3. What does it offer local people? What do they enjoy in their free time?

4 **12** Listen again and mark the statements true (T) or false (F).

1. Melbourne has great weather and many places of natural beauty.
2. It is known as Australia's architectural capital.
3. The arts are enjoyed by a small number of art lovers.
4. The summer is a good time for festivals.
5. Melbourne's Formula One motor race and tennis tournament are world famous.
6. Not many visitors know about the local sports.

5 Would you like to visit Melbourne after hearing this guide? What would you do there?

Grammar expressions of quantity

6 Turn to the audioscript on page 176. Find the examples of the items below. Make a note of which expressions have *of* after them and which don't. Then compare your list with your partner.

- expressions in the script that mean "many or much"
- expressions that mean "not many or much"
- expressions that mean "some"

▶ EXPRESSIONS OF QUANTITY

+ plural count noun
(not) many, (a) few, a (small) number of, several
+ noncount noun
(not) much, (a) little (of), a/an (large) amount of
+ plural count or noncount noun
a lot of, lots of, plenty of, loads of, lack of, (almost) no, (not/hardly) any, some, enough

For more information and practice, see page 161.

7 Look at the grammar box. Then read the pairs of sentences and answer the questions.

1 Which expression means "some" and which means "only a small number of"?
   a **Few** people will be familiar with it.
   b Melbourne may have **a few** gray days.
2 Can you use the same expression in both sentences?
   a In fact there are **hardly any** forms of artistic expression that are not represented.
   b In fact there are **almost no** forms of artistic expression that are not represented.
3 Which expression is used more often in affirmative sentences?
   a **Lots of** people around the world know the Australian Formula One Grand Prix.
   b But there **aren't many** people who know Australian Rules football.
4 Which expression is used with count nouns?
   a Art enjoys **an enormous amount of** support.
   b There are **a huge number of** smaller art spaces and venues.
5 Which expression is used in negative sentences?
   a There is **a lot of** information on what to do in Melbourne on the website.
   b There **isn't much** information about where to eat on the website.

8 Choose the correct option to complete each sentence.

1 A visit to the opera can cost *much / a lot of* money.
2 A reasonable *number / amount* of the winter festivals are free.
3 There is almost *no / any* rain in Melbourne at Christmastime.
4 There are *few / a few* tickets for the Australian Open Tennis available at the gate.
5 We saw *several / some* interesting street art at the Sweet Streets festival.
6 *Almost / Hardly* anyone attended the play.
7 Visitors show *a little / little* interest in dance.
8 There aren't as *many / much* differences between Melbourne and Sydney as people say.

9 Pronunciation **weak form: *of***

a 13 Listen and note how *of* is pronounced in these phrases.

a huge amount of support	a lot of information
a huge number of galleries	lots of people
a lack of natural attractions	

b Work in pairs. Practice saying these phrases where *of* is a weak form.

as a matter of fact	just the two of us
first of all	most of the time
in spite of that	of course
instead of me	that's nice of you

10 Work in pairs. Look at the charts on page 153 showing the results of a survey on Australians' participation in the arts. Complete the sentences using one word to describe what they show.

1 Overall quite a *lot* of Australians take an interest in the arts, but only a ________ participate creatively.
2 It seems that ________ of Australians read literature and a surprising ________ of them also write creatively.
3 There is certainly ________ lack of interest in the visual arts, with almost half of the population being involved in some way.
4 ________ attend concerts or musicals and ________ anyone did not listen to music at all.
5 The main reason for not participating is not having ________ time. But the ________ of money it costs to be involved and a ________ of opportunities are also important factors.

Speaking

11 Work in groups. Research your classmates' participation in the arts and then report your findings. Follow these steps:

- Each group must research ONE of the following: visual arts and crafts, theater and dance, reading and writing, music.
- Make a list of four or five questions to find out how people participate (creatively or receptively) and reasons for non-participation.
- Go around the class asking and answering questions.
- Come back to your group and share your results. Make conclusions, using expressions of quantity.
- Present your findings to the class.

4b Reverse graffiti

Listening

1 **14** Look at the statements about art. Do you agree with any of them? Listen to an artist's opinion and write down what he says about each one.

1 Art should be pleasing to the viewer.
2 Art should involve effort on the part of the artist.
3 Art should involve technical skill.
4 Art should have a social message or make a political point.

2 **14** Listen again. What are the roles of an artist and a viewer according to the speaker?

3 Work in pairs. Discuss what each of these types of artwork is.

graffiti landscape sculpture sketch

▶ WORDBUILDING suffixes

Some noun suffixes have no clear meaning (*-ment*, *-tion*). Others like *-scape* have a particular meaning: *cityscape, landscape, seascape, moonscape*

REVERSE GRAFFITI

When is cleaning walls a crime? When you're doing it to create art, obviously. A number of street artists around the world have started expressing themselves through a practice known as reverse graffiti. Inspired by the "clean me" messages that you see written on the back of some trucks, they find dirty surfaces and inscribe them with images or messages using cleaning brushes or pressure hoses. Either way, it's the same principle: the image is made by cleaning away the dirt.

Each artist has an individual style, but all artists share a common aim: to draw attention to pollution in our cities. The UK's Paul Curtis, better known as Moose, operates around Leeds and has been commissioned by a number of companies to make reverse graffiti ads.

Brazilian artist Alexandre Orion turned one of São Paulo's traffic tunnels into an amazing mural by scraping away the dirt. Made up of a series of white skulls, the mural reminds drivers of the effect their pollution is having on the planet. "Every driver sits in the comfort of a car, but they don't give any consideration to the price their comfort has for the environment and consequently for themselves," says Orion.

The anti-pollution message of the reverse graffiti artists confuses city authorities since the main argument against graffiti is that it spoils the appearance of both public and private property. This was what Leeds City Council said about Moose's work: "Leeds residents want to live in clean and attractive neighborhoods. We view this kind of advertising as environmental damage and will take strong action against any advertisers carrying out such campaigns." It seems that no action was taken against the advertisers—no fines or any other punishment—but Moose himself was ordered to clean up his act. Was he supposed to make all the property he had cleaned dirty again?

As for Orion, the authorities were annoyed but could find nothing to charge him with. They had no other option but to clean the tunnel—but only the parts Orion had already cleaned. The artist merely continued his campaign on the other side. The city officials then decided to take drastic action. They not only cleaned the whole tunnel but also every other tunnel in São Paulo.

Reading

4 What do you think about graffiti in cities? Do you think it improves or spoils the appearance of the urban landscape?

5 What do you think *reverse graffiti* is? Read the article and check.

6 Use the information in the article to complete these sentences. Use one word per space.

1 Reverse graffiti works by cleaning away the .... on walls.
2 The aim of the reverse graffiti artists is to highlight the problem of ....
3 Some reverse graffiti artists are paid to make images that act as ....
4 Orion made his message for ....
5 The local authorities in Leeds were .... by this new type of graffiti.
6 In São Paulo, the response of the authorities was to .... every tunnel.

7 Work in pairs. Discuss the questions.

1 Do you like this kind of graffiti?
2 If you were a city authority, how would you deal with reverse graffiti in your city?

Grammar **determiners**

8 Work in pairs. Look at the highlighted words in the article and decide if the nouns that come after each are singular, plural, or noncount.

▶ DETERMINERS

each, every, either, the whole + singular noun
all, both + plural noun
any, no + singular or plural noun
all, any, no + noncount noun

For more information and practice, see page 161.

9 Look at the grammar box. Answer the questions.

1 Which determiner emphasizes the individual?
  a **Every** artist has an individual style.
  b **Each** artist has an individual style.
  c **All** artists have an individual style.

2 Which determiner(s) talk about two things?
  a **Every** way, it's the same principle.
  b **Either** way, it's the same principle.
  c **Both** ways, it's the same principle.

3 Which sentence(s) about the action taken against advertisers are negative?
  a They took **no** action against them.
  b They didn't take **any** action against them.
  c Did they take **any** action against them?

10 Choose the correct option. Sometimes there is more than one possibility.

"*Every / all / each* child is an artist. The problem is how to remain an artist once he grows up. *Pablo Picasso, artist*

Every / all / each art is an imitation of nature. *Seneca, philosopher and writer*

Drawing is the honesty of the art. There is *any / no* possibility of cheating. It is either good or bad. *Salvador Dali, artist*

As an artist you want it *both / either / every* ways. You want it to have an immediate impact, and deep meaning as well. *Damien Hirst, artist*

Some days I produce something, other days nothing. *Each / Every / Either* way, I feel it's time well spent. *Anonymous, artist*

Science and art belong to *all / the whole / every* world, and before them vanish the barriers of nationality. *Goethe, writer*

Let *each / every / all* man exercise the art he knows. *Aristophanes, dramatist*

Do not fear mistakes; there aren't *no / any*. *Miles Davis, musician*"

11 Discuss the quotations. How do they fit with the definitions of art that you discussed earlier?

12 Complete the rules for an art prize with a determiner.

1 .... candidates are chosen for an exhibition they have given in the last year.
2 Candidates are nominated by the public or by the jury. .... way, the jury has the final say in the four who are shortlisted.
3 The aim of the prize is to celebrate .... innovation and young talent.
4 .... candidate is invited to display examples of their work at the exhibition.
5 .... artist over 50 years can enter.
6 The artists can use .... medium they like.
7 The winner receives $25,000. .... other shortlisted candidates get $5,000.

Speaking

13 Your city would like to commission a piece of art that would (a) improve the appearance of the downtown area; (b) be fun; and (c) attract visitors. Work in small groups and:

- discuss what you want and who should make it
- make a list of rules for the competition

14 Exchange your rules with another group. Then submit an idea for piece of art to be evaluated.

4c Hip-hop planet

Reading

1 Work in pairs. Look at the different music genres in the box. Discuss the questions.

1 How often do you listen to each type of music?
2 When you listen, do you pay much attention to the lyrics?
3 Do you identify strongly with this type of music?

blues	classical
country	hip-hop
jazz	pop
reggae	rock
soul	traditional / folk

2 Discuss what themes or attitudes you associate with hip-hop and rap music. Who do you think listens to this music? Then read the article and compare your answers with what the author says.

3 Read the article again quickly. Answer the questions.

1 What was the theme of the first rap song the author heard?
2 Aside from music, what are other artistic expressions of hip-hop culture?
3 What do the DJs do to create hip-hop's individual sound?
4 What is the appeal of hip-hop to middle-class children?
5 Why does Assane say that rap belongs to his country?
6 What does the author not like about hip-hop music?

4 Explain these phrases.

1 It sounded like a broken record (para 1)
2 the way you step over a crack in the pavement (para 2)
3 life on the other side of the tracks (para 4)
4 its macho pose (para 6)
5 the empty moral cupboard that we have left our children (para 7)

Critical thinking analyzing contrasts

5 This article is all about what hip-hop is and isn't. Find and underline sentences that tell you:

1 a what the author thought of rap music 26 years ago
b what he thinks now
2 a the environment in which rap music originated
b where it thrives now
3 a the message conveyed by the early rappers
b the message conveyed by successful hip-hop artists now
4 a that hip-hop culture can seem selfish
b that this selfishness in young people is not their fault

6 Work in pairs. Compare your answers, then write a short summary of the values of hip-hop culture, according to the author. Do you agree with him?

Word focus *cool*

7 *Cool* has a few meanings in English: (1) not warm; (2) stylish and fashionable; (3) calm; (4) OK. Which meaning does it have in the article (para 5) and in sentences 1–6?

1 I don't know what I've done to offend Liz. She was really **cool with** me when I spoke to her earlier.
2 It's not **cool** to arrive early at a party like that.
3 Jaime **lost his cool** completely when his computer froze.
4 That's a really **cool** jacket. Where did you get it?
5 I think she did very well to **keep her cool** with that customer. I would have gotten very angry with them.
6 Wait for the frying pan to **cool down** before you add more oil.

Speaking

8 Work in pairs. Look at the lyrics below. What themes and attitudes to life can you identify in each genre?

Country song

When you ain't got a friend to lean on
There are folks you can depend on
Home, that's where you turn to
Family won't turn their back on you
Yeah, it's all right there in your own backyard
They'll be waitin' when times are hard

Rock song

Ooh, be true to yourself
Don't let anyone put you down
If you feel you're getting tied
Then ride right on out of town
Don't be nobody's slave
Live your life—that's what I say

9 Look at the genres in Exercise 1 and discuss the questions.

1 What values does each genre project?
2 Do you have to believe these values to like the music?

HIP-HOP PLANET

BY JAMES MCBRIDE

I first heard rap in 1980, at a party in Harlem. It sounded like a broken record. It was a version of an old hit record called *Good Times*, the same four bars looped over and over. On top of this loop, a kid chanted a rhyme about how he was the best disc jockey in the world. It was called *Rapper's Delight*. I thought it was the most ridiculous thing I'd ever heard.

For the next 26 years, I avoided rap music the way you step over a crack in the pavement. I heard it booming out of cars and alleyways from Paris to Abidjan, but I never listened. In doing so, I missed the most important cultural event in my lifetime. No American music has exploded across the world with such force since swing jazz in the 1930s. This defiant culture of song, graffiti, and dance, collectively known as hip-hop, has permeated almost every society.

Hip-hop began in the mid-1970s, in an almost bankrupt New York City. The bored kids of the South Bronx and Harlem came up with a new entertainment. This is how it worked: one guy, the DJ, played records on two turntables. Another guy—or girl—served as master of ceremonies, or MC. The DJs learned to move the record back and forth under the needle to create a *scratch*, or to drop the needle on the record and play *a break* over and over to keep people dancing. The MCs rapped over the music to keep the party going. One MC sought to out-talk the other. Dance styles were created. Graffiti artists also emphasized the *I* because the music was all about identity: I am the best.

Initially, hip-hop artists produced socially-conscious songs that described life on the other side of the tracks, where people are denied the same opportunities as the rich. Grandmaster Flash's 1982 hit *The Message* is a perfect example. They describe a child who is born and raised in the ghetto, hating the world for his situation and all the things he cannot have.

These days most commercial rappers in America brag about their lives of crime and what fame and money have brought them, among which women seem to be just another material possession. For those from poor backgrounds, the life of a successful rapper has become an aspiration; for richer suburban kids, it is a symbol of something cool.

In poor urban communities around the globe, rap music is a universal expression of outrage at the injustice of the distribution of wealth. Its macho pose has been borrowed from commercial hip-hop in the US, but for most, the music represents an old dream: a better life. "We want money to help our parents," Assane, a nineteen-year-old budding DJ from Dakar in Senegal, tells me. "We watch our mothers boil water to cook and have nothing to put in the pot. Rap doesn't belong to American culture," he says. "It belongs here. It has always existed here, because of our pain and our hardships and our suffering."

That is why, after 26 years, I have come to embrace this music I tried so hard to ignore. Much of hip-hop, particularly the commercial side, I hate. Yet I love the good of it. Even if some of it embraces violence, hip-hop is a music that exposes the empty moral cupboard that we have left our children. They can hear it and understand it. The question is: can we?

brag (v) /bræg/ speak proudly about your achievements
defiant (adj) /dɪˈfaɪənt/ challenging or opposing another's authority
looped (adj) /lupt/ repeated without a break
out-talk (v) /ˌaʊt ˈtɔk/ talk longer or better than another

4d Personal tastes

Real life describing likes and dislikes

1 Do you like musicals? Which ones have you seen? Did you see them live or on film? Tell your partner.

2 🔊 **15** Listen to a conversation in which Tomas and Jae talk about the musical *The Lion King*. Put a check (✓) next to the items they both like and an ✗ next to those they don't.

ticket prices	☐	the music	☐
Disney comic characters	☐	the visual effects	☐
Elton John	☐	this production	☐
musicals in general	☐		

3 🔊 **15** Look at the box. Tell your partner which of the phrases Tomas used to express each like and dislike. Then listen again and check.

▶ DESCRIBING LIKES AND DISLIKES

Likes	Dislikes
I love…	I can't stand…
I'm a big fan of…	I'm not generally a fan of…
I'm really into…	I'm not very big on…
It is very inspiring.	…doesn't really do anything for me
It sounds right up my alley.	I never feel particularly/ especially inspired by…
I could watch / read / listen to… all day.	It doesn't really sound like my kind of thing.
	…really gets on my nerves
	I get a little tired of…

4 Work in pairs. Look at these sentences and say which words most naturally go in each space.

1 I'm not .... big on romantic comedies.
2 I get .... tired of reality TV shows.
3 I never feel .... inspired by science fiction books.
4 I'm not .... a fan of musicals.
5 Rap doesn't .... do anything for me.
6 I'm afraid opera gets on my ....

5 Work in pairs. Tell each other about something (a type of music, characters in a book or a movie, a particular ad) that you dislike. Use the phrases in Exercise 3 to help you. Do you share each other's dislikes?

6 Now work in groups. Each of you think of a musical, play, movie, concert, TV show, or exhibition you enjoyed recently. Describe it to the group and compare and discuss your likes and dislikes. Use the box to help you.

I'm a big fan of Star Trek and I loved the last movie!

Really? I can't stand science fiction!

4e You have to see this

Writing an online review

1 Read the online review of an exhibition by a recent visitor to London. Would you follow the recommendation? Why?

2 Answer the questions. Then compare your answers in pairs.

1 How are the following themes organized in the review? Put them in order (1–5).
- the recommendation
- an introduction
- the content of the exhibition
- the occasion of the visit
- where and when it is on

2 What information about the event does she include?
3 Is the tone of the review personal or impersonal?

3 Writing skill **personalizing your writing**

a Work in pairs. Look at the following features of personal and impersonal writing. Then find examples of the personal tone in the review.

Personal tone
- use pronouns
- use active verbs
- use contracted forms
- use phrasal verbs
- add personal details
- use conversational linking phrases (like *what's more*)
- share your feelings

Impersonal tone
- use pronouns
- use passive verbs
- use uncontracted forms
- use formal verbs
- avoids personal information
- use formal linking phrases (like *furthermore*)
- be objective in your judgments

http://www.travelreviews.com

I find that it's always worth checking out the parks when you visit a foreign city. Besides providing a welcome break, they can contain some interesting surprises. Last week, exhausted from visiting two museums and too tired even to think about shopping anymore, my friend and I took a walk in Kensington Gardens. I was so glad we did, because otherwise we'd have missed Anish Kapoor's mirror sculptures.

There are four of them, and rather than looking out of place as so many modern sculptures can, these really complemented their surroundings.

Sky Mirror, as its name suggests, is placed at an angle to reflect the changing sky. Another, Red Mirror, is also directed at the sky but has a red tint. The one I liked best was the C-Curve, a convex mirror that makes you see everything upside down. It was so funny to watch dogs and children approach it, trying to figure out what they were looking at.

The secret of this exhibition's success is that it makes you appreciate what is already a lovely park even more. It will be on display until March 30th. I'd definitely recommend taking the time to go and see it for yourself if you're in London. What's more, it's free!

4 Write a brief, personalized review of something for a website. Then exchange your review with another person in the class.

5 Read your partner's review. Check that it:
- makes you want to go and see this event.
- includes all the items described in Exercise 2 in their correct order.
- feels friendly and personal.
- includes features from Exercise 3.

4f Urban art

Video

Urban art is all about innovation.

Grammar verb + infinitive or *-ing*

4 Complete the sentences from the article.

1 Sheikh Rashid imagined .... a gateway to the world.
2 It was a dream Sheikh Rashid could not afford ....
3 In 1959, he asked .... him some money.
4 He helped .... the shopping capital of the Middle East.

5 Read the article again quickly and find:

1 two more verbs followed by the *-ing* form
2 two more verbs followed by infinitive
3 one more verb followed by somebody + infinitive
4 one more verb followed by the base form

▶ VERB + INFINITIVE	VERB + *-ING*
Verb + infinitive *He couldn't afford to build a new harbor.* **Verb + someone + infinitive** *He asked a friend to lend him some money.* **Verb + someone + base form** *He helped Dubai become a great city.*	**Verb + *-ing*** *He imagined building an amazing city.*

For more information and practice, see page 162.

6 Fill in the blanks with the right form.

1 The population of Dubai grew from half a million in 1990 to 1.5 million in 2008 and has kept on .... (grow) to this day.
2 Sheikh al Maktoum decided .... (make) Dubai the region's most important financial center.
3 Attracting foreign banks and companies involved .... (reduce) taxes for companies and individuals.
4 The expansion of the airport allowed .... (Dubai / become) the fourth busiest international airport in the world.
5 If you enjoy .... (shop), Dubai has over 70 shopping malls to choose from.
6 By planting 10,000 trees each year for the past four years, the city planners have managed .... (create) many green spaces.
7 The banking crisis made .... (construction / slow) down.
8 But it seems that Dubai can't help .... (build) more property and tourist attractions.

Vocabulary

7 Work in pairs. Make urban features by combining words in A and B.

A

green	high-rise
leisure	luxury
highway	pedestrian
shopping	waterfront

B

apartment	building
center	development
overpass	mall
spaces	zone

8 Complete the sentences with the correct forms of the verbs below. Then check your answers with your teacher.

convert	redevelop
demolish	ruin
modernize	transform

1 In the 1960s the local authority decided to .... the area as a shopping district.
2 This involved .... all the houses and making way for huge parking lots.
3 Even the residents seemed to accept that the area had to be ....
4 If you proposed .... houses into stores on such a big scale today, I don't think you would be allowed to do it.
5 The result was that they .... the city's character.
6 Now, 50 years later, the local authorities want to .... it into a mixed area again.

9 Replace the underlined words in the questions (1–6) with words from Exercise 8 that mean the same thing.

1 Have any old factories been <u>turned into</u> apartments or houses?
2 Is there an area of the town that has been <u>changed completely</u> in your lifetime?
3 Is there an area of the town that has been <u>damaged</u> by new development?
4 Do you have a transportation system that needs to be <u>brought up to date</u>?
5 What buildings were you sorry to see <u>knocked down</u>?
6 Is there a run-down area of the city that you would like to see <u>rebuilt</u>? How?

Speaking

10 Work in pairs. Ask and answer the questions in Exercise 9 about your own town.

5b The Kerala model

Listening

1 Look at the two photos taken in the Indian state of Kerala. Which of these adjectives could you use to describe each place shown?

exotic	fertile	gorgeous	hectic
prosperous	remarkable	tranquil	

2 16 Listen to an interview. What is surprising about the level of social development in Kerala?

3 16 Listen again. Are the sentences true (T) or false (F)?

1 The journalist went to Kerala to write an article.
2 Kerala has a lot of people in a small area.
3 One of the signs of Kerala's social development is the high level of education.
4 Women have a superior social position to men.
5 People in Trivandrum are too busy to be involved in politics.
6 One of the secrets of Kerala's success is the open-minded attitude of its people.

4 Convert these definitions to adjectives. Check your answers in the audioscript on page 177.

Having…
1 a good rate of literacy = *literate*
2 a good standard of living = ...-..........
3 a good education = ...-..........
4 good health = ...
5 a high level of culture = ...
6 strong interest in politics = ...
7 tolerance of differences = ...

▶ WORDBUILDING adverb + adjective

Adverbs and adjectives can be combined to describe people and things.
politically engaged, highly cultured

5 Work in pairs. Answer the questions.

1 What do you think is the main reason for Kerala's success as a society?
2 Could this kind of society work anywhere?

6 Pronunciation: rhyming words

a 17 Work in pairs. Words that rhyme end with the same sound. Match the words (1–8) with the word that rhymes (a–h). Then listen and practice saying them.

1 state	a faced
2 low	b plane
3 head	c opt
4 course	d though
5 main	e weight
6 stopped	f force
7 none	g fun
8 waste	h said

b Look at these words. Can you think of a word that rhymes with each?

break foot height signed walk word

Grammar: verbs with *-ing* and infinitive

7 Match each verb in bold to the correct meaning (a or b).

1 Have you **tried visiting** India?
2 I'm **trying to show** how remarkable Kerala is.
a attempting something
b experimenting with something

3 I was meaning to **go on to tour** other parts.
4 The students **went on protesting** for four days.
a continuing an action
b a change of situation

5 It was **meant to be** a vacation.
6 Usually that would **mean** people **having** a fairly poor quality of life.
a describing intentions
b describing what is involved

7 I don't **regret changing** my plans.
8 No land is wasted, which I **regret to say** is not always the case in some developing countries.
a apologizing for what you are about to say
b saying you are sorry about a past event

9 **I remember going** there in the 1990s.
10 Please **remember to send** me a copy.
a describing memories
b talking about things that need to be done

11 We **stopped to visit** an Indian journalist I know.
12 Keralites never **stop debating**.
a ending something
b the reason for stopping

▶ VERBS WITH *-ING* AND INFINITIVE

Verbs with two meanings
remember, go on, stop, mean, try, regret + *-ing* and infinitive

Verbs with no change in meaning
prefer, continue, hate, like, love, start + *-ing* and infinitive

For more information and practice, see page 163.

8 Look at the grammar box. Then choose the correct form.

1 No one knows how long Kerala will be able to go on *to maintain / maintaining* this model society.
2 This is the journalist's impression of Kerala. You would have to try *to live / living* there yourself to see if it was the reality.
3 I regret *to tell / telling* you that getting there by plane is really expensive.
4 If you stopped *to see / seeing* some other places in India on the way, it would make it more worthwhile.
5 But that would also mean *to plan / planning* your trip more carefully.
6 The interviewer remembers *to visit / visiting* beautiful beaches and lagoons.

9 Complete the interview using the correct form of the verbs in parentheses.

Interview

WHAT INTERESTED YOU IN KERALA IN THE FIRST PLACE?

Well, I remember [1] .... (read) an interesting article about it about 15 years ago and I meant [2] .... (visit) and see for myself, but I only managed to go last year.

AND WHAT DID YOU FIND? WAS IT THE PERFECT MODEL THAT MANY PEOPLE HAVE SAID IT IS?

I think what they have achieved is amazing. The government implemented a number of measures to try [3] .... (improve) people's quality of life and on the whole, they have succeeded.

FOR EXAMPLE?

The most important is land reforms. In the 1960s, they stopped [4] .... (allow) landlords to charge rent to tenant farmers. This meant [5] .... (give) the land back to the people, mostly peasants, who worked on it.

SO POOR PEOPLE BENEFITTED?

Certainly. At the same time, the government also started [6] .... (invest) heavily in education, so poor people not only became better off, they also became better educated.

AND WHAT ARE THE NEGATIVE EFFECTS OF ALL THIS? THERE MUST BE SOME.

No system is perfect, I regret [7] .... (say). The problem in Kerala is that the economy is still largely based on agriculture. And someone who leaves school with a good education probably doesn't want to go on [8] .... (work) in the fields. So even though they prefer [9] .... (live) in Kerala, they often move to another more industrially developed state in India, or even abroad, to get a decent job.

Speaking

10 Work in pairs. Ask and answer the questions on page 155 to find out how happy your society is. Then compare your answer with another pair. Were people's answers very different? If so, why?

5c Sustainable development?

Reading

1 Work in pairs. Look at the photo on page 63 of the Mekong River in Laos before a hydroelectric dam project. How do you think the dam affected the lives of the people living near the river?

2 Read the article quickly and check your answers from Exercise 1. In what other ways did the dam affect people's lives?

3 Answer the questions based on the article.

1. Who helped to finance the project?
2. Why was this surprising?
3. How much electricity will it generate?
4. Who will use the electricity?
5. How many local people are affected?
6. What will happen to the local people?
7. Who says life is better now for local people?
8. Why do environmentalists think life for local people could get worse?

4 Complete the statements based on the article.

1. The dam flooded a big area and created a huge ________ . (para 1)
2. The World Bank would like the project to be a ________ that everyone can admire. (para 2)
3. The people from the flooded area should have better ________ in the future. (para 5)
4. Without their farmland, locals will have to find new ways to ________ a ________ . (para 5)
5. The people now have ________ that they didn't have before, like electricity, sanitation, and clean water. (para 8)
6. Changing the environment so dramatically has a big effect on the local ________ and ________ . (para 10)

Vocabulary *re-*

5 Underline all the words in the article beginning with *re-*. Then circle the verbs that mean "to do something again." Form nouns from them.

> ▶ **WORDBUILDING prefix *re-* with verbs and nouns**
>
> verb: *redevelop*
> noun: *redevelopment*

Critical thinking **fact or opinion**

6 Work in pairs. This article contains a mixture of facts and opinions about the benefits of the Nam Theun 2 hydroelectric dam. List the facts and opinions about the project's impact on the:

- local economy
- local people
- environment

7 Look back at the article. What told you when an opinion was being given rather than a fact? Tell your partner.

8 Compare your answers with another pair. Do you think that the dam has brought more benefits than disadvantages to Laos?

Word focus *pick*

9 Work in pairs. Find two phrases in the article using the word *pick* and discuss what they mean. Then do the same for the phrases in bold below.

1. I think it's easy to **pick holes** in the World Bank plan, but at least they are trying to do the right thing.
2. Can I **pick your brain** for a moment? I'm not sure my facts are right.
3. Sales of electricity to Thailand were slow at first but they**'re picking up** now.
4. He feels that he **is being picked on** by everybody.
5. I asked him to **pick me up** from the airport.
6. We offer a range of services—you can **pick and choose** what you want.

Speaking

10 Work in pairs. What is the impact on people and the environment in the following development projects? How do you deal with this sensitively? Discuss and make lists.

- helping a city damaged by a hurricane
- building a high-speed railway line between two cities
- moving people from a poor and depressed area in a city to a new town

SUSTAINABLE DEVELOPMENT?

Kai Kensavaong will never again walk along the muddy lanes of Sop On, the village in southern Laos where she was born. Her old home now lies at the bottom of a reservoir created to feed a hydroelectric power plant, the first to be funded by the World Bank for over twenty years. "I'll never forget that place," says the 41-year-old villager. "It was my home. I picked my first bamboo stalks there."

The World Bank stopped financing hydropower projects in developing countries twenty years ago because of criticism that such projects were harming local communities and the environment. But Nam Theun 2—a 127-foot-high (39 m) dam on the Mekong River that generates over 1,000 megawatts of electricity—is the showpiece for the bank's new policy of supporting sustainable hydropower projects. For Laos, it is part of a longer-term strategy to revitalize the economy and become the battery of Southeast Asia.

The bank says that lessons have been learned from projects in the sixties and seventies, when people were forced to resettle and whole areas of forest or agricultural land were flooded. When it comes to clean energy, the bank thinks hydropower is the best option, offering the best solution to the 1.5 billion people without access to electricity.

In 2010, Nam Theun 2 brought \$5.6 million in sales of electricity, and it is estimated that during the next 25 years it will generate around \$2 billion in revenue to Laos, one of Asia's poorest countries, since most of the electricity will be exported to its power-hungry neighbor, Thailand. The government has promised that this money will be spent on reducing poverty and renewing and improving the country's infrastructure.

Seventeen villages in the flooded area have now been rebuilt and the 6,200 people, mostly farmers, who lived in them have been retrained to make a living from the reservoir. The power company has promised to double their living standards within five years. According to the World Bank, 87 percent of those resettled believe life is much better than before, since they now have electricity, sanitation, clean water, new roads, and greater access to schools and health care.

"In the old village, things just weren't convenient," said Tiea, 25, one of the relocated villagers. "It wasn't a pretty place, the houses weren't very nice, and we didn't have power. In the new village, we have electricity, we can see better."

But the old criticisms remain. Environmental and human rights groups warn that the dam will have a negative impact on water quality and fish, and that the local people who were relocated after the area was flooded may not be able to support themselves economically in the future.

"People are happy with these new amenities, but the real problem is how to restore sustainable livelihoods for communities who used to rely on the natural resources—forests, fish, and grazing lands for their animals—now that they've lost these," says Ikuko Matsumoto, program director for the environmental group, International Rivers.

In addition to the 6,200 villagers already rehoused, activists also point out that there are over 110,000 people in riverside villages downstream from the dam whose lives will have to change because of the new river ecosystem. They claim that these people will have to deal with issues like flooding, decline of the fish population and poor water quality. How quickly they will pick up new skills is uncertain.

But the World Bank says it is responsive to these problems. A 1,500-square-mile (4,100 km) protected area has been established around the dam to safeguard flora and fauna. It admits, though, that rebuilding the lives of the villagers is not a short-term process, and that everyone is trying to learn and readjust as they go along.

5d Evaluating a project

Real life making decisions

1 Work in pairs. What kind of development would most improve your town? Choose three items and number them (1–3) in order of importance.

a new arts center (theater, music, film, fine art)
a new rec (recreation) center
a new shopping mall
better local stores
better public transportation
fewer cars (pedestrian zones, bike trails)
more (affordable) housing
more green spaces

2 **18** Listen to a meeting of some bank employees who are discussing a project they have funded and complete the notes.

1 Amount of loan	The bank lent the local government $________.
2 Purpose of loan	To help redevelop a ________ in the city.
3 Aims of project	To give local residents a nicer park and some ________ facilities.
4 Progress so far	They have cleaned the area up, planted ________, laid new ________. They have also built the ________ and the children's ________.
5 Other work	They have built a ________ and bought a sculpture for $________.
6 Needs	A new loan of $250,000 to complete the ________ courts and ________ course.

3 **18** What do the bank employees decide to do about the new loan? Do they all agree?

4 **18** Complete the sentences in the box with the phrases the speakers use to give their opinions and to agree and disagree. Then listen again and check.

MAKING DECISIONS

What do you think we should do?
What's your view / opinion?
If you [1] ________, that's completely wrong.
Personally, I think that's absurd.
I don't think we [2] ________ give them another cent.
I find it amazing / ridiculous that he said that.
I think we should / we ought to give them the benefit of the doubt.
[3] ________ be too hasty. / We shouldn't be too hasty.
We need [4] ________ whether they are in the spirit of the original aims of the project.
That really [5] ________ the opinion of the local residents.
The [6] ________ see it, it's probably a good thing.
I'd [7] ________ with that.
That's right.
I agree.
Is everyone OK / happy with that?
Exactly.
Are we all [8] ________?
That [9] ________ to me.

Speaking

5 Work in pairs. Read the report on page 153 about another project which the bank is financing and consider these points.

- name of project
- date started
- original goals
- action taken and money spent
- results (positive and negative)
- next steps and money needed

Decide together if you think the bank should lend more money for this project. Discuss your decision with another pair and try to come to an agreement with them.

5e Big cities, big problems

Writing an opinion essay

1 Work in pairs. Why do you think people want to live in big cities? Make a list of the reasons. Do you think their lives are better there?

2 The chart shows the percentage of the world's population living in cities. What problems do you think this creates?

3 Look at the title of the opinion essay and then read the answer. What is the opinion of the writer?

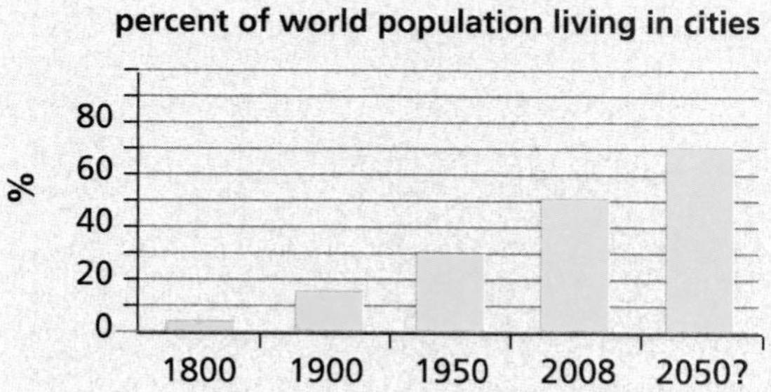

Our cities have become too big. The problems they create outweigh the benefits.

In 1800, only two percent of the world's population lived in cities. Over the last 20 years, more and more people have moved to cities looking for work and a better life. As a result, more than half the world's population now live in cities and that number is expected to grow. Cities are monuments to the amazing organizing abilities of human beings. However, in some cases, they also have many social, economic, and environmental problems. The question is: do the problems they create outweigh their benefits?

Cities exist because they are more convenient places to live. Jobs, schools, and hospitals are all close to home. There is a wide choice of people to socialize with and good choices for entertainment.

On the other hand, there also seems to be more crime, more poverty, and more pollution, often in a particular area, making things even worse. But this is not so surprising, if you think about it. The same problems exist in the countryside or in smaller towns, but they are not so concentrated. Because of this, they are noticed less.

As long as the population of cities does not grow more quickly than the services available to it, cities can solve a lot of our problems. They keep the population from spreading into the countryside. In addition, they provide jobs and a more interesting life. The problem with cities is not how big they are, but how well managed they are.

4 Does this opinion essay follow the standard format?

Introduction → Arguments for → Arguments against → Conclusion

5 An introduction can take different forms. Which of these does the writer use?

- a dramatic example of the problem
- a story about the problem from the writer's own experience
- statistics that illustrate the seriousness of the problem
- a quote from someone famous about the topic

6 Writing skill **linking words**

a Look at the linking phrases below. Then underline other examples of each type in the essay. Compare your answers with your partner.

Adding an argument	Introducing a contrasting fact	Explaining the consequences
Furthermore,	Then again,	Consequently,

b Complete the sentences with a linking phrase.

1 Certain cities in the world have become especially popular. ...., we have seen the emergence of megacities with over ten million inhabitants.

2 A lot of people find a better standard of living in big cities. ...., you can also find very poor people living in them.

3 .... to being convenient for people, cities are also convenient for business.

7 Write an opinion essay about the statement below. Then compare your answer with your partner. Did you use the same arguments?

In our modern lifestyles, we have lost our sense of community. We need to return to a simpler way of life.

8 Read your partner's essay and check the following:

- Do you find the arguments convincing?
- Is it organized in clear paragraphs?
- Does it follow the format suggested in Exercise 4?
- Does it use one of the introduction techniques suggested in Exercise 5?

5f Aquarium on Wheels

Video

The program really means a lot to me because I want to major in marine biology.

Before you watch

1 Work in groups. Look at the title of this video and the photo and discuss the questions.

1 Why do you think the video is called *Aquarium on Wheels*?
2 Do you think aquariums can teach children about more than just sea life?
3 What might the program teach young people?

2 Work in pairs. Mark what you think you will see.

a kid dressed as a monkey			a computer
a crocodile	a diver	a fish tank	a frog
a necklace	seashells	a tiger	a toy snake

While you watch

3 Watch the video and check your answers from Exercise 2.

4 Watch the first part of the video (to 02:17). Choose the correct option to complete the sentences.

1 The students in the video are:
 a employees of the Aquarium on Wheels program.
 b visitors to the National Aquarium.

2 The students want to teach about:
 a recycling. b conservation.

3 The students perform a play about:
 a snakes. b monkeys.

4 The children laugh because the actor says that:
 a fighting is going to make his hair look messy.
 b he doesn't have any leaves to eat.

5 Aquarium administrators want to give students:
 a training in marine biology.
 b lessons for life.

5 Watch the second part of the video (02:18 to the end). Answer the questions.

1 What kind of skills do the students need?

....

2 What haven't the people in their family done?

....

3 What does DejaNé Jones say is the most important thing the program has taught her?

....

4 What did performing the play teach them?

....

5 What does George Faulk want to be?

....

6 Why is the program personally important to Martha Schaum?

....

After you watch

6 Roleplay **an interview with Martha Schaum**

Work in pairs.

Student A: Imagine you work for a local newspaper. Use the information below to prepare questions to ask Martha Schaum about the Aquarium on Wheels program.

Student B: Imagine you are Martha Schaum. A reporter from a local newspaper is going to interview you. Look at the information below and think about what you are going to say.

- the overall objectives of the Aquarium on Wheels program
- who is involved with the program
- what the student employees have been doing
- what the program gives the student
- what Martha gets out of the program personally

Act out the interview, then change roles and act out the interview again.

7 At the end of the video, the narrator says: "The Aquarium on Wheels program is having a powerful impact on more than just the rain forests." What does that mean? Why do you think the program is so successful?

8 Work in groups and discuss these questions.

1 What kind of education about the environment do young children in your country receive? Is it effective?
2 The overall goal of the Aquarium on Wheels program is to entertain and educate. Do you think these two aims are compatible? Can you think of examples that meet both aims successfully?

advantageous (adj) /ˌædvənˈteɪʤəs/ having a good effect
camouflage (n) /ˈkæməˌflɑʒ/ something an animal uses to make it difficult to see
major (v) /ˈmeɪʤər/ get a college degree in
mess up (v) /ˈmes ˈʌp/ make something look disorganized
overall (adj) /ˈoʊvərˌɔl/ general
poison dart (n) /ˈpɔɪzən ˈdɑrt/ a small arrow covered with poison at one end which is fired from a long tube by blowing

UNIT 5 REVIEW

Grammar

1 Work in pairs. What is the main industry in your town or city? How has this affected the character of the city?

2 Read the interview and answer the questions.

1 What is the new industry that has emerged?
2 How does this resident feel about it?

3 Complete the interview with the correct form of the verb: *-ing*, infinitive or base form.

I = Interviewer; R = Resident

I: So, are you enjoying [1] ______ (live) here again after a fifteen-year absence? Has Berlin changed a lot since you were last here?

R: Of course. There has been a huge amount of development. They have kept on [2] ______ (build) and [3] ______ (redevelop) since the early nineties. In many ways that is great for the city, but I regret [4] ______ (say) that its character has changed, and not for the better.

I: What do you mean by that?

R: Well, there are as many as 9 million tourists a year. It's as if the city government has decided [5] ______ (turn) Berlin into a vacation destination.

I: But surely tourists are a good thing? If they stopped [6] ______ (come), the city would lose a lot of jobs and income. I heard that tourism will help [7] ______ (create) 50,000 new jobs.

R: I'm not anti-tourist. I understand that tourism means [8] ______ (earn) good money, but a lot of this money goes straight to private companies. I think the city should ask tourists and tourism companies [9] ______ (pay) a tax for visiting Berlin. Then this money could be invested in real jobs for residents.

I CAN	
use verbs with *-ing* and infinitive	☐
use verbs with both *-ing* and infinitive but with different meanings	☐

Vocabulary

4 Match the words (1–6) with their meaning (a–f).

1 convert	a bring up to date
2 spoil	b change completely
3 modernize	c rebuild
4 demolish	d damage
5 transform	e turn into
6 redevelop	f destroy

5 Work in pairs. Use a different verb in each space.

1 Green spaces can really ______ a city.
2 In the 1970s and 1980s, there was a tendency to ______ older buildings downtown and replace them with high-rise buildings.
3 It's a good idea to ______ downtown areas into pedestrian zones.
4 People complain that the character of many famous cities has been ______ by ______ them with luxury apartments and expensive stores.

6 Discuss with your partner if any of the items in Exercise 5 are features of your city. Do you agree with the statements? Why?

I CAN	
talk about the different features of a city	☐
describe changes in a city	☐

Real life

7 Work in pairs. Complete each opinion with a verb.

1 What do you ______ of the idea to restore the downtown area to the way it was 200 years ago?
2 I ______ it amazing that no one has thought of doing it before.
3 If you ______ me, it's not a good idea.
4 No, that doesn't ______ right to me either.
5 The way I ______ it, if it's good for the local economy, then it's a good thing.
6 I think it ______ on what local people want.
7 Yes, I'd ______ along with that.

8 Work in small groups. Decide if it is better to restore old buildings or knock them down and start again.

I CAN	
reach a decision by expressing opinions and agreeing or disagreeing	☐

Speaking

9 Work in pairs. Tell each other about a large development project you know about (transportation, redevelopment, new town, sports or recreation complex). Cover these points:

- the project's benefits
- whether it is sustainable or not
- who supports the project; who opposes it
- your opinion

Unit 6 Alternative travel

The Hotel de Glace, Quebec, Canada; the only ice hotel in North America
Photograph by Ralph Lee Hopkins

FEATURES

1 Look at the photo. What do you think there is to do in this hotel? Would you like to stay here? Why?

2 Work in pairs. Choose the correct option(s). Then ask each other the questions.

1 How much *vacation / days off* do you get each year?
2 When you make a hotel reservation, do you usually ask for a room with a *sight / view*?
3 Do you generally take a lot of *suitcase / luggage* when you travel, or do you prefer to travel light?
4 What is your favorite kind of *scenery / countryside*: the ocean, forest, mountains, or desert?
5 Do you generally enjoy the *travel / trip* as much as actually getting there?
6 Which *airplane / airline* do you prefer to fly with?
7 On your last vacation, how long did it *take / last* to get to your destination?

6a Staycations

Speaking

1 Work in pairs. Ask each other these questions about your capital cities and their attractions.

1 Can you name five important tourist attractions?
2 How many have you visited?
3 Have you ever taken a bus tour or walking tour of the city?
4 Have you ever been to a famous market in the city?
5 How often do you visit the city's main museums or galleries?
6 Do you know the name of a good, reasonably-priced hotel in the city?

2 Are there parts of your local area that you haven't ever visited or feel that you don't know? Would you consider taking a vacation there? Why?

Reading

3 Read the blog. Are the sentences true (T) or false (F)?

1 Staycationers always sleep at home.
2 Staycationers go out and do different activities during their staycation.
3 Staycations have all the stresses of normal travel.
4 Staycations simulate traditional vacations.

4 Now use the information in the blog to complete these statements.

1 Staycations got started because...
2 They are good for the local economy because…
3 Some people think that visiting local attractions isn't as exciting as…
4 Without leaving New York, Karen Ash was able to have a…

STAYCATIONS

You probably don't like the term "staycation." Neither do I. But don't let that bother you. As a concept, staycations are a pretty good idea. Maybe you've already had one, but didn't know what it was called. Staycations don't just mean staying in and relaxing at home. They involve getting out more by taking day trips to see local sights. If you don't want to stay home, you can vacation locally—for example, at a local campsite.

Staycations first became popular after the financial crisis of 2008, when people were looking for ways to cut back on their spending. Apart from the savings, let's not ignore the other benefits: you don't have any of the problems associated with travel, such as packing, long drives, delays at airports, and so on; and you put money back into the local economy, by eating out, for example.

Some staycationers who base themselves at home like to follow a set of rules, such as setting a start and end date, planning their activities ahead of time and avoiding routine. You don't have to do these things, but it helps to create the feel of a traditional vacation. Others, aware that a visit to the local zoo may not match the thrill of foreign travel, take it a step further. Take, for example, Karen Ash, whose story appeared in the *Wall Street Journal*.

A resident of New York, Ash decided not to go to Japan, as she had originally planned, but instead took a weeklong Japanese vacation in her own city. This included buying postcards and souvenirs at a Japanese market, admiring bonsai plants, eating ramen (even speaking Japanese when ordering), all without leaving New York. Her itinerary also involved joining in at a traditional Japanese tea ceremony, attending a taiko drumming concert, and watching Japanese soap operas on DVD. I don't think many people would want to take this much trouble to create their staycation, but you get the idea!

Vocabulary phrasal verbs with *in* and *out*

5 Work in pairs. Find two phrasal verbs in the article with *in* and two with *out*. Discuss what they mean.

6 Complete the sentences using *in* and *out*.

1 I'd like to try ______ that new restaurant downtown. I've heard it's excellent.
2 Should we eat ______ tonight? We've got food.
3 I'm going to drop ______ on Uncle Joe and see how he is feeling. He's stuck at home with a broken leg and he is probably really bored.
4 All I seem to do is work and sleep these days. I need to get ______ more.
5 My daughter stayed ______ until 3 a.m. last night. I was really worried.
6 Please fill ______ this form with your name, address, and passport number.

> **WORDBUILDING phrasal verbs with *in* and *out***
>
> Some verbs can be used with both *in* and *out*. Sometimes they give opposite meanings and sometimes they give different meanings. Other verbs may only be used with either *in* or *out*.
>
> *eat in, eat out; drop in, drop out; join in, ~~join out~~*

7 Ask each other the following questions.

1 Do you feel you get out enough? If not, what would you like to do more of?
2 How often do you eat out?
3 What do you usually do in the evenings, if you are staying in?
4 If you saw some people in the park playing volleyball, would you watch or join in?
5 How late were you allowed to stay out when you were fifteen years old?
6 Do you like to try out new types of food?
7 Do you like it when people drop in on you, or do you think they should be invited to come to your house?
8 What is your ideal weekend night like? Do you go out or stay in?

Grammar *not*

8 Underline these examples in the article and comment on the position of *not* in each case:

1 a negative infinitive (para 4)
2 a negative sentence using *want* (para 1)
3 the opposite of *must* (para 3)
4 a negative sentence using *think* (para 4)
5 a negative sentence using *let* (para 2)

> **NOT**
>
> **Negative infinitive**
> *It's cheaper not to go abroad.*
>
> ***want***
> *I didn't want to stay in…* *I ~~wanted not to~~ stay in…*
>
> ***must not* and *don't have to***
> *You must not book a vacation without comparing prices first.* (Note that in British English, the contracted form *mustn't* is commonly used in place of *must not.*)
> *You don't have to spend a lot of money to enjoy your vacation.*
>
> ***hope* and *think***
> *I hope it doesn't rain.* *~~I don't hope it rains.~~*
> *I don't think that's right.* *~~I think that's not right.~~*
>
> ***let's***
> *Let's stay home this year. Let's not go abroad.*
>
> For more information and practice, see page 163.

9 Look at the grammar box. Then make each sentence express the opposite idea using negatives.

1 Let's spend a lot of money on a foreign vacation.
2 I want to stay in a big modern hotel.
3 Staycations can replace foreign vacations.
4 I hope the hotel is near the river.
5 I told them to wait until the last minute.
6 We must go swimming—if you want to, that is.

10 Look at these tips from a travel magazine. Choose the correct option.

> Let's [1] *don't forget / not forget* that the main reason for choosing a staycation is to save money. For example, if you [2] *don't want to spend / want not to spend* a lot on eating out, just take a picnic with you when you go on a day trip. It [3] *must not / doesn't have to be* a cheap picnic; you can still treat yourself to a few luxuries.
>
> Try [4] *to not choose / not to choose* only activities that cost money. One idea is to plan a two- or three-day walk and take a tent with you. If you [5] *don't think you'll enjoy / think you don't have to enjoy* camping, then look up some motels you could stay in instead.
>
> The most important thing is to be adventurous. The fun of any vacation is discovering new places and there is no reason why a staycation should be any different. I [6] *hope it isn't / don't hope it's* a disappointment!

Speaking

11 Work in small groups. Plan a five-day staycation in your own area or the area you are studying in. Try to give the staycation a theme, like the foreign theme in the article. Make a short itinerary of at least five activities.

12 Work with another group. Compare your staycation ideas. Have a class vote on which staycation sounds the most fun and practical.

6b Voluntourism

Listening

1 Work in pairs. What do you think the saying below means? Do you have a similar saying in your language? Do you think it's true?

"A change is as good as a rest."

2 🔊 **19** Voluntourism is when people travel to a foreign location to work for free. Look at the photo. What sort of volunteering do you think people do here? Listen and check.

3 Which of the statements best summarizes Katie Samuel's opinion of what a good volunteer vacation should be?

a a working vacation where you learn practical and useful skills
b a cultural experience where both the visitor and the host benefit
c an enjoyable way to help others less fortunate than yourself

4 🔊 **19** Listen again and complete these sentences with one word per space. Then discuss what each expression means.

1 You probably thought that kind of vacation was for eighteen-year-olds in **their** ______ **year**.
2 Wouldn't people who only get **a few weeks** ______ **a year** prefer a more relaxing option?
3 This should be **a** ______ **travel experience**, not just **a work** ______.
4 In return, the locals take them for ______ **walks**, which are like mini-safaris.
5 They have to pay for their flight and **their** ______ **expenses**.
6 The CRTP helps to restore **cultural** ______ **sites** around the world.

5 Work in groups. Discuss the questions. Then tell the class.

1 What do you think of this type of vacation?
2 Should people have to pay to volunteer?
3 What other ways can you think of to get close to local people on a vacation?

Grammar negative and tag questions

6 There are various ways of phrasing a question. Look at these examples (1–4) and match each one to the answer the speaker wants (a–c).

1 Have you ever thought of doing a little building work during your vacation?
2 You probably thought that kind of vacation was for eighteen-year-olds, didn't you?
3 Wouldn't most people prefer a more relaxing option?
4 It's not really a vacation as we know it, is it?

a Doesn't expect a particular answer (*yes* or *no*)
b Expects the answer to be *yes*
c Expects the answer to be *no*

7 Work in pairs. Find more examples of questions that expect a particular answer in the audioscript on page 177.

Elephants are often the victims of poaching; a project in Kenya helps local people find other ways to make a living.

> **NEGATIVE and TAG QUESTIONS**
>
> **Open questions (no confirmation of opinion demanded)**
> *Do you like visiting new places?*
> *Yes, now and then.*
>
> **Negative questions**
> *Don't you like visiting new places?*
> *No, not at all.*
>
> **Tag questions**
> *You like visiting new places, don't you?*
> *Yes, I love it.*
> *You don't like visiting new places, do you?*
> *No, you're right. I don't.*
>
> For more information and practice, see page 164.

8 Look at the grammar box. Convert these open questions into negative or tag questions that fit the answers.

1 Do you like the idea of volunteer vacations? (tag question)

....?

Yes, I do, very much.

2 Do you think it's an interesting idea? (negative question)

....?

No, I don't.

3 Have you been on a volunteer vacation? (tag question)

....?

Yes, two years ago.

4 Did it seem strange to pay money in order to work? (negative question)

....?

No, not really.

5 Will you be going again this year? (tag question)

....?

No. We're taking a staycation this year.

9 Pronunciation intonation in questions

a 20 Look at the grammar box. Listen to the sentences and answer the questions.

1 Does the speaker's intonation rise or fall at the end of an open question?
2 Does the speaker's intonation rise or fall at the end of a negative question?
3 Does the speaker's intonation rise or fall at the end of each tag question?

b 21 Work in pairs. Practice saying the converted questions in Exercise 8 with the correct intonation. Then listen and check your pronunciation.

10 The Great Continental Divide is a biking and hiking trail that crosses North America from Mexico to Canada. Read this telephone conversation and convert the sentences in bold into negative or tag questions. Then check your answers with your teacher.

A: Hi, I'm interested in helping out on the Great Continental Divide this summer. My friend did four days last summer. [1] .... **(I / can / work / for / just a few days)**
B: Absolutely. Anything from two days to two months.
A: That's great. I have about a week in June. How much does it cost to take part?
B: It's free.
A: Sorry? [2] .... **(I / have to / pay / for / my accommodation)**
B: No, it's completely free. You just have to register.
A: [3] .... **(I / can / do / that / online)**
B: Sure, you can. It's on our website. [4] .... **(you / have / visited / our website)**
A: Yes, I took a quick look. And where on the trail can I work?
B: New Mexico, Montana, Wyoming…
A: [5] .... **(you / have / got / something / in Colorado)** That's where I live.
B: Yes, we do. We have opportunities in Winfield.
A: [6] .... **(and / you / provide / training / first)**
B: It's on-the-job training, unless it's very specific. We're looking for a chef at the moment. [7] .... **(you / want / to be / a chef)**
A: No. I just want to help build some trails.

Speaking

11 Ask negative or tag questions to try to persuade others of your opinions about these items.

- beach vacations
- experiencing local culture
- traveling alone
- trying out local food
- volunteer vacations
- working abroad

6c Unusual places to stay

Reading

1 Work in pairs. Make a list of what you look for in a vacation destination (comfort, a beautiful setting, modern facilities). Then compare your list with another pair.

2 Read part of a travel magazine's guide to unusual places. Answer the questions.

1. Which seem like comfortable places to stay?
2. Which seem to have the most disadvantages?

3 Read the article again. Choose the correct option to complete the sentences.

1. Karosta's own description of its hotel:
   a is surprising. b is not truthful.
2. The writer thinks the cost of a night in prison:
   a is too high. b is about right.
3. For a long time after the gold rush Virginia City:
   a was uninhabited.
   b was a rich town.
4. The cabins at the Nevada City Hotel are:
   a all newly built.
   b a mix of old and new.
5. The caves of Sassi di Matera have always been:
   a lived in. b used to store things.
6. The new owners have tried to keep the original:
   a furniture. b feel of the caves.
7. In a lot of art hotels the art is not:
   a very good. b very prominent.
8. The different rooms at the Propeller Island City Lodge are decorated:
   a in a dramatic way.
   b in a similar way.

4 All these words describe parts of a building. Find them in the article and discuss their meaning with your partner. Use a dictionary if necessary.

balcony	balustrade	corridor
earth roofs	saloon	vaulted ceilings

5 Which of these places would you prefer to stay in? Why? Tell your partner.

Critical thinking **claims and justifications**

6 Each of these hotels claims to offer an authentic experience. For each hotel, say what the experience is, which facts support this claim, and which facts, if any, don't support it.

Hotel	Claims to be...	Supporting facts	Contradictory facts

7 Work in pairs. Discuss the questions.

1. Does it matter that some of the claims the hotels make are not always justified?
2. Does it make you less likely to trust them?
3. Does it make you less likely to stay there?

Word focus *mind*

8 Work in pairs. Find two expressions with the word *mind* in the text. Discuss whether they are nouns or verbs and what they mean. Then work out what these other expressions with *mind* mean.

1. I am **of two minds** about whether to stay at a hotel or drive home.
2. If you **change your mind** about coming with me, let me know before Friday.
3. I'm sure you can think of a solution if you **put your mind to it**.
4. Sorry I haven't got back to you about the weekend. I've had a lot **on my mind** lately.
5. Sorry, I know I've heard his name before but my **mind's gone blank**.

9 Write three sentences with different phrases with *mind*, but leave a blank where the phrase should be. Exchange sentences with another pair and fill in the blanks.

Speaking and writing

10 Work in small groups. Create your own idea for an unusual place to stay. Discuss:

- where the hotel is
- how your hotel is different
- whether it should be luxurious or basic
- what facilities you can offer that fit with the theme

11 Write a short description of it. Then present your idea to the class. Vote for which one sounds the most interesting.

Unusual places to stay

PRISON HOTELS Built in 1905, Karosta naval jail in Latvia was originally home to mutinous Russian sailors. In the 1970s, it housed political prisoners. In direct contrast to most hotel publicity, the website describes Karosta proudly as "unfriendly, unheated, and uncomfortable." They are not lying. This is more of a jail experience than a hotel stay. "Reception" is a dark corridor where a former prison guard explains the rules to you (no luggage except a toothbrush, no attempts to escape), and then fires his gun in the air to show you he is serious. After a meal of bread and sweet Russian tea, "guests" are given five minutes to bathe before making up their own beds from wooden benches and thin mattresses. Sound unpleasant? It is. But for $12 per night, what do you expect?

PERIOD HOTELS Would you like to experience life in America's Wild West 150 years ago? Virginia City, Montana, a former gold-rush town, was a ghost town until it was restored in the 1950s for tourism. Owned largely by the state government, the town now operates as a large open-air museum. Nearby is the Nevada City Hotel and cabins where you can hang up your Stetson hat and enjoy life as a cowboy. The rooms feature period Victorian furniture, and downstairs the saloon has a true Wild West feel. The cabins look extremely rustic from the outside—two even have their original earth roofs—but inside they have large double beds and private bathrooms. Bear in mind that if you book mid-week, you might be disappointed because the city only comes to life on weekends, when actors in period costumes play sheriffs, cowboys, and gold prospectors.

CAVE HOTELS If you had more primitive accommodation in mind, try the caves of Sassi di Matera on the toe of Italy, inhabited since the Bronze Age. During the Renaissance, they developed into more sophisticated rooms with stone walls, vaulted ceilings, and balustrades. But more recently they were the poor homes of peasants who lived there with their animals until as late as 1952. Now, however, they have been renovated to provide hospitality in a historical setting. Although visitors to Le Grotte Della Civita must do without television or fridges, the rooms are comfortably furnished with antique furniture and period terracotta tiles. The owners wanted the caves to feel as authentic as possible, so they built the furniture into the walls and left in place the iron rings where peasants tied up their animals. Prices start at $300 per night.

ART HOTELS A modern art gallery is a place where you can lose yourself in an artist's vision of the world. A hotel is essentially a place where you can spend the night, in either more or less comfort, according to your budget. As its advertising promises, Propeller Island City Lodge in Berlin manages to combine the two. Housed in a former apartment block, the hotel is a collection of individually designed rooms—the upside-down room, the all-orange room, the mirror room—which are often so extreme that you have no choice but to get into the spirit of it. In some art hotels, you can forget the art and simply enjoy the comfort of your surroundings. That's not the case with Propeller Island. The rooms can be small and claustrophobic (although some have balconies) and often you have to share a bathroom with other guests. But if you don't mind that, it may be the next best thing to spending the night in a gallery.

6d Couch surfing

Real life getting around

1 Work in pairs. Take one minute to read this description of couch surfing. Then discuss how couch surfing works. Is it something you would do? Why?

2 You are going to listen to a conversation between a couch surfer and a host. Look at the box. Who do you think says each expression?

3 **22** Listen to the conversation. Check your answers from Exercise 2.

4 **22** Listen again. Complete the expressions.

> **GETTING AROUND**
>
> I'm coming in by [1] ________ .
> I wanted to pick you up, but [2] ________ .
> That's [3] ________ , but I can find my own way.
> How do I get to [4] ________ ?
> You could just catch [5] ________ .
> Alternatively, you can hop on [6] ________ .
> Look out for the [7] ________ on your right.
> It's only a twenty-minute [8] ________ .
> The easiest thing is to [9] ________ .
> I'll come out and [10] ________ .
> If I get held up, I'll [11] ________ . But otherwise, expect a call around six thirty.

5 **Pronunciation intonation in sentences with two clauses**

a **23** Listen for these two sentences with *but*. Notice how the speaker's intonation rises at the end of the first clause, indicating that they have not finished speaking.

I wanted to pick you up, but my car's in the garage that day.
You could just catch a taxi, but it's about eleven miles from downtown.

b Practice saying these sentences using the same intonation.

1 I'll try to be home by six, but I can't promise I will.
2 Normally it's a ten-minute drive, but the road work has made it longer.
3 I can't make it today, but I'll come tomorrow.
4 It's nice of you to offer, but we can find our own way.
5 The bus is cheap, but the train is much quicker.

6 Work in pairs. Take turns playing the roles of couch surfer and host. As the guest, call your host and ask about the best way to get to his/her home from another city.

Originally the idea of a New Hampshire student who emailed 1,500 students at the University of Iceland asking if he could spend the night on their couches, couch surfing is now an established worldwide practice. This is how it works. When you have made your travel plans, you contact people on the couch-surfing network by email to find out if they can offer you a bed for the night in the places you are going to visit. There's no fee. The only obligation on your part is to be able to offer a place to stay at your home when someone asks in the future. Aside from being free, the benefit is that you meet people with local knowledge. If you're lucky, some might even become long-term friends.

6e A disappointed customer

Writing a letter of complaint

1 Have you ever had a bad experience on vacation that caused you to complain? What happened and what was the outcome?

2 Read this complaint and answer the questions.

1 Why is the customer unhappy?
2 What does she want the hotel to do about it?
3 Does her complaint seem justified?

> 44 Ascot Street
> New Haven, CT 06511
>
> Sweet Hotel Group
> Via Central 150
> Miraflores
> Lima, Peru 15001
>
> Dear Sir or Madam:
>
> I am writing to express my dissatisfaction with my stay at the Grau Hotel on April 12. I made a reservation through another website which was offering one night for two people with dinner for $110. However, when we arrived at 5:30 p.m., we were informed that there was no table available in the restaurant and that we could find another restaurant in town.
>
> We got a strong impression that because we used a discounted offer, we did not receive the same level of hospitality as regular, full-paying guests. The situation was both embarrassing and inconvenient. After some discussion with the staff, we were able to have dinner at the hotel restaurant, but much later than we wanted to, at 9:30 pm. No one apologized for this.
>
> Given the circumstances, compensation is not my principal concern. Rather, I would ask you to investigate the matter thoroughly to ensure this does not happen to other guests.
>
> Sincerely
>
> Ann Dunhill

3 Work in pairs. Formal letters follow certain conventions. Answer the questions.

1 What is the correct position for each address?
2 Where is the reason for writing mentioned?
3 Where is the request for action?

4 Writing skill **formal language**

a Find the formal words or phrases in the letter that say the following:

1 to say I was unhappy
2 we were told
3 a cheap deal
4 after we talked to
5 what worries me most
6 look into
7 make sure

b Convert the phrases in bold in these sentences into more formal language. Use the letter to help you.

1 We **want** to **tell you how unhappy we were** with the standard of the food on the cruise ship.
Example:
We wish to express our dissatisfaction with the standard of the food on the cruise ship.
2 I **told** the receptionist that I **had booked the room** for two nights, not one.
3 After **I'd talked to** the manager, she **said she was sorry** and promised to **look into** the problem. **But** no action was taken.
4 I expected the safety of the guests to be what the staff **were most worried about**.
5 Given the **trouble** this caused us, we expected to **get some money back**.
6 The manager said no other rooms were **free**, but if the opportunity **came up**, she'd move us.

5 Read the situation and then write a letter of complaint to the hotel.

You recently stayed at a small hotel in downtown Chicago. During the night, you were awakened by some noisy people in the room next door. You went down to the reception desk to tell a member of the hotel staff, but no one was there. You are angry and upset that no one was on duty during the night.

6 Exchange letters and read your partner's letter. Use these questions to check their letter.

- Does it begin with the reason for writing?
- Does it end with what action is expected?
- Does it use rhetorical or other types of questions to be persuasive?

6f East Timor

Video

East Timor: for the intrepid few, an emerging tourism destination with unspoiled natural beauty

Before you watch

1 Work in groups. Look at the photo of East Timor and discuss the questions.

1 What do you know about East Timor?
2 Why do you think the caption says that East Timor is "for the intrepid few"? What does this suggest about the country?

2 What do you think you will see in this video? Check the items below.

a a person sunbathing on a tropical beach
b builders renovating a damaged building
c a group of people pulling in fishing nets from the sea
d tourists having drinks in a hotel bar

While you watch

3 Watch the video and check your answers from Exercise 2.

4 Watch the first part of the video (to 00:45). Complete the conversation between a journalist (J) and Ann Turner (A).

J: Hi Ann, where do you work?
A: 1 ....
J: Why did you first come to East Timor?
A: 2 ....
J: When did you decide you wanted to stay?
A: 3 ....
J: What four things impressed you most?
A: 4 ....
J: How many fish species are there?
A: 5 ....
J: Why is there such a huge diversity of fish species here?
A: 6 ....

5 Watch the second part of the video (00:46 to the end). Answer the questions.

1 What is the main problem on East Timor?
....
2 How long has East Timor been independent?
....
3 What happened after people in East Timor voted for independence?
....
4 What is the government worried about?
....
5 What policies is the government working on?
....
6 What should people who want to start a tourism business in East Timor do?
....

6 Watch the whole video again. Number the quotes in the order you hear them.

a The subsequent recovery effort has been painfully slow.
b Welcome to East Timor, one of the world's newest countries.
c It faces an age-old predicament: how to make the most of its natural assets without destroying them.
d East Timor is a former war zone.
e We are still developing policies and regulations.

After you watch

7 Roleplay talking about a new project

Work in pairs.

Student A: Imagine you are a foreigner living in East Timor. You want to build a small beach hotel. Look at the ideas below. Think about what you are going to say to a government official.

- what you hope to do
- how you will protect the environment
- how your hotel will benefit the local economy

Student B: Imagine you are an East Timor government official. Look at the information below. Think about what you are going to tell a business person.

- You are interested in attracting tourism but you also want to protect the environment.
- Find out how the beach hotel will do both.

Act out the conversation. Then change roles and act out the conversation again with a new business. Decide whether the business is a good idea or not.

8 Work in groups and discuss these questions.

1 Which areas of your country attract tourists?
2 How does tourism contribute to the economy of your country?
3 What impact does it have on natural assets?
4 Do you think the government does enough to protect the natural assets of your country?

asset (n) /'æset/ a valuable possession
emerging (adj) /ɪ'mɜrʤɪŋ/ in the process of becoming
expatriate (n) /eks'peɪtriət/ someone who lives in a foreign country
infrastructure (n) /'ɪnfrəˌstrʌkʧər/ basic services that are necessary for a community to function
intrepid (adj) /ɪn'trepɪd/ brave, willing to take risks
meager (adj) /'migər/ small
militia (n) /mə'lɪʃə/ an armed group
rampage (v) /'ræmpeɪʤ/ behave in a wild and violent way
ruin (v) /'ruɪn/ destroy
unspoiled (adj) /ʌn'spɔɪld/ in a natural state

UNIT 6 REVIEW

Grammar

1 Work in pairs. Look at the photo. What kind of tourist attraction do you think this is?

2 Read the conversation and see if you were right. Then complete it using phrases with *not*.

M = Meka; P = Pauline

M: You're planning to go to Mexico for your vacation, [1] ________?

P: That was the plan, but I've [2] ________ (decide / go) now. I thought to myself, You're always traveling to exotic places. Why [3] ________ (you / explore) your own country?

M: That's interesting. That's called a staycation, [4] ________? You'll certainly save a lot of money.

P: Well, I hope so. But I [5] ________ (want / stay) at home. I'm going to travel around the north of France. Giverny, the garden where Monet painted his water lilies, is one place I'd really like to go. I [6] ________ (hope / rain) a lot.

M: Where are you going to stay? Or [7] ________ (decide) yet?

P: I'll take a tent with me, but I [8] ________ (think / I will use) it all the time. Let's [9] ________ (be) too ambitious! I'll stay in guest houses sometimes.

M: Well, I think it sounds like a great idea. It means you [10] ________ (must / worry) about visas and changing money and all.

3 What is Pauline's next vacation going to be? Why?

I CAN	
use *not* correctly with *hope*, *think*, *want*, *let*, *must*, and *have to* in the infinitive	☐
make negative questions and negative tag questions	☐

Vocabulary

4 Put the correct preposition in each space.

1 Do you prefer to cook for yourself or do you generally eat ________ when you're on vacation?
2 Do you like to try ________ new food?
3 Do you generally join ________ with group activities and organized excursions or do you prefer to do things alone?
4 If you had two weeks ________, how far would you travel?
5 Have you ever had to fill ________ an immigration form?
6 Do you stay ________ later than usual when you're on vacation?

5 In pairs, ask each other the questions above.

I CAN	
use phrasal verbs with *in* and *out*	☐
talk about vacations and travel	☐

Real life

6 Match each phrase in list A with its ending in list B.

A	B
I'm coming in	in traffic.
The easiest thing is to hop	my own way.
I'll pick you up	ride.
I'll call if I get held up	to your house?
Look out for the Hoover building	by train.
I can easily find	on a bus.
It's only a ten-minute	on your right.
How do I get	from the station.

7 Tell your partner how to get to a well-known meeting point in your town by public transportation.

I CAN	
describe the best way to get from one place to another	☐
ask for directions and travel advice	☐

Speaking

8 Work in pairs. What do you look for when choosing a vacation destination? Tell each other which of these matters more to you and why:

- the comfort OR the experience
- the journey OR the destination
- familiarity with the place OR not knowing anything about it
- relaxation OR being active

Unit 7 Natural resources

This photo taken half above, half under water shows fishermen on an Indonesian coral island.
Photograph by David Doubilet

FEATURES

1 Work in pairs. Look at the photo. How many natural resources can you identify?

air	soil
animals	sunlight
fossil fuels (coal, oil, gas)	trees
minerals	water
plants and fruits	wind

2 Match the words (1–5) to their definitions (a–e). Then discuss which words apply to the natural resources in Exercise 1.

1 abundant	a nature can replace what is used
2 exhaustible	b in plentiful supply
3 inexhaustible	c can be used up
4 renewable	d difficult to find
5 scarce	e will never be used up

3 The three Rs of saving natural resources are: Reduce, Reuse, and Recycle. What examples can you give of each of them? Do you do any yourself?

7a Water conservation

Speaking

1 Work in pairs. Why do we need to save water when over 70 percent of the Earth's surface is covered by water? Read the article and see if your answer was similar.

So what if people waste a lot of water—we've got enough, don't we? Well, we may have a lot of ocean water, but we are using fresh water faster than nature can replace it. So instead we are forced to recycle waste water, cleaning it and then piping it into people's homes. That process requires a lot of energy—running a tap for five minutes uses the same energy as burning a 60-watt light bulb for fourteen hours—and a lot of money. Also, when underground natural water reservoirs (or aquifers) get low, they can become contaminated with high concentrations of natural minerals like arsenic, or man-made chemicals from the ground. To prevent this, we need to keep these reservoirs well-stocked. Here's where our water goes:

A six minute shower	15 gallons (55 liters)
A hamburger	660 gallons (2,500 l)*
A serving of goat meat	11 gallons (42 l)
A bar of chocolate	372 gallons (1410 l)
A serving of chicken	153 gallons (580 l)*
A cup of coffee	36 gallons (135 l)
Flushing the toilet	2 gallons (8 l)
500 sheets of paper	6,000 gallons (22,500 l)
A slice of bread	11 gallons (40 l)
1 lb (½ k) of clean wool	22,500 gallons (85,000 l)

* in the case of the farm animals, only a few gallons were drunk by the animals or used in processing; the majority of the water went into the grain they were fed during their lives.

2 Look at the facts and answer the questions.

1 Are you surprised by any of the facts? Why?
2 What are the best ways to save water?

Listening

3 **24** Listen to speakers from the United Kingdom, the United Arab Emirates, the United States, and Mexico talking about water. What does each say about:

1 their own attitude toward water use?
2 what will happen if water is not conserved?

4 **24** Listen again and answer the questions.

Speaker 1
1 How does Liam describe Manchester?
2 What does he do when he brushes his teeth?
Speaker 2
3 What is the problem with desalinating water?
4 What is Gemal researching?
Speaker 3
5 How has the Colorado Delta changed in the last 100 years?
6 What is the river water used for?
Speaker 4
7 What practical water saving measures does Carmen do at home?
8 What does she suggest about other people's attitudes toward water use?

5 Are there similar situations in your country?

Grammar **mixed conditional sentences**

6 Work in pairs. Look at the *if* sentences (1–6). Answer the questions (a–c).

a Which sentences describe present situations and present consequences?
b Which describe past situations and past consequences?
c Which are a mixture of the two?

1 If we had known the facts, we would not have wasted so much water in the past.
Example:
B. *We didn't know the facts in the past, so we wasted a lot of water in the past.*
2 If I had been brought up in Saharan Africa, I would be more aware of my water use.
3 If we used less water, we wouldn't have to use so much energy treating it.
4 If not for desalination, this country would not have been able to develop.
5 If you had visited the area around the old delta in Mexico 100 years ago, you would be shocked to see it now.
6 If more people thought and acted like me, things would not have come to this point.

A world of its own

Madagascar, the world's fourth largest island, at over 225,000 square miles, is a unique place that has been blessed with exceptional riches. Roughly 90 percent of its flora and fauna is found nowhere else on the planet. The spectacle of its carrot-shaped baobab trees and ghostly lemurs makes even the most well-traveled visitors wide-eyed with amazement and delight.

But its rare beauty hides the desperate situation of its people. The typical Madagascan lives on about a dollar a day, even though you would not guess this from the cheerful and optimistic Malagasy, the island's main ethnic group. Since the first humans arrived in Madagascar some 2,300 years ago, loggers and developers have destroyed nearly 90 percent of the island's original forest habitat, harvesting it for timber or burning it down to create room for crops and, more recently, cattle.

Considering that Madagascar's population is growing by three percent a year, this tension between rich land and poor residents is increasing daily. Alarmed ecologists have named Madagascar a biodiversity hot spot, deploring the practice of slash-and-burn agriculture. In 2002, the global environmental community rejoiced when green-friendly Marc Ravalomanana was elected president. But only seven years later, in the spring of 2009, the military replaced Ravalomanana with a former radio disc jockey who seemed to have little interest in protecting the environment.

Needing money, the new government reversed a ban on the export of precious hardwoods, making it legal to sell wood from trees which had already been cut down or had fallen during the cyclones that regularly hit the island. Yet in reality they did little to control the loggers who continued to rob the forests of new wood. The main targets of this environmental crime are the rosewood and ebony trees. The wood from these majestic trees is in high demand: in China, it is used to make exotic imperial-style furniture for the new middle class; in Europe and America, it is a valued material in the manufacture of expensive musical instruments.

The locals are caught in a trap. Poverty and the high value of rosewood—at $3,000 per cubic meter it is ten times as valuable as oak—have driven them to cut down trees that are traditionally considered sacred. It is dangerous and back-breaking work. Using hand axes, in a few hours they bring down a tree that has stood tall for many centuries. Then they cut the trees into logs and drag them several miles to the nearest river.

The rare hardwood trees are not the only casualties. In order to transport the heavy rosewood logs downriver, rafts must be built from other wood. For each raft, the loggers cut down four or five lighter trees near the river, causing the earth to erode and silt up the rivers. Animals' habitats have also been disturbed, putting their survival at risk.

In this bleak landscape, one man's work offers hope. Olivier Behra, who first came to Madagascar from France in 1987, believes that the only solution is to give local people economic alternatives. Almost single-handedly, he has stopped deforestation in the Vohimana forest by encouraging the locals instead to collect medicinal plants, which they never imagined had any monetary value, and sell them overseas. The village lemur hunter has been retrained as a guide for tourists obsessed with lemurs. The same tourists also pay to visit the wild orchid conservatory that Behra has set up. Can small-scale and sensitive initiatives like this compete with the rosewood mafia of Madagascar? Only time will tell.

MADAGASCAR IN NUMBERS

FOURTH-LARGEST island in the world after Greenland, New Guinea, and Borneo

22 MILLION people from 18 different Asian and African ethnic groups living here

90 PERCENT of its flora and fauna is found nowhere else on Earth

70 different species of lemur found only on Madagascar

300 YEARS: the time it takes a rosewood tree to reach maturity

Number 1 producer of vanilla in the world

27,000 TONS of ebony and rosewood exported in 2009, much of it illegally

7d The climate change debate

Real life making your point

1 Work in pairs. What causes climate change? Is it man-made or a natural phenomenon? Use the expressions below to help you.

CO_2 emissions	natural weather cycle
fossil fuels	the greenhouse effect
global warming	

2 25 Listen to four people discussing climate change. Which two people would change their habits to help prevent climate change?

Speaker 1: Elena ☐ Speaker 3: Jim ☐
Speaker 2: Anne ☐ Speaker 4: Rick ☐

3 25 Listen again. Complete the expressions (1–6) that the speakers use to make their points.

▶ MAKING YOUR POINT

Giving examples
Take..., for example...
Let me give you an example...
Imagine [1] ________ hair...

Stressing a point
The point is that...
I, for one, [2] ________ in how I pollute...
Look, there's no doubt that [3] ________...
To be honest with you,...

Rejecting an argument
I don't accept that.
I used to believe [4] ________, but...
Yeah, but that's not the point.
I (don't) believe it simply because [5] ________.

Challenging the question itself
The whole starting point for this debate is wrong.
We're approaching this debate all wrong by saying [6] ________ problem.

4 25 Discuss which of the techniques (a–e) each speaker used to make a point. Listen again and check.

a humor
b challenging the question itself
c speaking clearly and slowly
d illustrating with examples/stories
e anticipating counter-arguments

5 Which technique did you find most effective? Which technique do you prefer yourself? Tell your partner.

6 Pronunciation sentence stress

a 26 When making their point, each speaker uses word stress to emphasize the important words. Listen to this example.

I don't know and I'm not sure **anyone** knows for sure. (2 words)

b 27 Underline the words which you think are most stressed. Then listen and check.

1 We don't know that we're causing it, but some people say we might be... (2 words)
2 ...scraping ice off the inside of my windows rather than the outside. (2 words)
3 Regional temperatures may be lower, but average global temperatures keep on rising. (2 words)
4 Because it's not just an environmental problem. It's an economic problem, a social problem, even an ethical problem. (4 words)

7 Work in pairs. Choose one of the solutions to climate change given below. Work out arguments in favor of this solution. Think about the techniques you will use to make your point and the examples you could give. Then debate another pair who have a different solution.

The solution to climate change is:
- reducing energy use by inreasing fuel prices
- paying poor countries to protect their forests
- finding a technological solution to cool the Earth (like putting millions of tiny mirrors in space to reflect the sun's rays)
- getting all countries to sign an international agreement to limit CO_2 emissions

7e Waste of energy

Writing a letter to the editor

1 Do you ever read the letters section of newspapers, local or national? Have you ever written a letter to the editor yourself?

2 Read the letter. Answer the questions.

1 Who wrote the letter?
2 Why did they write it?
3 Do you find it persuasive? Why?

Financial News **Published: March 20**

To the Editor:

James Anderson (Travel section, March 15) writes about the waste of energy in hotels: overheated rooms, lights left on all night, towels used once and washed. He is right, but why stop with hotels? Wouldn't it be better to mention all the other mindless waste that characterizes modern life?

In the morning, I walk downtown past stores whose doors are wide open, blowing hot air into the street. At night, I walk home past fully-lit, empty office buildings, when the workers have already left; past enormous flashing screens where advertisers try to go one better than the competition. At the supermarket, I take my frozen vegetables from open freezer bins. My children leave their computers on when they go out, and their phone chargers plugged in with no phone on the other end (though they should know better).

All this waste illustrates two simple facts. First, that energy is too cheap and we had better increase its price substantially to make people more energy-conscious. Second, that no one really considers the public interest anymore.

Just as it is in the public interest that we have speed limits on our roads—though some of us may not like it—so would we be better off if we were forced by our government to conserve energy.

V. Dupeyrat
Head of Energy Services
DEF Energy, Seattle

3 Work in pairs. How is the letter organized? Match the functions (a–d) with each paragraph. Discuss whether they could be organized differently.

a Examples that illustrate the problem
b A recommendation or call to action
c The reason for writing
d A summary of the problem

4 **Word focus *better***

Underline all the phrases using the word *better* and match them with the definitions (a–e) below. Compare answers with your partner.

a not be so stupid
b in an improved (often economic) situation
c more useful or desirable
d improve on the effort of another
e really ought to

5 **Writing skills giving vivid examples**

a What does the writer say about lights and towels to illustrate his argument?

b Find more examples of energy waste in the first two paragraphs.

6 Look at this list of things that annoy people about modern life. Expand three of them to explain what is annoying about it, as in the example. Then compare with your partner.

Example:
magazines that… *are full of news about celebrities*

airlines which…
cell phones that…
TV shows about…
supermarket food that…
computer programs which…

7 Write a short letter (150 words) to the editor, talking about one of the items in Exercise 6. Make sure you include the same elements as in the sample letter. Then exchange letters with your partner. Do they agree with the way you feel?

8 Read your partner's letter. Use these questions to check their letter. Is it correctly organized?

- Does it use enough examples?
- Does it end with a summary?
- Is it persuasive?

7f Galapagos energy

Video

Naturalist Charles Darwin once called the Galapagos "a little world within itself."

Before you watch

1 Work in groups. Look at the photo and discuss the questions.

1 What do you know about the Galapagos Islands? Make notes about:
a their location.
b the population.
c what the islands are famous for.

2 What do you think Darwin meant when he called the Galapagos "a little world within itself"?

2 Complete the video summary with words from the glossary below.

The Galapagos Islands are home to many unique species of plants and animals. However, recently human beings have invaded this tropical [1] ________. Tourism has [2] ________ and workers from the [3] ________ have followed. This has created pollution from vehicle [4] ________, the energy people use, and the trash they produce, which harms the islands. Now, [5] ________, corporations, and the government are working to minimize human impact.

While you watch

3 Watch the video and check your answers from Exercises 1 and 2.

4 Watch the first part of the video (to 02:41) and answer the questions.

1 Why did the animals on the Galapagos evolve into unique species?
____

2 What do people always say about the islands?
____

3 What do the volcanic eruptions tell scientists?
____

4 How long have humans been living on the islands?
____

5 What is one positive aspect of tourism?
____

6 What happened after the recent oil spill?
____

5 Watch the second part of the video (02:42 to the end). Mark the things you see.

a bird with a blue beak	a bicycle	boats
a bird with a red beak	black sandals	a bus
a recycling bin	a motorbike	a seal
a blue dress	a pink T-shirt	a turtle

6 Watch the second part again and answer the questions.

1 What is the goal of the program that international organizations and the Ecuadoran government are working on?
____

2 What four examples of conservation projects does the video show?
a ________
b ________
c ________
d ________

After you watch

7 Roleplay an interview with Leopoldo Bocheri More

Work in pairs.

Student A: Imagine you are going to interview Leopoldo Bocheri More. Read the information below and prepare a list of questions.

Student B: Imagine you are Leopoldo Bocheri More. A journalist is going to interview you. Look at the information below and think about what you are going to say the journalist.

- the problems the Galapagos have
- what the government is doing
- what other help is needed

Act out the interview. Then change roles.

8 Work in groups and discuss these questions.

1 What natural areas in your country have been adversely affected by human activity?
2 What can be done to protect such places?

conservationist (n) /ˌkɑnsər'veɪʃənɪst/ a person who works to preserve nature
contaminant (n) /kən'tæmɪnənt/ something that pollutes
emissions (n) /ɪ'mɪʃənz/ smoke and gas from machines
haven (n) /'heɪvən/ a place people or animals can escape to
leak (n) /lik/ liquid or gas that escapes through a hole
mainland (n) /'meɪnˌlænd/ a large area of land that is not an island
oil spill (n) /'ɔɪl ˌspɪl/ when oil accidentally escapes from the place it is stored
old-timer (n) /'oʊld 'taɪmər/ a person or animal who has lived in a place for a long time
pristine (adj) /prɪs'tin/ in perfect condition
relic (n) /'relɪk/ something left over from the past
revenue (n) /'revəˌnu/ money earned
run aground (v) /'rʌn ə'graʊnd/ hit rocks or the bottom of the sea
skyrocket (v) /'skaɪˌrɑkɪt/ to go up very quickly
wake-up call (n) /'weɪk ʌp ˌkɔl/ a warning to pay attention

UNIT 7 REVIEW

Grammar

1 Work in pairs. Do you think that young people are more or less aware of the need to conserve resources than their parents' generation?

2 Read part of a blog discussing young people's attitude toward resources. What kind of things are they aware of? And not aware of?

3 Complete the text with the correct form of the verbs.

The younger generation seems very aware of global problems with natural resources. If you ask them about the rain forests, for example, they [1] *will say / would say*: "Oh, I wish people [2] *stopped / would stop* cutting them down. They're destroying the planet."
But on a personal level, they don't seem to be so aware. For example, it seems they would rather [3] *leave / left* the computer in sleep mode than [4] *turn / turned* it off. If the central heating was on too high, they [5] *would be / would have been* more likely to open a window than turn it down!
We parents are partly to blame for this. If we [6] *were / had been* stricter with our children when they were young, they [7] *would know / would have known* how to act now. I wish that they [8] *had / had had* more energy-saving education at school. As parents, we'd all rather schools [9] *teach / taught* these things because when we try, our children just think we are nagging!

I CAN	
hypothesize about present and past situations using mixed second and third conditionals	☐
express wishes and preferences about the past and future with *wish*, *if only*, *would rather*	☐

Vocabulary

4 Work in pairs. Find the odd one out in each group of words. Explain why it doesn't fit.

1 conserve, waste, save, preserve
2 natural, abundant, scarce, inexhaustible
3 oil refinery, oil slick, oil rig, oil tanker
4 sunlight, minerals, air, wind
5 majestic, tall, obsessed, desperate

5 Work in small groups. Think of two natural resources that are scarce. Discuss what we can do to protect them.

I CAN	
talk about natural resources	☐
use nouns, verbs, and adjectives about using and conserving natural resources	☐

Real life

6 Work in pairs. Which speakers (1–5) agree with this sentence and which disagree?

We should force developing countries to consume resources more carefully.

1 "Worry about developing countries? I have enough trouble remembering to turn off the lights!"
2 "The point is that the developed nations have used resources as they wished, so why shouldn't developing countries do the same?"
3 "If a rich person in India wants to own four cars and a mansion, who am I to say he can't?"
4 "I know you'll say that it's *everyone's* duty not to waste resources, but I don't accept that."
5 "It's not about what's fair; it's about what's necessary. We all need to conserve."

7 Which technique (a–e) does each speaker use to make their point?

a humor
b challenging the question itself
c using emphasis
d using examples/stories
e anticipating counter-arguments

8 Choose one of the techniques in Exercise 7 and make your own point about the need to conserve resources.

I CAN	
use different techniques to make my point in a debate	☐

Speaking

9 Work in small groups. Discuss the following issues.

- a regret you have about harming the environment
- a consequence of not protecting natural resources in your area
- an action to help conserve a natural resource

Unit 8 The news

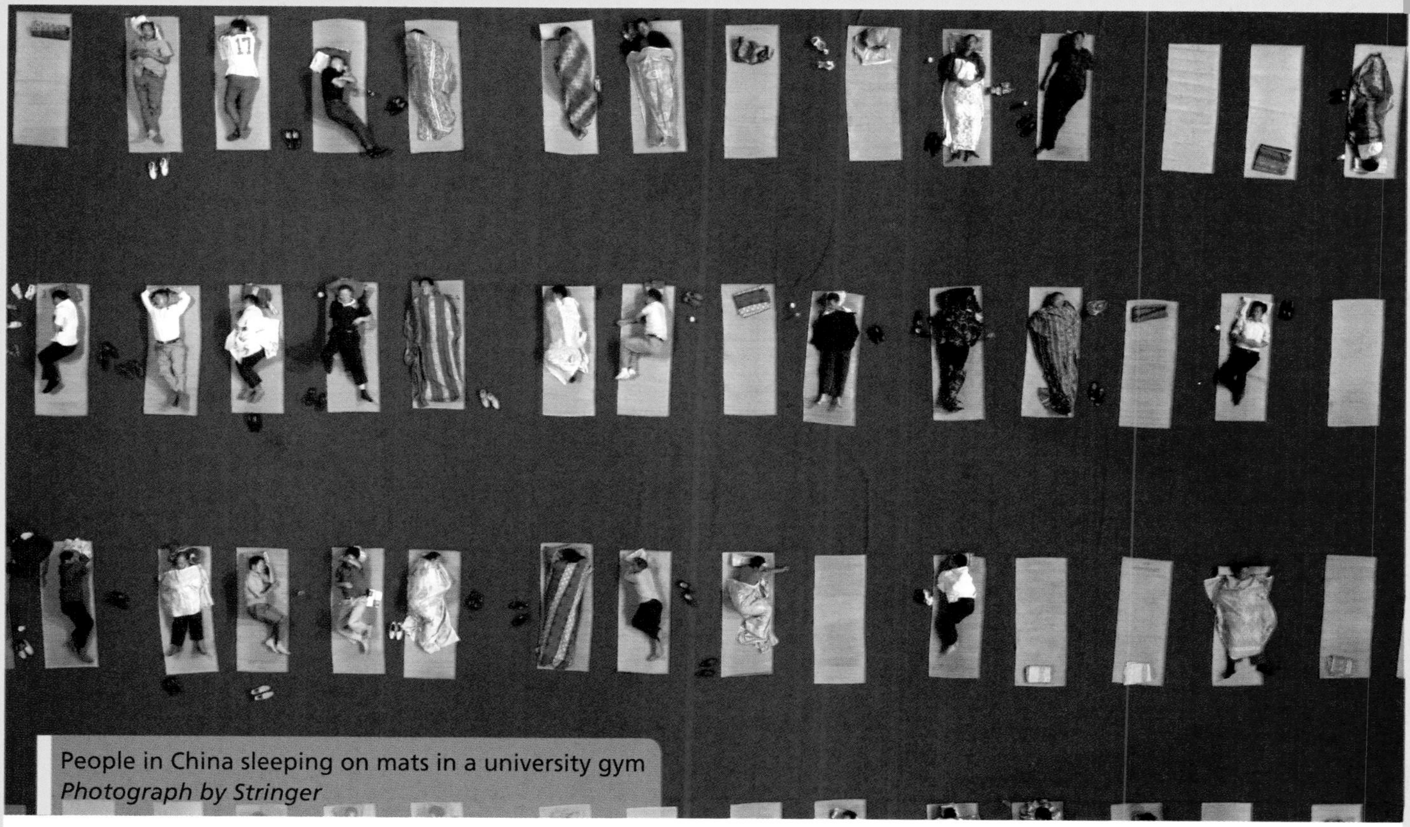

People in China sleeping on mats in a university gym
Photograph by Stringer

FEATURES

1 Match the phrases to complete these English sayings about the news. What sayings about news do you have in your language?

1 Good news…	a is good news.
2 Bad news…	b doesn't sell.
3 No news…	c travels fast.

2 Work in pairs. Look at the photo and caption. Why do you think these people are sleeping in the gym? Think of a news story to explain the photo. Share your answers with the class.

3 Do the following fall into the category of hard news (serious, urgent) or soft news (less serious, not urgent)? Discuss.

- a column with celebrity gossip
- a local news story about a new housing development
- an editorial about a political scandal
- business news about interest rates
- a travel feature about Nicaragua
- a science news story about a cure for Alzheimer's disease

8a A life revealed

Vocabulary photography

1 Read the quotations. Find the following:

- 3 words that mean *a photograph*
- 2 words for parts of a camera
- 3 verbs that describe what a camera does with an image

2 Which is your favorite quotation? Why?

> A picture is worth a thousand words. *- Fred R. Barnard*
>
> What you have caught on film is captured forever… it remembers little things, long after you have forgotten everything. *- Aaron Siskind*
>
> There is one thing the photograph must contain: the humanity of the moment. *- Robert Frank*
>
> Look and think before opening the shutter. The heart and mind are the true lens of the camera. *- Yousuf Karsh*
>
> I see no reason to record the obvious. *- Edward Weston*
>
> A great photographer takes 100 shots and keeps just one. *- Anon*
>
> Seeing and composing the beauty is what separates the snapshot from the photograph. *- Matt Hardy*

Reading

3 Work in pairs. Look at the two photos and discuss the questions. Then read the article and check your answers.

1 Have you seen either of these photos before?
2 Where are these people from?
3 How old are they?
4 What is the relationship between them?

4 Complete these sentences by finding the contrasting facts in the article.

1 Sharbat Gula let McCurry take her picture, even though…
2 The picture became world famous, even though…
3 McCurry recognized 29-year-old Gula immediately, even though…
4 Gula does not complain about her life, even though…

A LIFE REVEALED

She remembers the moment the photographer took her picture. The man was a stranger, but he asked if he could, and she agreed to let him take it. She had never been photographed before and, until they met a second time seventeen years later, she was not photographed again.

The photographer, Steve McCurry, remembers the moment too. It was 1984 and he was recording the lives of Afghan refugees in a camp in Pakistan. She was staring out of the school tent and he admits thinking at the time that the picture would be nothing special. Yet the "Afghan girl," as the portrait is now known, became one of the most iconic images of our time. McCurry used her intense expression, so untypical of an average, carefree twelve-year-old girl, to warn us not to ignore the victims of war, especially its young victims.

In 2002 National Geographic persuaded McCurry to return to Pakistan to look for the girl. After showing her photo around the refugee camp, he found a man who had known her as a child and knew where to find her. He offered to get her from her home in the Tora Bora mountains and after three days returned with Sharbat Gula, a woman perhaps 29 years old. McCurry knew at once that this was her.

Time and hardship had erased her youth. Her skin was weathered. Yet her eyes still burned with the same intensity. Her brother explained the story of their lives, blaming the war for forcing them and many other Afghans out of their homeland. When Sharbat was six years old, they fled to the mountains, hiding in caves and begging people to give them food and blankets. She married when she was sixteen and now her time is occupied with bringing up her three children, cooking, cleaning, and caring for them. Yet she does not complain about having a hard life. More amazingly, she is not aware of the impact that the photo of the young Sharbat with her sea-green eyes had on the world.

iconic (adj) /aɪˈkɑnɪk/ well-known and admired everywhere

Grammar reporting verbs

5 Look back at the article and complete these sentences using reporting verbs. Note the form that follows the reporting verb in each case.

1 She **agreed** ________ him take her picture.
2 He **admits** ________ at the time that the picture would be nothing special.
3 McCurry used her intense expression to **warn** us ________ the victims of war.
4 In 2002 National Geographic **persuaded** McCurry ________ to Pakistan.
5 He **offered** ________ her from her home in the Tora Bora mountains.
6 Her brother **blamed** the war ________ them out of their homeland.
7 They **begged** people ________ them food and blankets.
8 She does not **complain** ________ a hard life.

6 Work in pairs. What is being reported in Exercise 5? Discuss what the person actually said at the time. Then compare answers with another pair.

1 She agreed to let him take her picture.
Yes, you can take my picture.

▶ REPORTING VERBS

Verb + infinitive
She agreed to let him take her picture.

Verb + someone + infinitive
National Geographic persuaded McCurry to return to Pakistan.

Verb + -ing
He admits thinking at the time that the picture would be nothing special.

Verb + preposition + -ing
She does not complain about having a hard life.

Verb + someone + preposition + -ing
Her brother blamed war for forcing them out of their homeland.

For more information and practice, see page 167.

7 Look at the grammar box. Use the verb given to report each of these statements.

1 You've taken some amazing photos!
She ________. (complimented)
2 You should think seriously about doing this professionally.
She ________. (encouraged)
3 You are far too modest about your own talents.
She ________. (accused)
4 Why don't you take a better photograph?
She ________. (suggested)
5 I'll also introduce you to my friend, who is a wildlife photographer.
She ________. (promised)
6 In fact, I'm sorry I haven't introduced you to him sooner.
She ________. (apologized)
7 You really should enter that photo competition in National Geographic.
She ________. (urged)
8 I can lend you my camera, if you don't think yours is good enough.
She ________. (offered)

8 Complete the article about the ethics of taking photos of other people. Put the verbs in the correct form. (You may need a preposition.)

Photographers who take pictures without their subject's knowledge are accused [1] ________ (be) sneaky or even unethical. A photographer who uses a telephoto lens to take a picture of someone at home cannot deny [2] ________ (do) wrong—they invaded someone's privacy. Newspaper reporters are often criticized [3] ________ (do) this kind of thing, not that it stops them.

But isn't this the same as taking pictures of strangers without permission? They haven't said it's OK for you [4] ________ (take) their picture. Maybe they would feel uncomfortable if you asked them [5] ________ (pose) for a shot; they might even refuse [6] ________ (let) you do it.

A lot of photographers insist [7] ________ (be) invisible so that their shots are more natural. They object [8] ________ (ask) their subject for permission first because this would spoil the moment. But I disagree. I always advise photographers [9] ________ (talk) to their subjects first. In fact, I strongly recommend [10] ________ (get) to know their subjects' story, because it gives the shots more meaning.

Speaking

9 Work in small groups and discuss the questions.

1 Do you like having your photo taken? Why?
2 What is the best way to get a good photo of someone?
3 Do you ever take photos of people you don't know? How do you approach this?
4 Have you ever felt uncomfortable about taking a photo of someone you didn't know?

8b And finally...

Vocabulary the feel-good factor

1 News programs often like to end with a good news story. Look at the adjectives that describe how this type of story can make people feel and match each one to a definition.

amusing	appealing	charming	encouraging
inspiring	odd	optimistic	quirky

1 ...., ...: hopeful
2 ....: makes one smile or laugh
3 ....: shows what people can achieve
4 ...., ...: unusual or strange
5 ...., ...: delightful

▶ WORDBUILDING forming adjectives from verbs

We can add *-ing* to many verbs to form adjectives.
amuse → amusing, encourage → encouraging

2 Work in pairs. Think of an example of a good news story you have heard recently. Tell your partner. Use one of the adjectives in Exercise 1.

I saw a really inspiring local news story on TV about a five-year-old boy who raised money for his sick sister by...

Listening

3 **28** Listen to four feel-good news stories and complete the summaries.

1 People thought that the ...., but they were wrong because .... As a result in the future we will see ....
2 Researchers believe they have found .... When people took ...., the result was that ....
3 The world's largest .... says they have invented .... But doctors ....
4 Costa Rica is .... because it has .... Countries like .... on the other hand, ...

4 Work with a student from another group and retell the stories to each other. Which story did you find the most optimistic? Quirky? Inspiring?

Grammar passive reporting verbs

5 Look at these two examples of passive reporting verbs and answer the questions.

It *was thought* that the large blue butterfly was extinct.
It *is estimated* that 20,000 large blue butterflies will be seen this summer.

1 What do/did people actually say or think?
2 When do/did they say or think this?

▶ PASSIVE REPORTING VERBS

Typical reporting verbs
say, think, believe, report, consider, know, estimate, expect, claim

***It* + *is* + passive reporting verb + *that* + sentence...**
It is thought that people are more healthy these days. (present report of present event)
It is thought that people were less healthy in the past. (present report of past event)
It is thought that people will be healthier in the future. (present report of future event)

***It* + *was* + passive reporting verb + *that* + sentence...**
It was thought that the butterfly was extinct. (report and event at same time in past)
It was thought that the butterfly had disappeared. (past event before past report)
It was thought that the butterfly would not return. (past report of a future event)

For more information and practice, see page 167.

6 Work in pairs. Look at the grammar box. Then look at the audioscript on page 179 and underline more sentences with passive reporting verbs. For each one decide:

- when the reporting happened
- when the reported event happened

1 ....

2 ....

3 ....

4 ....

5 ....

6 ....

7 ....

7 Transform these sentences into passive reporting sentences using *it*.

1 People report: "Large blue butterflies are everywhere now."
Example:
It is reported that large blue butterflies are everywhere now.
2 30 years ago people said: "The large blue butterfly is a common species."
3 People said: "Hunters caused the butterfly to die out."
4 The announcer said: "People thought the butterfly was extinct."
5 I said: "I take zinc and I haven't had a bad cold in a year."
6 In the past people thought: "Costa Rica is a poor country."
7 Scientists claim: "Taking zinc helps if you have a cold."
8 They said: "None of the previous experiments has been conclusive."
9 Experts claimed: "Eating the new chocolate will improve your health."
10 But people know: "Eating too much chocolate is actually bad for you."

8 Look at these other news items and facts and make sentences using the passive reporting verbs given. Tell your partner whether you think each one is true or not. Then check your answers on page 155.

1 It / believe / that chewing gum when you peel onions / prevent / you from crying.
2 It / say / Google's name / come / from "googol," a number with 100 zeros.
3 It / know / that laughing regularly / increase / life expectancy by up to ten years.
4 In 2008, it / report / that air pollution in the US / fall / by 40 percent since 1980.
5 It / claim / recently that scientists studying the zebrafish / discover / a way for the human heart to heal itself.
6 In 2011, it / report / that a man whose house had been crushed by a huge rock in the New Zealand earthquake /sell / the rock for $10,000.

Writing and speaking

9 Work in groups of three and prepare a feel-good news story. Choose a theme of your own or one from the list below. Then write the story together, using at least two passive reporting verbs. When you have finished, practice reading it aloud. Then each person should join a new group of three and read their stories to the other students.

- a person rescued by an animal
- the discovery of a valuable painting or antique
- a child's remarkable musical ability
- the invention of a new clothing fabric
- a couple who are celebrating their 90th wedding anniversary
- a dentist that people actually enjoy visiting

8c From hero to zero

Reading

1 Work in pairs. Look at the headlines below, as they appeared over several months. Discuss what you think happened.

HERO BA PILOT PETER BURKILL SPEAKS:
I THOUGHT WE'D DIE IN HEATHROW CRASH

"I AM NOT A HERO"
SAYS BA CRASH PILOT CAPTAIN PETER BURKILL

REAL HERO OF BA FLIGHT 38
IS COPILOT JOHN COWARD

HERO PILOT "FORCED OUT OF BA"

FALLEN HERO: THAT DAY CHANGED MY LIFE FOREVER

OFFICIAL REPORT SAYS ICE FAULT
CAUSED BA AIRPORT CRASH

2 Read the story quickly. Then check the sequence of key events with your partner. How did the story differ from your answer in Exercise 1?

3 Mark the statements true (T) or false (F).

1 Burkill's copilot was at the controls when the engines failed.
2 Some passengers were badly hurt.
3 At the time of the accident, Burkill was a single man who liked to enjoy himself.
4 Burkill's crew read BA's internal report.
5 Burkill was praised in the AAIB report.
6 He was too loyal to BA to work for another airline.

4 Complete the sentences with words from the article.

1 Burkill went from being a hero to being a (opposite of *hero*) *villain* . (para 1)
2 When the plane crash-landed, (incredibly) ________ it stayed upright. (para 2)
3 Perhaps his colleagues believed he was (no good at his job) ________ . (para 3)
4 The press portrayed Burkill as irresponsible: he (failed) ________ the people he was supposed to be responsible for. (para 4)
5 Burkill felt (completely unsupported) ________ by his colleagues. (para 5)
6 After the official report was published, Burkill was (given as a prize) ________ a medal for his actions. (para 7)

Critical thinking **different perspectives**

5 Each participant had a different perspective and a different motivation for acting as they did after the accident. Make notes to complete the table.

People involved	Their view of Burkill's role	Motivations for their actions
Peter Burkill	*he did what any pilot would have done*	*to clear his name and keep his job*
BA staff		
BA management		
AAIB*		
the newspapers		

*Air Accidents Investigation Branch

6 Who do you believe? Who do you think the newspapers' readers believed?

Word focus ***word***

7 Find four expressions in the article with *word*. Match each one with the definitions below.

1 make the final point in an argument and win it
2 news or a rumor starts to circulate
3 no evidence other than what two sides claim to be true
4 no news about something

8 Work in pairs. What do these other expressions with *word* mean?

1 "The new gallery is amazing. But **don't take my word for it**: go see for yourself."
2 "When my husband handed me the keys to a new car for my birthday, I was at a loss **for words**."
3 "The hotel doesn't advertise at all. It just relies on **word of mouth** to get new customers."
4 "I can't believe they're closing the library. They **gave their word** that they wouldn't."

Speaking

9 Work in groups. Discuss the media in your country.
1 How respectful are reporters towards politicians?
2 How balanced is the reporting of public scandals?
3 Are people interested in reading about the private lives of famous people?

Before you watch

1 Work in groups. Look at the photo and discuss the questions.

1 Where are the people in the photo?
2 Why do you think they are there?
3 What do you think the caption tells us about the people in the photo?

2 Mark the things you think you are going to see in this video.

a bear	a rollercoaster
a bulldozer	snow
clouds	sunflowers
drums	a sunrise
food vendor	umbrellas

While you watch

3 Watch the video and check your answers from Exercise 2.

4 Watch the video again and describe these things.

1 Mount Fuji

....

....

2 the fire and water festivals

....

....

3 the weather when Karen Kasmauski climbs the mountain

....

....

5 Watch the first part of the video (to 02:07). Are these sentences true (T) or false (F)? Correct the false sentences.

1 Karen Kasmauski is enjoying perfect weather for her photo shoot.
2 Karen thinks Japanese people worship Mount Fuji because it is so beautiful.
3 Mount Fuji is worshipped with fire and water festivals.
4 Karen starts her photo shoot in the forest at the base of the mountain.
5 You can buy crackers and cakes at Mount Fuji.
6 Climbing Mount Fuji is seen mostly as something tourists have to do.

6 Watch the second part of the video (02:08 to the end). Make notes about these things. Then compare your notes with a partner.

1 How Karen feels when she gets to the top.

....

....

2 How Mount Fuji was different in the past.

....

....

3 Managing Mount Fuji.

....

....

4 What happens at the end of the climbing season.

....

....

After you watch

7 Roleplay interviewing a National Geographic photographer

Work in pairs.

Student A: Imagine you are a photographer for National Geographic. You are going to be interviewed by an amateur photographer. Make notes about the items below.

Student B: Imagine you are an amateur photographer. You are going to interview a photographer for National Geographic. Prepare questions based on these items.

- lifestyle of a photographer
- the advantages and disadvantages of the job

Act out the interview, then change roles.

8 Karen Kasmauski says that climbing Mount Fuji is "a national bonding experience." What do you think she means? Are there any symbols of national unity in your country?

9 Work in groups and discuss these questions.

1 Are there any special places in your country where people like to go and take photographs?
2 What makes an interesting photograph for you: the place, the people, or what is taking place?
3 Is there any famous place in the world you would like to photograph? Why?

appease (v) /ə'piz/ keep a person or a thing calm
bento box (n) /'bentoʊ ˌbɑks/ a wooden or metal box, divided into compartments, used in Japan for storing a meal
bonding (n) /'bɑndɪŋ/ the process of becoming emotionally close to other people
bulldozer (n) /'bʊlˌdoʊzər/ a large machine that moves earth
conical (adj) /'kɑnɪkəl/ shaped like a cone
pilgrimage (n) /'pɪlgrɪmɪʤ/ a journey to a holy place
purification (n) /pjʊərɪfɪ'keɪʃən/ the process of making something clean
typhoon (n) /taɪ'fun/ a very strong tropical storm
vending machine (n) /'vendɪŋ məˌʃin/ a machine that sells things, for example, drinks or food

UNIT 8 REVIEW

Grammar

1 Work in pairs. Look at the photo of a new development. What do you think the designers are trying to create?

2 Read the news article below and see if you were right.

3 Complete the article with the correct form of the verbs. Use prepositions where necessary. Then check your answer to Exercise 1.

Big cities are often criticized [1] ________ (be) big polluters. But it is generally considered that Singapore [2] ________ (be) an exception to this rule. For a long time the government has encouraged developers and conservationists [3] ________ (think) of ways to increase the island's green spaces. Recently green groups suggested [4] ________ (turn) the old KTM railway corridor into a nature trail. But perhaps the most striking project is Gardens by the Bay, a futuristic park which includes eighteen Supertrees. When it is complete, it is said that each of the eighteen trees [5] ________ (be covered) in more that 200 varieties of plants.

The government invited various companies [6] ________ (submit) ideas for the project and this was chosen as the most exciting. A spokesman for the government complimented the designers [7] ________ (come) up with a "truly innovative" design. The Supertrees are between 80 and 160 feet tall and mimic the function of real trees, absorbing sunlight through photovoltaic cells and collecting rainwater. The photographer who took this picture admitted [8] ________ (feel) skeptical about the project until he saw it for himself. "It looks like something from the movie *Avatar*: almost too good to be real!"

I CAN	
report speech with reporting verbs and the correct dependent verb form	☐
report what is generally said or thought with passive reporting verbs	☐

Vocabulary

4 Work in pairs. Find the odd word out in each group. Explain your choice.

1 movie, photo, snapshot, picture
2 column, feature, scandal, editorial
3 inspiring, amusing, optimistic, encouraging
4 lens, shutter, flash, camera
5 urge, promise, encourage, persuade
6 objection, suggestion, proposal, recommendation

5 Work in pairs. Describe a news photo that had a big impact on you. What was the story behind the picture?

I CAN	
talk about photography	☐
relate feel-good news stories	☐

Real life

6 Put each phrase into the right category: reporting what someone said (R), expressing belief (B), or expressing disbelief (D).

1 They figure that half a million people came to the free festival.
2 I'd take that with a grain of salt.
3 Apparently, a lot more people came than expected.
4 I think the number has been blown out of proportion.
5 According to official reports, around 250,000 attended.
6 It seems that the organizers were only expecting 150,000.
7 You can take the organizer's word for it.
8 Don't pay attention to what the promoters say. They just want publicity.

7 Work in small groups. Discuss an event, local or national, people have been talking about recently. Tell each other what you believe to be the real facts.

I CAN	
report what I heard	☐

Speaking

8 Work in pairs. Create a short news item about an event in your class or institution. Include at least two verbs reporting what people said.

Unit 9 Talented people

A mahout (elephant driver) bathes his elephant.
Photograph by Robert Harding

FEATURES

1 Work in pairs. Match the words in the box to the definitions (a–g).

background	experience	knowledge	degrees
qualities	skills	talents	

a strong natural abilities
b abilities developed by practice
c (generally positive) characteristics
d certificates which show you have learned something
e what you've done in your life
f what you know
g your past in general (birthplace, education, places lived)

2 Look at the photo and the caption. What qualities, skills, knowledge, and experience do you think a mahout needs to do their job well? Discuss.

3 Make short notes on your own background, experience, knowledge, and talents. Then ask each other questions.

9a An ordinary man

Reading

1 Work in pairs. Look at the photo and read the title of the article. Do you know who Neil Armstrong is? Tell your partner what you know.

2 Read the article and say in what ways Armstrong was an ordinary man and in what ways he was extraordinary.

3 Read the article again. Answer the questions.

1 Why is Armstrong called "the ultimate professional"?
2 Who paid for his college and what did they get in return?
3 What motivated Armstrong?
4 What does "the rest is history" mean?
5 What did Armstrong do to avoid publicity after the Apollo 11 mission? Why?
6 According to Armstrong, who was responsible for the success of the Apollo 11 mission?

An ORDINARY man

Neil Armstrong, the most famous of the astronauts on Apollo 11, has been called the ultimate professional. He was hired to do a job. He did the job and then he went home and kept quiet about it. In 40 years, he gave two interviews. He died in August 2012. But how could the man who first set foot on the Moon, a hero to millions of people, have remained such a mystery?

People like Armstrong often develop their interests at a young age. He pursued a career built on a passion for flying that he developed during his childhood in the 1930s. He learned to fly before he had graduated from high school in Wapakoneta, Ohio. He then took courses in aerospace engineering at Purdue University in Indiana, sponsored by the United States Navy. In return, Armstrong served as a naval pilot for three years. He saw action almost immediately, flying 78 missions in the war in Korea.

He left the Navy in 1952, and two years later got a job with the Lewis Flight Propulsion Laboratory, where he flew experimental aircraft. He reached speeds of 4,000 MPH and altitudes of over 200,000 feet. When he decided to become an astronaut is not clear. Certainly, it was not his ambition to be famous. An extremely talented pilot, he wanted simply to push the boundaries of flight.

He was selected for a space training program in 1960, and shortly after, news began to circulate that NASA was looking for astronauts for their Apollo program. Incredibly excited, he applied for the job and was accepted in 1962. The rest, as they say, is history.

When the astronauts returned from the Apollo 11 Moon landing of July 1969, Armstrong was a worldwide celebrity and could have done anything he wanted: TV shows, public speaking, etc. Instead, he became a professor at the University of Cincinnati. On weekends, he went flying to get away from all the attention. He subsequently worked for two private avionics companies until he retired in 2002. In 40 years he only gave two interviews. Why did Armstrong avoid publicity? Certainly he felt fortunate to have had the chance to fulfill his dream, but he did not feel any more special than the thousands of people who worked on the Apollo space program. He was just the pilot.

Astronaut Buzz Aldrin photographed on the Moon by Neil Armstrong (visible in Aldrin's visor)

Vocabulary careers

4 Work in pairs. Find verbs in the article that collocate with each of these nouns. Then identify the different steps in Armstrong's career.

1 to ________ a career
2 to ________ a school or college
3 to ________ a course
4 to ________ in the Navy
5 to ________ an astronaut
6 to ________ a company
7 to ________, ________, ________ a job

WORDBUILDING verb (+ preposition) + noun collocations

pursue a career
graduate from a school/college

Grammar articles: *the* or no article?

5 Look at how *the* or no article are used in the paragraph. Match the words in bold (1–7) with the uses of *the* and no article (a–g).

Neil Armstrong, (1) **the most famous** of (2) **the astronauts** on Apollo 11, has been called the ultimate professional. He was hired to do a job. He did (3) **the job** and then he went (4) **home** and kept quiet about it. In 40 years, he gave two interviews. But how could (5) **the man** who first set foot on (6) **the Moon**, a hero to (7) **millions** of people, have remained such a mystery?

a to talk about an already mentioned thing
b to talk about something unique
c before a superlative adjective
d to talk about a specific thing or person
e to talk about specific things or people
f to talk about things or people in general
g before certain familiar places (like work)

6 Work in pairs. Find one more example of each use in the rest of the article.

▶ ARTICLES: *THE* or NO ARTICLE?

definite article
the + singular/plural count nouns, noncount nouns = specific things

no article
– + plural count nouns, noncount nouns = things in general
Note: We don't use *the* with most time expressions or place names. However, there are some exceptions.

For more information and practice, see page 168.

7 Find an example in the article of the following:

1 no article with:
a) a country
b) a subject of study
c) a month
2 *the* with:
a) a country
b) a professional group
c) a period of time

8 Complete these sentences by inserting *the* where necessary.

1 While flying for ________ Navy in ________ Korea, Armstrong had to eject into ________ sea when one of ________ wings on his plane was damaged.
2 Armstrong and Aldrin only spent one day on ________ surface of ________ Moon.
3 Armstrong retired from ________ NASA in ________ 1972, but he helped with ________ crash investigations in ________ later years.
4 ________ first investigation was in ________ May 1970 following an explosion on ________ Apollo 13.
5 ________ other investigation involved ________ space shuttle Challenger, which broke into ________ pieces over ________ Atlantic Ocean near ________ Florida.
6 In ________ nineties, Armstrong stopped signing ________ autographs, because ________ dealers were selling each for $1,000.

Speaking

9 Draw a path of your own (or a parent's) career. Begin with your interests as a child. Finish with future ambitions. If it is not an obvious linear progression, show how the direction changed. Then explain the path to your partner.

When I was a kid, I really liked to draw. But my parents wanted me to be a lawyer, so I started college for law in 2013.

But now you're in art school!

Yes… I hated it, so I took a year off and then dropped out!

9b Pushing the boundaries

Listening

1 31 Listen to an interview about the National Geographic Emerging Explorers program and answer the questions.

1. What is the aim of the program?
2. How does National Geographic help those selected?
3. What kind of fields do Emerging Explorers work in?

2 31 Are the sentences true (T) or false (F)? Listen again and check.

1. Emerging Explorers are people who are not yet fully established in their careers.
2. Emerging Explorers get money and publicity for their work in the magazine.
3. They generally have a scientific background.
4. Storytellers are explorers who record traditional stories from different cultures.
5. Alexandra Cousteau's father filmed other Emerging Explorers.
6. Alexandra is interested in how new technology can help to spread the environmental message.

Grammar relative clauses

3 Work in pairs. Look at the relative clauses in bold from the interview (a–e). Then discuss the questions (1–4).

a. Each year, between eight and fifteen explorers, **whose work is really outstanding**, are selected.
b. Emerging Explorers are generally people **who are at an early stage of their careers**.
c. National Geographic awards each one of them $10,000, **which is intended to go towards further research**.
d. The magazine is a place **where other interested people can read about their work**.
e. There are all these people doing important work out there in the various fields **that I have described**.

1. In which sentence is the relative pronoun the subject of the relative clause?
2. In which sentences does the relative clause explain who or what is being talked about?
3. In which sentences does the relative clause give extra information and how does the punctuation help you know this?
4. In which sentence could the relative pronoun be omitted?

▶ RELATIVE CLAUSES

Relative pronouns: *who* (*that*), *which* (*that*), *where*, *whose*
Subject: *She's the woman who won the award.*
Object: *That's the award which/that the woman won.*
OR *That's the award the woman won.*

Defining relative clause
This clause contains essential information for identification.
She's the woman who won an award for her photography.

Non-defining relative clause
This clause contains extra information, separated by one or two commas.
Her husband, who is also a photographer, accompanied her on the trip.

***that* or no pronoun**
The article (that) I read about her was good.

For more information and practice, see page 169.

4 Look at the grammar box. Then complete these sentences about Emerging Explorer Alexandra Cousteau by inserting the correct relative pronoun and any commas that are missing.

1. Alexandra Cousteau ________ is a conservationist believes water will be the most important issue of the 21st century.
2. Alexandra Cousteau ________ father was an oceanographer is a great advocate for environmental protection.
3. Cousteau says that the environmental movement uses communication tools ________ are old-fashioned.
4. She is currently planning an expedition ________ aim is to research different water ecosystems around the world.
5. She is currently working on a book ________ she hopes will teach people how to live on a "Water Planet."
6. The problem ________ she says was created by people is a problem ________ people can only solve by working together.

Grammar reduced relative clauses

5 An alternative to a relative clause is a reduced relative clause. Look at the participles in bold in these sentences. Which are active and which are passive?

1 We have so many different types of explorers, **chosen** from diverse fields.
2 There are all these people **doing** important work out there in the various fields.
3 That's the skill of the storytellers, **communicating** important facts about the planet.
4 She works as a conservationist, **trying** to persuade people to protect resources like water.
5 Alexandra Cousteau, **inspired** by her father's success as a storyteller, is researching ways in which the environmental community can use new media.

> **REDUCED RELATIVE CLAUSES**
>
> **Present participle**
> *researching*
> *She works at Harvard, ~~where she is~~ researching sharks. (active)*
> **Past participle**
> *researched*
> *It's a subject ~~which is~~ researched by only a few people.*
> (passive)
>
> For more information and practice, see page 169.

6 Look at the grammar box. Then rewrite the reduced relative clauses in Exercise 5 as relative clauses.

7 Complete the profiles of other Emerging Explorers below by inserting the missing information as a reduced relative clause where possible and if not, as a relative clause.

1 She has been called the real-life Lara Croft by the *New York Times*.
2 She cycled a distance of 700 miles.
3 They threatened to harm her.
4 He is fascinated by the truly big questions.
5 He plays music to take his mind off problems.
6 He spends his time diving into water caves deep under the ground.
7 The caves have been undisturbed for 3.5 million years.
8 Knowledge is provided by these dark and wonderful places.

8 Work in pairs. Circle the eight adjectives in the profiles that describe people's strengths and qualities.

9 Which of these people would you most like to meet? Tell your partner.

Speaking and writing

10 Think of someone you admire for the work they do. Write a short description of their achievements and qualities. In groups, read your descriptions and ask questions.

Kira Salak, [1] ______________, doesn't want to tell travel stories you have already heard. Independent and adaptable, she has traveled across Papua New Guinea on foot, and Alaska on a bicycle, [2] ______________. It is not easy traveling alone as a single woman in remote and dangerous regions. In Mozambique, she escaped soldiers [3] ______________. But she does not regret such experiences because she says they have helped her discover her strengths.

Stephon Alexander is a theoretical physicist [4] ______________ like "how did space and time begin?" It's an unusual job because you need to be not only analytical and patient, but also daring and a risk taker, because to answer such questions you have to make guesses. Often you can be completely wrong. But when you are right, he says, the feeling is amazing. The work can be mentally tiring, but Alexander is quite an easy-going type. He is also a jazz musician, [5] ______________.

Kenny Broad is an extreme explorer [6] ______________. These "blue holes," [7] ______________, are like time capsules, full of interesting scientific evidence about the way life on our planet has evolved. The caves are also important reservoirs of fresh water. An articulate and passionate speaker, Broad promotes the idea that by working together, scientists from different backgrounds can benefit from the knowledge [8] ______________.

9c The king herself

Reading

1 Work in pairs. Look at the title of the article. What is strange about the words *king* and *herself* together?

2 Read the article and put these events about Hatshepsut's life in the correct chronological order.

a Her mummy was discovered in a minor tomb.
b The monuments she built were destroyed.
c Thutmose III became pharaoh.
d She ruled Egypt as king for 21 years.
e Her mummy was identified and put in the Royal Mummy Rooms.
f She married Thutmose II.
g She was born, the eldest daughter of Thutmose I and Queen Ahmose.

3 What were the different roles that Hatshepsut fulfilled (like pharaoh)?

4 Choose the correct option (a–c) to complete the sentences.

1 Hatshepsut's mummy was not identified at first because it:
a was badly damaged.
b was not in a royal tomb.
c had another name with it.

2 Hatshepsut was very worried that people would:
a realize she was a woman.
b not think she was royalty.
c not remember her.

3 Thutmose III did not want people to know that Hatshepsut had been:
a king.
b queen.
c related to him.

4 Thutmose II's children consisted of:
a one son and one daughter.
b one son.
c one daughter.

5 According to tradition, the queen regent was supposed to:
a make offerings to the gods.
b help until the king was ready.
c be a politician.

6 In later statues and images, Hatshepsut appears male from:
a her body shape.
b the way she stands.
c the dress she wears.

Critical thinking weighing the evidence

5 Find evidence that supports each sentence (1–6). If the sentence is definitely true, write 100%. If there is no evidence, write 0%. Put percentages in between if it is not clear.

1 When Hatshepsut's sarcophagus was first found in 1903, it was empty.
2 The mummy called KV60a was Hatshepsut's body.
3 Hatshepsut wanted to produce a male heir, but failed.
4 Hatshepsut had a greater claim to become pharaoh than Thutmose III.
5 Hatshepsut wanted her subjects' approval.
6 The king in waiting, Thutmose III, was angry that Hatshepsut had assumed the role of king.

6 Work in pairs. Compare your scores and your evidence.

Word focus *long*

7 In the article, find these six phrases (1–6) with the word *long* and match each one to its definition (a–f).

1 at long last	a soon
2 as long as	b over a long period of time
3 long for	c after much waiting
4 long after	d provided that
5 before long	e much, much later
6 in the long term	f desire very much

8 Complete the sentences using phrases with *long*.

1 Hatshepsut clearly .... people to remember her.
2 The grand monuments she built ensured she would be remembered ....
3 .... people believed she had a divine right to be pharaoh, Hatshepsut felt safe.
4 Hatshepsut died in 1458 BC and ...., Thutmose III had destroyed most references to her as king.
5 Experts in hieroglyphs .... uncovered the truth.
6 Thutmose III ruled for another 34 years, ... Hatshepsut had died.

Speaking

9 Work in small groups. Say who you would expect to find doing these jobs: mostly men, mostly women, or an equal number of men and women. Give reasons.

company director	cleaner	nurse	teacher
IT technician	doctor	plumber	
machine operator	florist	secretary	
prime minister	lawyer	senior civil servant	

10 Look at the statistics on page 154. Which job in Exercise 9 fits in which category? Compare and discuss your answers.

THE KING *Herself*

Today she is in the Royal Mummy Rooms at the Egyptian Museum in Cairo, reunited at long last with her family of fellow pharaohs, with a sign saying she is Hatshepsut, the king herself (1473–1458 BC).

But in 1903, when the archaeologist Howard Carter found Hatshepsut's sarcophagus in the Valley of the Kings, it was empty. Had her mummy been stolen or destroyed? The truth only came out a century later when Egyptian scientists positively identified a mummy called KV60a, discovered more than a century earlier in a minor tomb, as that of Hatshepsut. None of the treasures normally found with pharaohs' mummies were with it. It was not even in a coffin.

For Hatshepsut, a pharaoh who did not fear death as long as she was remembered, the irony is great. As one of the greatest builders in one of the greatest Egyptian dynasties, she raised numerous temples and shrines. She commissioned hundreds of statues of herself and left accounts in stone of her titles, her history, even her hopes and fears. Inscribed on an obelisk at Karnak are the words: "Now my heart turns this way and that, as I think what the people will say. Those who see my monuments in years to come, and who shall speak of what I have done."

But following her death, her successor and stepson Thutmose III set about erasing her memory. At Deir el Bahri, at the temple designed to be the center of Hatshepsut's cult, her statues were smashed and thrown into a pit. Images of her as queen were left undisturbed, but wherever she proclaimed herself king, the destruction was careful and precise. Why?

Hatshepsut was the eldest daughter of Thutmose I and Queen Ahmose. But Thutmose also had a son by another queen, and this son, Thutmose II, became pharaoh when his father died. As was common among Egyptian royalty, Thutmose II married his sister, Hatshepsut. They produced one daughter; another, less important wife, Isis, gave Thutmose II the male heir that he longed for, but Hatshepsut was unable to provide.

When Thutmose II died not long after from heart disease, his heir, Thutmose III, was still a young boy. As was the custom, Hatshepsut assumed control as the young pharaoh's queen regent. And so began one of the most intriguing periods of ancient Egyptian history.

At first, Hatshepsut acted on her stepson's behalf, respecting the convention that the queen should handle political affairs while the young king learned the ropes. But before long, she began performing kingly functions, like making offerings to the gods. After a few years, she assumed the role of king of Egypt, supreme power in the land. Her stepson was relegated to second-in-command and "the king herself" proceeded to rule for an amazing 21 years.

What caused Hatshepsut to break so radically with the traditional role of queen regent? A social or military crisis? A desire for power? A belief that she had the same right to rule as a man? No one really knows. Maybe she felt, as a direct descendant of the pharoah Thutmose I, she had a greater claim to the divine line of pharaohs than Thutmose III. At first she made no secret of her sex—in images her body is unmistakably a woman's—but later she is depicted as a male king, with headdress and beard, standing imposingly with legs apart.

Her hieroglyph inscriptions have frequent references to "my people" which suggest that she knew she had broken with tradition and wanted her subjects' approval. Whatever their opinion was, there is no doubting the frustration of Thutmose III. After Hapshepsut's death, he took his revenge, wiping his stepmother's reign as pharaoh out of history. But in the long term it is she, the king herself, who achieved the greater fame.

coffin (n) /ˈkɔfɪn/ a box in which a dead body is put to be buried
commission (v) /kəˈmɪʃən/ to order and pay for something to be made
divine (adj) /dɪˈvaɪn/ related to God
heir (n) /eər/ a successor

9d Right for the job

Real life describing skills, talents, and experience

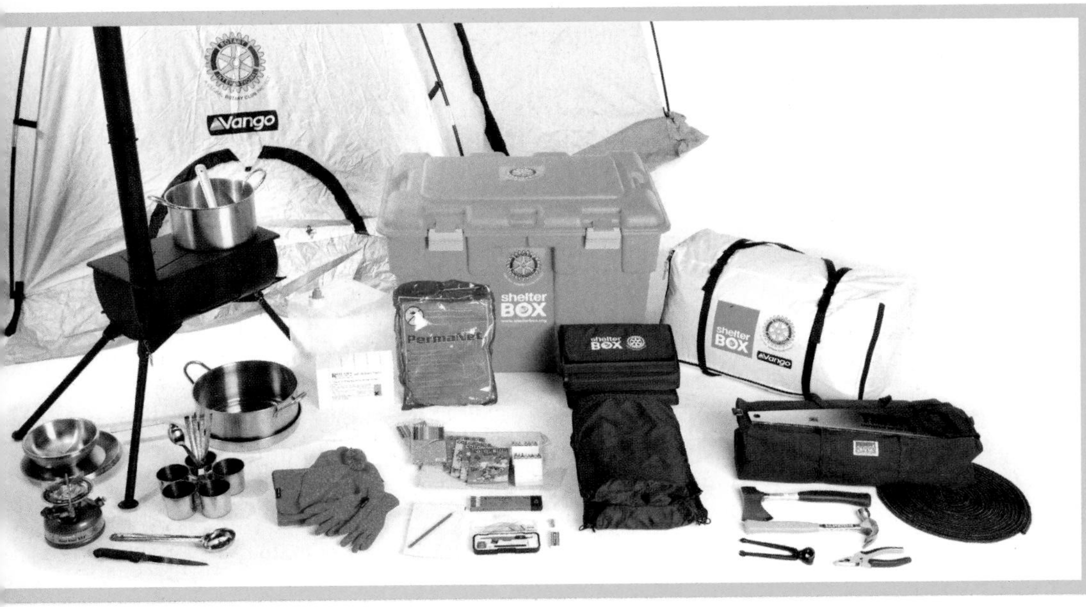

Shelterbox is a charity which sends boxes of essential items needed in an emergency—a tent, tools, cooking utensils, a water purification kit—to places where disasters, such as earthquakes and floods, have struck. Boxes are prepared in the US and delivered immediately by Shelterbox employees to anywhere in the world where they will help save lives.

1 Read the description of Shelterbox. What kind of organization is it and what service does it offer?

2 32 Listen to someone being interviewed for a job at Shelterbox. Answer the questions.

1 What aspect of Shelterbox's work is the candidate interested in?
2 What is the interviewer concerned about?

3 32 Look at these phrases from the interview describing the candidate's suitability for a job. Note the prepositions used in each case. Then listen to the interview again and complete each one.

DESCRIBING SKILLS, TALENTS, AND EXPERIENCE

I'm familiar with your work because I have a friend who [1] ....
I'm really interested in [2] ....
I specialized in [3] ....
I think I would be well-suited for [4] ....
I'm good at coping with [5] ....
I have quite a lot of experience [6] ....
I'm pretty good with [7] ....
I'm comfortable with all [8] ....
I'm serious about wanting to [9] ....
I need to become more knowledgeable about [10] ....

4 Work in pairs. Discuss: did the candidate do a good job of selling himself to the interviewer?

5 Pronunciation difficult words

a 33 The spelling of a word in English is not always a clear indication of its pronunciation. How confident are you that you can pronounce these words from the interview? Mark each word confident (✓), somewhat confident (?), and not confident (×). Then listen and check.

although	comfortable	environments
foreign	knowledgeable	months
specialized	suited	world

b 34 Listen to and spell eight more words.

6 Work in pairs.

Student A: Choose one of the jobs below that interests you and think about the skills, talents, and experience you have that would help you do it. Try to convince Student B why this would be a good job for you.

Student B: Interview Student A for the job. Then swap roles.

- a travel guide for walking tours
- a sales assistant in a children's bookstore
- an outreach director for a charity that helps the homeless
- an assistant to a cameraman who makes films about plants and wildlife

9e Professional networking

Writing an online profile

1 Do you use any professional networking sites? Why?

2 Read the profile and summarize in no more than nine words what this person's main skills and qualities are. How effective was his profile in putting across the key points?

3 Read the tips on how to write a profile on a professional networking site. Put a check mark (✓) next to each tip that has been followed, a cross (✗) next to those which have not, and a question mark (?) if the tip has only been partly followed.

> Tips:
> 1 Include a personal photo and recommendations from others.
> 2 Give a heading and summary so that readers can get the main idea quickly.
> 3 Say what you're doing now.
> 4 List all the places where you have worked or studied; someone from there may be looking at your profile!
> 5 Job titles may mean nothing to others, so always describe what you did in each job.

Profile

Tom Vasquez
Managing Director of EverReady Learning

Location: Chicago, IL
Industry: Online learning
Current: Developing innovative e-learning program for the car industry

Past

- Head of development, Faheys Educational; responsible for new products
- Editorial Director, York Books; published *Learning in the 21st Century*
- Director of Business Studies, Carston University

Education: Stanford University

Summary
Learning is my passion. I specialize in the design and management of online learning programs for industry, but I am also a writer, editor, blogger, educator, and business consultant. My work has brought me into contact with many companies and I am now skilled at identifying and responding to the learning needs of any business sector, from cosmetics to car-making. If my experience has taught me one thing, it's that learning is the key to improvement for all of us.

4 Writing skill writing in note form

a Look at these four phrases from the profile. Which are proper sentences? Which are written in note or shortened form? Why is this?

1 responsible for new products
2 Learning is my passion.
3 published *Learning in the 21st Century*
4 Developing innovative e-learning program for the car industry

b Insert the necessary words (pronouns, articles, auxiliary verbs) to show what the phrases in note form would look like as full sentences.

c Convert these statements from other profiles into a shorter, more concise form by deleting the unnecessary words.

1 I worked as a personal assistant to the Marketing Director.
2 I am currently writing an article for *National Geographic* magazine.
3 I was in charge of organizing corporate social events.
4 I took the official photos for the Boston Ballet.
5 I am working for various charities.
6 I was hired to raise money for a local college.

5 Write your own short professional profile, similar to the one above. Think about the message you would most like the reader to be left with. When you have finished, exchange profiles with another member of the class. Read them once quickly and tell each other your main impression.

6 Read your partner's profile again. Check the following points:

- Has the profile been laid out correctly?
- Have the tips in Exercise 3 been followed?
- Has note form been used in places to make the profile more concise?

9f Queen of Egypt

Video

She has a reputation for beauty, power, controversy, and ultimately, tragedy.

Before you watch

1 Work in pairs. Make notes about what you know of Cleopatra.

- who she was
- when and where she ruled
- important events in her life

2 You are going to watch a video about the story of Cleopatra. Write down three kinds of images you think you might see which help to tell this story.

While you watch

3 Watch the video and check your ideas from Exercises 1 and 2.

4 Watch the video again and answer the questions.

1 Why was Cleopatra forced from power?

....

2 How did she first meet Julius Caesar?

....

3 How did Cleopatra's relationship with Caesar help her?

....

4 Why did Octavian go to war with Mark Antony and Cleopatra?

....

5 In what year and what battle was Mark Antony beaten?

....

6 How did Mark Antony die?

....

7 How did Cleopatra die?

....

5 Match the sentence beginnings (1–7) with the endings (a–g). Then watch the video again to check.

1 Julius Caesar arrived in Alexandria
2 Cleopatra's relationship with Caesar kept Rome
3 After Caesar's murder
4 Cleopatra and Antony shared
5 Mark Antony's Roman rival, Octavian
6 Cleopatra spread numerous
7 Antony's followers carried him to Cleopatra

a from taking direct control of Egypt.
b false rumors of her death.
c where he died in her arms.
d in pursuit of a rival Roman general.
e her position became uncertain.
f went to war against them.
g a hunger for power.

After you watch

6 Roleplay **first meeting with Caesar**

Work in pairs.

Student A: Imagine you are Cleopatra. You arrive in Caesar's court hidden in a rug. You need to charm Caesar so that he will help you become queen again. Read the information below and make notes.

Student B: Imagine you are Caesar. Cleopatra arrives in your court hidden in a rug. Read the information below and make notes.

- how you feel (surprised, excited, curious)
- what you want from the other person
- how you can help the other person
- what you decide to do

Act out your meeting, then change roles and act out the meeting again.

7 At the end of the video, the narrator says: "Cleopatra lives on in history through her personal story of love and tragedy." Why do you think her story has lasted for so long? Do you think her story teaches us anything about love and power today?

8 Work in groups and discuss these questions.

1 Do you think Cleopatra was an admirable woman? Why?
2 Are there any similar characters in the history of your country?
3 Would you like to have lived in Cleopatra's time? Why?

charmed (adj) /ʧɑrmd/ fascinated by
controversy (n) /ˈkɑntrəˌvɜrsi/ disagreement about something
court (n) /kɔrt/ the place where a ruler lives and works
distort (v) /dɪsˈtɔrt/ change something from its normal shape
dynasty (n) /ˈdaɪnəsti/ a family that rules a country for several generations
grief (n) /grif/ great sadness
infuriate (v) /ɪnˈfjʊriˌeɪt/ make very angry
overjoyed (adj) /ˌoʊvərˈʤɔɪd/ extremely happy
pursuit (n) /pərˈsut/ the act of chasing someone or something
rival (n) /ˈraɪvəl/ a person or group that competes with another
rug (n) /rʌg/ a small carpet
seize (v) /siz/ take by force

UNIT 9 REVIEW

Grammar

1 Complete this text with *the* where necessary.

Constance Adams has had an unusual career path. She studied [1] ________ architecture at [2] ________ Yale University before working as an architect in [3] ________ Berlin and [4] ________ Japan. She then joined [5] ________ Johnson Space Center in [6] ________ US, where she helped design TransHab, a module for [7] ________ International Space Station. The idea of [8] ________ module was to provide [9] ________ living quarters for [10] ________ astronauts during their stay in [11] ________ space. In [12] ________ 2005 she became a National Geographic Emerging Explorer.

2 Complete the text with relative pronouns in 1–5 and present and past participles in 6–10.

Adams explains that the TransHab module was intended to be a habitat for a crew of six astronauts, [1] ________ mission was to reach Mars. The team had to design a module [2] ________ would be only 14 feet in diameter when it was launched. But once in space it needed to be three times that size to house the six astronauts [3] ________ lived there. So they made a structure [4] ________ could inflate and unfold in space to become a three-level "house" [5] ________ astronauts could eat, sleep, and work.

The outer shell of the module, [6] ________ (compose) of over twenty layers of different materials, had to resist the space debris [7] ________ (hit) the spaceship all the time. This debris can hit the spaceship seven times faster than a bullet, [8] ________ (cause) great damage. The outer layers were made of a kind of foam [9] ________ (use) in chairs and cushions. The inner shell was made of Kevlar, a material [10] ________ (wear) by soldiers and police for body protection.

3 Work in pairs. Discuss what was special about the module's size, shape, and materials.

I CAN
- use *the* and no article ☐
- use relative clauses and reduced relative clauses ☐

Vocabulary

4 Complete the sentences with these nouns and the correct form of the verbs.

background	become	do	experience
pursue	graduate	knowledge	degree
quality	serve	skills	take

1 My main academic ________ is in physics and I got it when I ________ from Duke University.
2 I have a lot of ________ organizing things. I ________ in the army for four years.
3 I think my main ________ is that I'm adaptable. I can ________ many different jobs.
4 I have good computer ________ . I ________ a course in advanced computing last year.
5 My ________ —both my parents are scientists—meant scientific research was a natural career for me to ________ .
6 My ________ of astrophysics helped me to ________ a space scientist.

5 Work in pairs. Use the nouns and verbs to describe your own skills and experience.

I CAN
- talk about my experience and skills ☐
- describe my career path ☐

Real life

6 Put the correct preposition into each space.

1 I'm familiar ________ most design software.
2 I specialized ________ mechanical engineering.
3 I think I am well-suited ________ working abroad.
4 I'm good ________ people.
5 I'm good ________ persuading people.
6 I'm serious ________ pursuing a career in art.
7 I'm not very interested ________ sitting all day.
8 I am pretty knowledgeable ________ mechanics.

7 Work in pairs. Tell each other about a job that would be right for you and one that wouldn't.

I CAN
- describe what kind of work I am suited for ☐

Speaking

8 Work in small groups. Describe the work of someone you admire. Include these points:

- a description of their qualities and talents
- what they have achieved

Unit 10 Customs and behavior

Two generations of Chinese visitors visit Beijing's Forbidden City.
Photograph by Nigel Swinn

FEATURES

1 Work in pairs. Look at the photo. What is it about the behavior of the younger tourists that surprises the older pair?

2 Look at the quotation below. Discuss what you think it means. Do manners make you a better person, or more socially acceptable—or both?

"Manners maketh man." *William of Wykeham (1324–1404)*

3 Complete these phrases about manners with words from the box. Check your answers with your teacher. Then discuss whether you think these things are important to teach children. What would you add?

chew	courtesy	inappropriate	interrupt
offensive	point	well-behaved	stare
talk	slouch		

1 Don't __________ with your mouth full.
2 Don't __________ when grown-ups are speaking.
3 Don't __________ or __________ at people.
4 Don't __________ gum.
5 Don't wear clothes that are __________ or __________.
6 Be polite, __________-__________, and show __________ to others.

10a Cruel to be kind

Reading

1 Work in pairs. Answer the questions.

1 What is happening in the photo?
2 How would you describe the mother's attitude: strict, intense, something else?
3 How strict were your parents? Are you happy that they were this way or not?

2 Work in small groups. Which of these things should parents control strongly? A little? Which should the child decide?

- watching TV
- playing computer games
- practicing a musical instrument
- going out to play with friends
- doing homework
- choosing what subjects to study at high school
- choosing extracurricular activities

3 Read the article and find out who "tiger mothers" are. How do their attitudes to the first five items in Exercise 2 compare to Western attitudes?

4 Does the writer approve of the "tiger mother" approach to child-rearing? Do you?

Vocabulary **raising children: verbs**

5 Work in pairs. Look at the pairs of verbs below and discuss the difference between them. You will find the first verb in each pair in the article.

1 *bring up* and *educate* children
2 *praise* and *reward* good behavior
3 *rebel against* and *disobey* your parents
4 *push* and *discipline* yourself
5 *give in to* and *spoil* your children
6 *nag* and *pester* someone
7 *shame* and *punish* someone

CRUEL TO BE KIND

Is there a right way to bring up children? Some parents read guides to find an answer, many just follow their instinct. Whatever they do, a doubt always remains: could I have done a better job?

A recent contribution to the subject is Amy Chua's controversial book *Battle Hymn of the Tiger Mother*, which describes the approach to child-rearing of an ambitious Chinese parent living in the West. According to Chua, Western mothers are far too soft on their children. She says they are always praising their children for every effort they make, even if the result is coming last in a race or playing a piano piece badly. These are the kind of parents who will give in to their children's demands to go out and play rather than do their homework, if they protest loudly enough.

The "tiger mother" method is very different and the key is total control. Tiger mothers will accept nothing less than perfect grades in every subject—failure to achieve these is just proof that children have not worked hard enough. They will encourage not with praise and reward, but by punishing and shaming. Chua told her daughter that she would give her doll's house to charity if she failed to master a difficult piano piece. She even rejected a homemade birthday card because her daughter had drawn it in a hurry.

But that highlights another difference, says Chua, which is directness and honesty. A tiger mother will not hesitate to tell her children that they are lazy, whereas Western parents are always telling their children not to worry, that they will do better next time, even if they think they have been lazy.

The constant nagging of the tiger mother, the banning of TV and computer games, seems harsh, but perhaps it works. Chua's children have not rebelled, and they don't resent their strict upbringing. They regularly get the top grades at school and are proficient at violin and piano —stereotypical symbols of success, critics would say. By contrast, children with more freedom and more laid-back parents will often lack self-discipline and will fail to push themselves to achieve more.

Grammar habitual actions: present tenses, *will*

SIMPLE PRESENT, PRESENT CONTINUOUS, and *WILL* FOR REPEATED ACTIONS

Simple present
Some parents read guides to find an answer.

Present continuous with *always*
She says they are always praising their children for every effort they make.

will
These are the kind of parents who will give in to their children's demands.

For more information and practice, see page 169.

6 Work in pairs. Look at the sentences in the grammar box. Which tense is used to describe:

1 typical behavior?
2 a habit which the speaker finds annoying?
3 a simple fact or general truth?

7 Find and underline:

1 an example of tiger mothers' typical behavior; an example of typical behavior of Western mothers' children.
2 a simple fact about Chua's children.
3 something Chua finds annoying about Western mothers.

8 Complete these comments by underlining the correct verb forms. Sometimes there is more than one possibility. Then discuss which ones you sympathize with and which you don't.

1 My parents *will always tell / are always telling* me to practice the piano and it just makes it a chore.
2 In my experience, children *will do / do* as little work as they can. So you have to make them do it.
3 Children *will want / want* to be loved. It's also true that they *will perform / perform* much better in a loving and secure environment.
4 All parents *will hope / hope* that their children will be successful, but they *won't always admit / aren't always admitting* it to their children or even themselves.
5 You have to have a different approach with different children. Some *will respond / respond* better to gentle encouragement; others *will need / need* to be pushed and challenged.
6 I don't like parents who *will always try / are always trying* to be friends with their children. There are too many parents who *will buy / buy* their children presents and let them do what they want just to get on their good side.

9 Read the anecdotes below and put the verb in the right form. Then check your answers with your teacher.

I've seen this kind of situation so many times in Mexico when children 1 .... (beg) their parents for some candy. At first the parent 2 .... (say) no. So then the child 3 .... (pester) and pester until the parent finally gives in—which they always do. It's against all the rules of parenting.

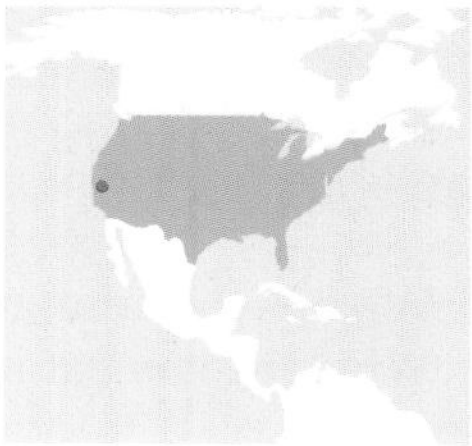

I teach in a school in San Francisco where we have quite a lot of ethnic Chinese and Japanese kids. By and large, they 4 .... (do) what you tell them. But the other kids 5 .... (always / misbehave). You have to tell them ten times to sit down.

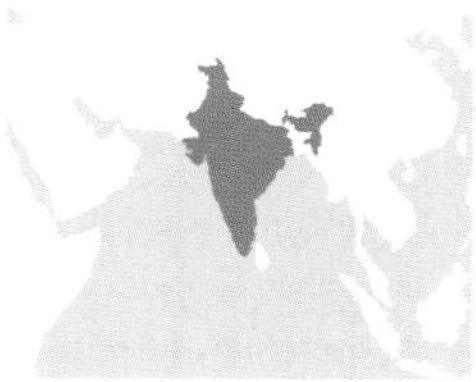

Where I live in India, it is common for young children to work. Kids still 6 .... (depend) on their parents, but they have a different attitude toward responsibility. Just as children in every culture 7 .... (play) naturally, so children in India naturally 8 .... (assume) responsibility for working and earning money.

Speaking

10 Work in pairs. Discuss the situations in Exercise 9. How familiar is each one to you? Does the behavior seem right or wrong?

11 Think of three more examples of children's and parents' behavior in your country: a simple fact about the way children or parents behave; an example of typical behavior; an example of behavior that annoys you or seems wrong.

12 Describe your examples to another pair. Are they similar to theirs?

10b A matter of taste

Listening

1 What is the strangest thing you have ever eaten? Why did you eat it? What did it taste like?

2 **35** Listen and answer the questions.

1 Where is the Nochmani tribe from?
2 What do they eat mostly?
3 How do they make sure there is enough of this food?

3 **35** Listen again and choose the correct word or phrase to complete the statements.

1 We live in an age when people are very .... what they eat.
 a nervous about b conscious of
 c careless about
2 In the past it was thought that the Nicobar Islands contained ....
 a no inhabitants b no fresh water
 c no fish
3 The Nochmani didn't want to eat ....
 a sweets and cakes b meat
 c any of the food they were offered
4 Insects have a lot of .... in them.
 a carbohydrates b vitamins
 c protein
5 The speaker thinks we could all benefit from eating ....
 a less meat b more insects
 c alternative types of food

4 What do you think of the diet of the Nochmani? Do you think what we eat is just a matter of habit? Why? Can we learn to eat anything if we have to, or are there some things we can never eat?

Grammar *used to, usually, be used to,* and *get used to*

5 Match each verb form in bold (1–5) to the meaning (a–e).

1 We **didn't use to worry** so much about food.
2 People **usually need** mammals in order to live.
3 The Nochmani **were not used to eating** meat.
4 If you **are used to** something, you prefer it.
5 We should **get used to eating** insects.

a refers to something that was strange or abnormal for someone
b refers to something that happens regularly or is generally the case
c refers to learning to cope with something difficult or unfamiliar
d refers to what someone did regularly in the past, but doesn't do anymore
e refers to something that is normal and not strange

▶ *USED TO, USUALLY, BE USED TO,* and *GET USED TO*

Past habits	**Present habits**
used to + infinitive	*(not) usually* + simple present
I used to eat...	*I usually eat...*
I didn't use to eat...	*I don't usually eat...*
Did you use to eat?	*Do you usually eat?*
Familiar (and unfamiliar) habits	**Habits that are becoming familiar**
be used to + noun or *-ing* form	*get used to* + noun or *–ing* form
I am used to (eating) Italian food.	*I am getting used to (eating) American food.*
I am not used to...	*I am not getting used to...*
Are you used to... ?	*Are you getting used to... ?*

For more information and practice, see page 170.

6 Look at the grammar box and then choose the right form to complete sentences 1–9 in A, B, and C. Note that we use *be used to* and *get used to* for things that are not strange or difficult to do.

A In China, people [1] *do not usually finish / didn't use to finish* everything on their plate, because it is a sign that they have not had enough to eat. Visitors from the West find it difficult to [2] *be used to / get used to* this, because they [3] *usually eat / are used to eating* everything to show that they like it. When a Chinese host sees their empty plates, he [4] *usually assumes / is used to assuming* that they want more.

B Fifty years ago, people in the US [5] *used to sitting / used to sit* down for meals with their families each evening. Families nowadays [6] *usually eat / used to eat* together only three times a week, because busy lives and TV get in the way. But it is believed that if more families could [7] *be used to dining / get used to dining* together, it would strengthen family relationships.

C Eating a traditional English breakfast of eggs, bacon, and sausages [8] *used to be / was used to being* a common thing in the UK. A big breakfast was important because people [9] *didn't use to eat / weren't used to eating* so many snacks during the day.

7 Put the verb in the most appropriate form to complete these sentences.

1 We .... (eat) out a lot, but restaurants are so expensive that we don't anymore.
2 I .... (have) a tuna salad sandwich for my lunch.
3 I .... (take) sugar in my coffee, but now I have a sweetener. It took a little while to .... (get used to) the taste, but now I can't tell the difference.
4 When I was staying with my friends in Iowa, we ate at six o'clock in the evening. It was strange, because I .... (eat) much later.

8 Are any of the sentences in Exercise 7 true for you? Have you had similar experiences? Discuss with a partner.

I also used to eat out a lot, but now I try to get home for lunch.

Not me, I usually buy a sandwich... not tuna, though!

9 In pairs, ask each other these questions.

1 What is something you have gotten used to doing recently?
2 Do you usually do your homework in the mornings or the evenings?
3 Are you used to eating dinner with your family or do you usually eat on the go?
4 What is the best way to get used to a new place?
5 What is something that you used to do that you don't do anymore? Why did you stop?
6 What is something that you are used to doing that you wish you could change? Why?

Vocabulary and speaking

10 Work in pairs. Place these four items of food into the correct category. Think of two more items for each category. Then compare your list with another pair.

breakfast cereal   chocolate bars
rice   yogurt

dairy products (like milk)	processed food (like frozen peas)	staple foods (like potatoes)	snacks (like potato chips)

11 Complete these sentences with information about eating habits in your country. Go around the class and exchange your information with at least three other people. Then work with your partner. Tell each other the two most memorable statements you heard.

1 When I was growing up, a lot of families used to...
2 The main staple food is... People aren't used to eating...
3 For breakfast, people usually...
4 I think visitors find some of our eating customs strange, because they are not used to...
5 People in my country don't usually eat...
6 Young people find it difficult to get used to...

10c A universal language

Reading

1 Work in pairs. Put the actions in the box into the correct category of body language. Then demonstrate the actions to each other. What is the meaning of each?

a handshake	standing with arms crossed
biting your bottom lip	waving
sitting back in your chair	
smiling	

posture: ....

gesture: ....

facial expression: ....

2 Read the article. Which sentence best summarizes the author's view?

a We need to learn how people from different cultures use body language.
b The differences in body language between cultures are small but important.
c There are more similarities than differences in body language between cultures.

3 According to the writer…

1 Making comparisons between cultures can be:
a fun. b useful.
c dangerous.
2 Standing too close to someone of another culture can:
a cause arguments. b cause discomfort.
c be a serious insult.
3 A lot of the facts given in travel guides are:
a very important. b wrong.
c not of much practical help.
4 Looking away from the speaker is a sign of:
a sadness. b boredom.
c both.
5 To avoid making mistakes in body language with other cultures, people need to be:
a sensible. b sensitive.
c both.
6 Differences in body language between people start at:
a an individual level. b a cultural level.
c an emotional level.

4 With your partner, demonstrate to each other:

- the two gestures described in paragraph 3
- the two greetings mentioned in paragraph 4
- the body language associated with boredom and anger described in paragraph 6

5 Do you agree with the writer's view about cross-cultural communication? Is your culture one that generally shows its emotions or not?

Critical thinking **sources**

6 The article gives a lot of information about body language and customs. But how do you know how reliable this information is? Underline the examples of different cultures' body language and customs in the article.

7 Work in pairs. Find the author's source for each example. Mark the source according to this scale:
3 = very credible; 2 = quite credible;
1 = incredible; and 0 = no source.

Word focus ***common***

8 Match the meanings of the word *common* (1–2) with the sentences (a–d).

common (adj)
1 something usual or normal
2 something that is shared by two or more people

a It is quite common in European countries to sit with your legs crossed.
b The things that we all have in common…
c There are also common factors when people are bored.
d If we all just apply a little sensitivity and common sense,…

9 Now do the same for these expressions.

e In a negotiation, always try to find common ground between you and the other party.
f It is a common misconception that English people drink only tea, not coffee.
g Don't worry about mispronouncing my name; it's a common mistake that everyone makes.
h It's common knowledge that many Asian cultures use chopsticks, not knives and forks.

Speaking

10 Work in pairs. Describe the following customs in your country. Then compare your answers with another pair. How similar were they?

- The most common form of greeting
- Common gestures that visitors are not used to
- Common eating customs
- Common misconceptions foreigners have about your country

A universal language

People love to compare and contrast. In most parts of England, you buy your bus ticket on the bus. In France, you buy it at a metro station. In Australia, you can buy it at a newsstand. We all find this kind of comparison entertaining. Books on cross-cultural communication exploit our curiosity by focusing on differences between people around the world, including the significance of their body language.

Proxemics, the study of different standards of personal space, is one example. How close I stand when speaking to people depends not only on my relationship to them, but also on my culture. This is important because if people are not used to standing as close as I do when we are talking, they might feel uncomfortable. Statistics tell us that the average distance at which two people stand in a social context—neighbors chatting, for example—is somewhere between 4 and 11 feet. In Latin cultures (like South America and Italy), and also in China, this distance tends to be smaller, while in Nordic cultures (like Sweden and Denmark), people usually stand farther apart.

The messages sent by your posture and gestures is another case in point. For example, it is quite common in European countries to sit with your legs crossed and the top foot outstretched. But, as I know from personal experience, people in Arab countries hardly ever sit this way because they might show you the bottom of their shoe, which is a serious insult. It is said that in the Philippines, people often greet each other by raising their eyebrows quickly. In the US, this is a sign of surprise.

Such information fills the pages of guide books, but I would really question the usefulness of what are presented as must-know facts. Clearly it is important to know a little about eating customs, tipping, and the rules concerning basic greetings—whether you should bow or shake someone's hand. But beneath the surface, we are not so different. Many signs are universal in the emotions that they communicate. Focusing on them is a much more profitable route than focusing on our differences.

Smiling is the best known sign, but not the only one. Behaviorists have proven that all over the world, people show sadness in a similar way. The face falls, the mouth becomes downturned and the eyes begin to look glassy. The person will probably look down or away and seem distracted.

There are also common factors when people are bored. They will look at other things, their feet will begin to move restlessly indicating that they want to escape, and they will tap their fingers or scratch their heads. Anger can also be read quite easily: the facial muscles tense up, often causing people to frown; the eyes stare, fixing themselves on the target of their anger; blood rushes to the face, turning it red. If the anger is great, the body will also tense up as if preparing itself for a physical fight.

Understanding these universal signals and reacting appropriately is the real key to cross-cultural communication. If we all apply just a little sensitivity and common sense, we are unlikely to cause lasting offense by making the wrong gesture or invading a stranger's personal space. Of course, some cultures show their emotions more openly and others prefer to keep them more hidden. But isn't that also the case within cultures, from one individual to another?

frown (v) /fraʊn/ to lower your eyebrows, causing lines to appear on your forehead
scratch (v) /skrætʃ/ to move your fingernails backwards and forwards across your skin
stare (v) /steər/ to look intensely and for a long time at something
tap (v) /tæp/ to hit something lightly with a finger or hand

10d A pre-wedding ritual

Vocabulary weddings

1 What pre-wedding customs or events are traditional for the bride-to-be in your country?

2 Work in pairs. Look at the words related to weddings and answer the questions.

bride	groom	bachelorette party
bachelor party	veil	

1 Which word means a pre-wedding party for the man? And for the woman?
2 Which word means the woman on her wedding day? And the man on his?
3 Which word means a piece of fine cloth that covers the woman's face?

▶ WORDBUILDING word pairs

Some words have a natural partner or make a matching pair.
bride and *groom*, *host* and *guest*

Real life describing traditions

3 36 Listen to the description of a traditional pre-wedding henna night in eastern Turkey. Then complete the first four phrases in the box below.

▶ DESCRIBING TRADITIONS

1 It takes place ....
2 It marks the ....
3 It is an occasion for ....
4 It symbolizes the ....

It's traditional / customary for this to be done by...
Typically / As a rule / Usually the women from...

Describing the sequence of events
The ceremony begins with the...
Then,... / After that,... / Next,... / Finally,...

While this is happening / During this part, the guests...
After / Once the bride's head has been...
On the morning of the wedding, a...

4 37 Listen to the rest of the description. Number the items in the order they occur.

a A child presents the hennaed coin to the groom.
b The bride's head is covered with a red veil.
c The guests sing separation songs.
d The bride's hands and feet are hennaed.
e A gold coin is put into the remaining henna.
f The henna is prepared by the daughter of another couple.

5 38 Retell the events to each other using the linking words in the box to help you. Then listen and compare.

6 Pronunciation the letter *s*

a 39 Listen to these words and for each one say if the letter *s* is pronounced /s/ or /z/. Note the spellings that produce each sound.

custom	dress	friends
music	suppose	weddings

b 40 Work in pairs. Practice saying the words, then listen and check. Think of three more words for each sound. Then compare words with another pair.

across	eastern	lose	place
rings	single	spends	surprise

Speaking

7 What special events take place before or after a wedding in your country? Describe one using the box to help you. Think about:

- when it takes place
- the sequence of the events
- its significance
- any special symbols used

8 Working in small groups, describe these customs to each other. When each person has finished their description, ask them questions.

10e Business customs

Writing an informal email (2)

1 Imagine you are about to go on a business trip to a country you haven't visited before. What would you want to know about the customs there?

2 Read the first email. What is Paul asking for? What is he worried about?

3 Read Dominic's reply. Which pieces of advice should calm Paul's worries?

> Hi Dominic
>
> Good to see you briefly the other day. Forgot to tell you I'm going to China next week. Not sure what to expect. I know you have experience doing business there. Don't want to make any mistakes with any potential business partners. Could you let me know what I should be particularly aware of?
>
> Thanks,
> Paul

> Hi Paul,
>
> Glad to hear you're going to China. Think you'll enjoy it. Is it Shanghai? Let me know. Maybe I can fix you up with a couple of contacts. Anyway, my advice:
>
> - Take plenty of business cards; Chinese people will always give you theirs (make sure you read them carefully). It's embarrassing not to give one in return.
> - Keep the name and address of your hotel on you at all times. Visitors are always getting into trouble because they can't remember where they're staying.
> - The Chinese love their food and are very proud of it. They'll offer you some unusual dishes. Be adventurous and be grateful!
>
> Good luck and talk to you soon,
> Dominic

4 Writing skill elision in informal writing

a Look at the two emails again. Underline four phrases in the first email and four in the second email where words have been omitted to save time.

b Rewrite the sentences and phrases by inserting the missing words to make them more formal.

Example:

It was good to see you the other day.

c Convert these sentences into a more economical style by removing unnecessary pronouns, auxiliary verbs, or the verb *be*.

1 I hope we can meet up soon.
2 It was too bad that you didn't get the job.
3 I'll be back next Tuesday night.
4 This is my address in New York…
5 I will look forward to hearing all about it.
6 It went pretty well, didn't it?

5 Write a response to this email.

> Hi there,
>
> Wondered if you could help. I'm flying over next week to meet some clients. Will have to take them out to dinner and talk to them a little socially. Can you give me some advice about how things are done over there? Eating customs, what to talk about, etc. Sorry to ask, but very grateful for any information you can provide.
>
> Thanks!
> Sara

6 Work in pairs. Exchange emails. Read your partner's reply and answer the questions.

- Is it written in an informal style?
- Has the writer given some useful tips?
- Is the content short and to the point?
- Has the writer used some elision?

10f Eating insects
Video

Larry Peterman is a candy man on a mission.

Before you watch

1 Work in groups. Look at the photo and discuss the questions.

1 What do you think a candy man is?
2 How does the photo make you feel? Do you think most people would feel the same as you?
3 What do you think Larry Peterman's mission is?

2 Work in pairs. Think about the candy you used to eat when you were a child. Describe them to your partner.

3 You are going to watch a video about eating insects. Answer these questions.

1 Which countries include insects in their diets?
2 Do you think eating insects is a new habit?
3 Are insects good for you?
4 Is producing insects better for the environment than producing meat?

While you watch

4 Watch the video and check your answers from Exercise 3.

5 Watch the video again. Number the foods in the order you see them.

a banana, cream, and cockroach dessert
b salt-water taffy
c lollipop with cricket
d cricket cocktail
e mealworm-covered apples
f stir-fry
g caramels
h caterpillars

6 Answer the questions.

1 Where is Hotlix?

....

2 How long has Larry been trying to get Americans to eat insects?

....

3 According to Larry, why do most Americans not like eating insects?

....

4 How many species of insects are eaten around the world?

....

5 How does Larry compare insects to wine?

....

After you watch

7 Roleplay **a meal at Larry's restaurant**

Work in groups of three.

Student A: Imagine you are Larry. Prepare an interesting insect menu. Then give the menu to your customers. Explain what each dish is and answer their questions.

Student B: You don't like the idea of eating insects but are prepared to try. Ask Larry about the menu and order your meal. Also ask Larry why he is so interested in promoting insect foods.

Student C: You love the idea of eating insects. Order a meal.

Act out the conversation, then change roles. Prepare a different menu.

8 At the end of the video, Larry predicts that gourmet insects will have "snob appeal." What do you think that means?

9 Do you think Larry will eventually win people over to eating insects? Why?

10 Work in groups and discuss these questions.

1 Are there any unusual dishes or foods in your country?
2 What types of foods do people in your country avoid eating generally? Why?
3 Are there any foods you don't like? Why?

advocate (n) /'ædvəkɪt/ a person who supports something
brim (v) /brɪm/ be full of
bug (n) /bʌg/ insect
munch (v) /mʌntʃ/ eat
niche (n) /niʃ/ a specialized business opportunity
revolting (adj) /rɪ'voultɪŋ/ disgusting
snob (n) /snɑb/ a person who thinks he or she is better than other people
swat (v) /swɑt/ hit

UNIT 10 REVIEW

Grammar

1 Work in pairs. Look at the photo. What do you know about the eating habits of the Spanish: when they eat, what they eat?

2 Read the paragraph from a travel guide. What times are Spanish meals?

3 Underline the correct forms.

People visiting Spain for the first time can find it difficult to [1] *be used to / get used to* the eating customs of the Spanish. It's not so much the food itself, but the timing of the meals that visitors [2] *aren't used to / don't get used to*. I [3] *was used to living / used to live* in Cadiz, and I actually liked the way they did things. Breakfast is a light continental affair—just a roll and some coffee usually—eaten between 8 and 9:30 a.m. The main meal of the day is lunch, which people [4] *are used to eating / usually eat* sometime between 1 and 3:30 p.m. Quite a few of the shops, museums, and galleries [5] *close / are closing* around this time, because the locals like to take time over lunch. They [6] *are always resting / will rest* for a short time afterwards, although the traditional afternoon siesta is not as common as it [7] *was used to being / used to be*. People eat late in the evening—rarely before 9 p.m.—and on the weekend, the locals often [8] *aren't eating / won't eat* before 11 p.m. or even midnight.

I CAN
- use *used to, be used to,* and *get used to* correctly
- talk about habits and typical behavior with simple present, present continuous, and *will*

Vocabulary

4 Work in pairs. Which word doesn't belong in each group? Explain your choices.

1 punish, discipline, nag, spoil
2 educate, bring up, look after, raise
3 encourage, shame, praise, reward
4 bread, cheese, rice, pasta
5 sit back, shake hands, wave, point
6 interrupt, stare, smile, chew gum
7 well-behaved, offensive, polite, courteous

5 Tell each other what postures, gestures, or facial expressions you often use and in what situations.

I CAN
- talk about bringing up children
- talk about eating habits
- talk about body language

Real life

6 Work in pairs. Find the correct ending from list B for each phrase in list A.

A	B
It marks	people give adult presents to the child.
It takes place	the moment when a child becomes an adult.
It is an occasion	the child to stand up and give a short speech.
It symbolizes	the parent walking into the hall with the child.
It's customary for	people in the audience can also say some words.
Typically the ceremony begins with	on the child's 16th birthday. for celebration.
After the child's speech	leaving childish things behind.

7 Tell your partner about a special celebration in your country and the traditions that surround it.

I CAN
- describe traditions and customs at special events

Speaking

8 Work in small groups. How is children's upbringing these days different from when you were a child? Look at the quote. Do you agree with this speaker?

My parents were quite strict. They used to expect us to do jobs around the house. I think children these days have it much easier, although they are always complaining that their parents expect a lot from them.

Unit 11 Knowledge and learning

Students processing their DNA at a museum learning lab
Photograph by Rajat Bansal

FEATURES

1 Work in pairs. Match each technique of acquiring knowledge or learning (1–4) to a definition (a–d). Which technique are the students using in the photo?

1 by authority
2 by observation
3 by reasoning
4 by trial and error

a experimenting
b using logic
c judging from what you see or hear
d reading or listening to an expert

2 Match these phrases with their definitions.

1 You have **a basic grasp** of chemistry.
2 You need **to find out** when the paper is due.
3 You're working with a tutor **to pick up** some test-taking tips.
4 You need to read through your notes and **process** them before writing your paper.
5 You're not sure what the right answer is, but you chose A because of a **gut feeling**.

a You are going to learn some strategies from an expert.
b You need to learn the date.
c You understand the fundamental principles.
d You need to internalize and reflect on the information.
e You picked an answer based on instinct.

3 Intuition is something we know without having to learn it. Tell a partner about a time when you used your intuition to make a decision.

11a Knowledge conservation

Reading

1 Work in pairs. Look at the photo in the article below of a botanist in the field. What does a botanist do?

2 List the plants or plant products you use on a daily basis. Then compare your list with another pair. Which uses did your lists have in common?

Example: *cotton in my clothes*

3 Read the article and answer the questions.

1. How is Maria Fadiman's interest in plants different from that of a traditional botanist?
2. Where does she work?
3. What two uses of plants are mentioned in the article?

4 What does the article say about:

1. the way Fadiman collects knowledge from local people?
2. the way that local people often pass their knowledge on?
3. the way Fadiman passes her knowledge on to her students?

5 Do you think that Fadiman's idea of recording traditional plant knowledge is useful? Why? What knowledge has been passed down to you by your parents or grandparents? Tell your partner.

> **▶ WORDBUILDING IDIOMATIC EXPRESSIONS**
>
> Often there are idiomatic expressions that can replace basic verbs like *think, realize*
>
> *It struck me that... = I realized that...*

KNOWLEDGE CONSERVATION

Dr. Maria Fadiman is an ethnobotanist: she studies how people use plants. "Looking at plant conservation without including people is a fantasy," she says. "The focus of my work is finding a balance where people use resources in a sustainable way."

It struck Fadiman early on that this was what she wanted to do. "I was born with a passion for conservation and a fascination with indigenous cultures," she explains. "Ethnobotany lets me bring it all together. On my first trip to the rain forest, I met a woman who was in terrible pain because the people in her village weren't able to remember which plant would cure her. I saw that traditional plant knowledge was being lost, and at that moment I knew conserving this kind of knowledge was what I wanted to do with my life."

Visiting the Ecuadoran rain forest, Dr. Fadiman was amazed at the variety of plants. "It looked like one big, green mish-mash," she says. "But the people who lived there were able to pick out the right plants for medicine and could distinguish not only the plants that were safe to eat, but also the right part of each plant."

The problem often is that such knowledge is stored only in local people's minds and it is passed down from generation to generation. Fadiman managed to persuade inhabitants of the Ecuadoran rain forest to let her record the information in written form. "They are excited by this idea because suddenly their knowledge is valued."

But conservation doesn't just mean protecting indigenous plants. If bringing in non-native plants, including cash crops like coffee, is beneficial to people and the environment, then that's fine too. In the Galapagos Islands, where overfishing was a real problem, environmentalists like Fadiman succeeded in getting local people to think about alternatives, like growing coffee.

By forming close relationships with local people and joining in with their way of life, Fadiman has inspired her own students at Florida Atlantic University. Students who couldn't easily absorb facts and statistics said they were able to engage much more easily with the subject when they heard her stories of going to the river to brush her teeth or sitting around a cooking fire.

indigenous (adj) /ɪnˈdɪdʒənəs/ native to a particular country or area

mish-mash (n) /ˈmɪʃˌmæʃ/ a confusing mixture or collection of things

Grammar *could, was able to, manage to,* and *succeed in*

6 Work in pairs. Underline the sentences in the article where the following forms (1–6) are used. Then match each form to the uses (a–c). Note that some forms can have more than one use.

1 *could*
2 *was / were able to (do)*
3 *couldn't*
4 *wasn't / weren't able to*
5 *managed to (do)*
6 *succeeded in (doing)*

a to describe success in a task on a particular occasion in the past
b to describe a general ability in the past
c to describe an inability to do something in the past

> ▶ ***COULD, WAS ABLE TO, MANAGE TO, AND SUCCEED IN***
>
> ***could*** **+ base form**
> *He could tell which plants were safe.*
>
> ***couldn't*** **+ base form**
> *I couldn't remember the name of the plant.*
>
> ***was / were able*** **+ infinitive**
> *We were able to learn a lot from the local people.*
> *He wasn't able to explain how he knew it was right.*
>
> ***manage*** **+ infinitive**
> *After two hours climbing, we managed to reach the top.*
>
> ***succeed in*** **+ *-ing***
> *We succeeded in finding a guide to take us.*
>
> For more information and practice, see page 171.

7 Look at the grammar box. Then complete the sentences.

1 In the past, people could ______ (distinguish) plants more than they can now.
2 Recently, a group of children who were asked where cotton came from weren't able ______ (say) whether it was from an animal or a plant.
3 People were able ______ (use) this knowledge to find food and medicines.
4 They also managed ______ (work) out which plants were good for certain purposes.
5 But they didn't always succeed ______ (pass) this knowledge on to the next generation.
6 So people couldn't ______ (keep) some of this knowledge from being lost.

8 Underline the correct form in each of these sentences. Sometimes both forms are possible.

1 By specializing in ethnobotany, Fadiman *was able to combine / succeeded in combining* an interest in plants with her interest in people.
2 She also studied geography, which meant she *could look at / managed to look at* people and the land.
3 In Ecuador, Fadiman *could record / managed to record* plant data that hadn't been written down before.
4 In Yucatan, Mexico, local women taught Fadiman how to weave, something that she *wasn't able to do / didn't manage to do* before.
5 On a recent trip to Ecuador, she *could visit / was able to visit* a lot of places in a short time by using a helicopter rather than buses and canoes.
6 Fadiman was impressed by how indigenous people *were able to make / succeeded in making* use of the plants around them.

Vocabulary **learning**

9 Work in pairs. Find pairs of words in this group with the same meaning.

absorb	acquire	be ignorant of
connect with	engage with	grasp
inspire	motivate	not know
pick up	take in	understand

10 Complete these sentences about your own learning at school using one of the forms in the grammar box. Ask and answer these questions.

1 Which teachers ______ (inspire) you at school?
2 What kind of facts ______ (absorb) most easily?
3 Which subjects ______ (engage with)?
4 ______ (pass) all your exams?
5 What knowledge ______ (acquire) that has been useful in later life?
6 Was there anything that ______ (not / grasp) that you wished you did now?

Speaking

11 Work in pairs. Think of a subject you know a lot about. How did you acquire that knowledge? Have you managed to record or pass it on in any way?

11b Memory

Speaking

1 Work in pairs. Look at the picture below for ten seconds. Then turn your book over and list the objects you can remember.

2 Compare your results with another pair. What techniques did you use to remember the items?

Items left at the Vietnam Memorial, Landover, Maryland

Listening

3 What things do you commonly forget? Which failures of memory annoy you the most?

4 **41** Listen to the first part of a talk on memory by a psychologist and note the common failures of memory that he mentions. Were any of them the same as yours?

5 **42** Listen to the rest of the talk and answer the questions.

1 What is AJ good at remembering?
2 How does she feel about her good memory?
3 Why are people's memories not as good as they used to be?

6 **43** Complete each statement with the missing word. Then listen and check.

1 AJ's memory is stimulated by .... in the same way that our memories can be stimulated by certain ....
2 Having a good memory should make people feel more ....
3 Our memories are selective: they remember mostly .... things and .... things.
4 We should be .... for all the things that our memories hide.
5 Technology has become "our .... memory."
6 Now medical science is trying to address the problem of .... memory.

7 Work in pairs. Discuss how much you rely on your internal memory to remember things as compared to aids such as Post-it notes, your computer, or diaries. Do you agree with the speaker that our memories are getting worse?

Grammar **future in the past**

8 **44** Listen to the first part of the talk again and complete the first half of these sentences with the correct verb forms.

1 You ________ to make a comment at a meeting and then...
2 You ________ to send a friend a card for his birthday, but then...
3 You recognized someone in the street and ________ spoken to her, but...
4 You promised you ________ mail a letter for someone and two days later...
5 You ________ to write down a great idea you had, but when you found a pen and paper,...

9 Work in pairs. What happened next in each case? Were any of these actions completed? Why?

10 Choose the right verb form to complete this description of another memory patient.

One interesting patient couldn't form new memories. He could only remember events before 1960. I [1] *was going to interview / would interview* his doctor about how someone with no memory managed to cope with daily life, but she suggested I interview him instead.
Our appointment [2] *was supposed to be / would be* at 2 p.m., but it made no difference since he lived only in the present. I [3] *would tell / would have told* him my name and why I was there, but I realized there was no point: [4] *it was going to mean / it would have meant* nothing to him. So I began by asking him about his past and he talked about his time as a child during the Second World War. Then the telephone rang. When he came back, I [5] *was about to ask / would ask* him to continue, but I realized he had completely forgotten our earlier conversation. I thought he [6] *was about to be / would be* frustrated by this but not at all. He seemed happy for not being burdened by memory.

▶ FUTURE IN THE PAST

going to* and *about to
I was going to call you, but I forgot.
I was about to call you, but I was interrupted.

would* and *would have
He said he would call me.
I would have called you, but I didn't have your number.

supposed to
He was supposed to call you. Did he forget?

For more information and practice, see page 172.

11 **45** Look at the grammar box. Transform these original plans into future in-the-past forms. Then listen and check your answers.

1 "I'm going to ask Sanjip to come."
I ________ , but I asked Kumar instead.
2 "She's supposed to be in Cairo this week."
She ________ in Cairo this week, but she's sick.
3 "I'll definitely send you the original."
He promised he ________ me the original, but he sent me a copy.
4 "We will be there by ten o'clock."
We ________ there by ten o'clock, but the train didn't get in until eleven fifteen.
5 He's about to announce that he will retire.
He ________ , but now he thinks he'll stay another year.
6 "The city planners will build a new shopping mall downtown."
The city planners ________ a new shopping mall downtown, but residents opposed it.

12 Pronunciation **contrastive sentence stress**

a **45** Work in pairs. Underline the words in each sentence in Exercise 11 that highlight the contrasting facts. Listen again and check. Then practice saying each sentence.

b Complete each of these sentences with a contrasting idea. Underline the words in the sentence that highlight the contrast. Then say your sentences to your partner. Ask them which words they thought were stressed.

1 I was going to order a steak, but…
2 They were supposed to be going on vacation, but…
3 I would have driven, but…
4 He said he would wait for me, but…
5 We were about to buy a new TV, but…

Speaking

13 Work in pairs. Choose a situation below. Think of a good excuse to explain why it happened. Then change pairs and explain your excuse again.

- You were 30 minutes late for an important business meeting and didn't call to say so.
- You borrowed someone's car and were supposed to return it the following day, but they had to call you to find out where you were.
- It was a close friend's birthday two days ago. You didn't send a card or get them a present.

11c A clever bird

Reading

1 Work in pairs. Do you know a domestic animal which is particularly intelligent? How does this intelligence show itself?

2 Read the article and say how Alex the parrot's intelligence showed itself.

3 Mark the sentences true (T), false (F), or not answered (NA).

1 People are right to believe that animals have thoughts and emotions.
2 Pepperberg's idea was to let Alex communicate to her how he saw the world.
3 Pepperberg didn't want people to think she had chosen Alex for his intelligence.
4 Alex showed that he could distinguish between colors and shapes but not numbers.
5 Pepperberg concluded that cognitive skills were necessary for survival in the wild.
6 Alex felt very proud of his ability to communicate in English.

4 In pairs, discuss if you were surprised by Pepperberg's results, and why.

Critical thinking **reinforcing ideas**

5 Often when writers express an idea, they reinforce it, to make sure the reader understands, by:

- saying the same thing in other words
- giving examples
- quoting someone who also made this point

Find and underline the ideas expressed below by the author. Note how each one is reinforced.

1 How can we find out if animals can think?
2 Pepperberg's idea was to ask the parrot for his thoughts.
3 Researchers had no confidence in her idea.
4 She wanted to get inside the parrot's head.
5 Alex's cognitive abilities are not typical of all animals.
6 Alex's cognitive abilities are necessary to cope with his environment.
7 Alex worked through various mental tests.
8 Alex behaved like a bored teenager.

6 Which method of reinforcing an idea did you find the most effective?

Word focus ***learn***

7 Work in pairs. Find these three expressions in the article with the word *learn*. Discuss what each one means.

1 learn as you go along
2 learn by heart
3 learn the hard way

8 Look at the expressions in bold with *learn* in the sentences below and figure out what each one means from its context. Which one means the same as "learn the hard way"?

1 If you work with an experienced chef, you can **learn some tricks of the trade**.
2 You're not ready to design the new brochure. You have to **learn to walk before you can run**.
3 It's **never too late to learn**. My grandfather took up the piano when he was 73.
4 I've **learned my lesson**. I'm never going to try to build a piece of furniture again without reading the instructions first.
5 I hate it too, but we're going to have to **learn to live with it**.
6 You'd think that the government would **learn from its mistakes**, but it never does.

9 Choose two of the expressions from Exercise 8 and use them in sentences about your own learning experiences. Read your sentences to your partner, omitting the expressions with *learn*. Can your partner figure out the missing expressions?

Speaking

10 Work in pairs. Take the quiz on page 154 to find out what type of learner you are. The answers are on page 155.

11 Work in small groups. Discuss how your learning style affects your language learning. What things can you do to learn more effectively? Look at the ideas below and add any others you can think of:

- watching English-language movies with subtitles
- reading stories (in English newspapers, books, magazines) and retelling them
- keeping a vocabulary book and drawing illustrations of each new word

A clever bird

How does a scientist find out to what extent an animal is capable of thinking? What evidence is there that it is able to acquire information about the world and act on it, learning as it goes along?

In 1977, Irene Pepperberg, a recent graduate of Harvard University, decided to investigate the thought processes of another creature by talking to it. In order to do this, she would teach a one-year-old African gray parrot named Alex to reproduce the sounds of the English language. "I thought if he learned to communicate, I could ask him questions about how he sees the world."

Pepperberg bought Alex in a Chicago pet store. She let the store's assistant choose him because she didn't want other scientists to say that she had deliberately chosen an especially smart bird. Given that Alex's brain was the size of a walnut, most researchers thought Pepperberg's communication study would be futile. "Some people actually called me crazy for trying this," she said.

But with Pepperberg's patient teaching, Alex learned how to imitate almost 100 English words, including the names of food. He could count to six and had learned the sounds for seven and eight. But the point was not to see if Alex could learn words by heart. Pepperberg wanted to get inside his mind and learn more about a bird's understanding of the world. She couldn't ask him what he was thinking about, but she could ask him about his knowledge of numbers, shapes, and colors.

In one demonstration, Pepperberg placed Alex on a wooden perch in the middle of the room. She then held up a green key and a small green cup for him to look at.

"What's the same?" she asked.

Without hesitation, Alex's beak opened: "Co-lor."

"What's different?" Pepperberg asked.

"Shape," Alex said. His voice had the sound of a cartoon character. But the words—and what can only be called the thoughts—were entirely his. Many of Alex's cognitive skills, such as his ability to understand the concepts of "same" and "different," are rare in the animal world. Very few animals share these skills. But parrots, like humans, live a long time in complex societies. And like humans, these birds must keep track of the dynamics of changing relationships and environments.

"They need to be able to distinguish colors to know when a fruit is ripe or unripe," Pepperberg explained. "They need to categorize things—what's edible, what isn't—and to know the shapes of predators. And it helps to have a concept of numbers if you need to keep track of your flock. For a long-lived bird, you can't do all of this with instinct; cognition must be involved."

In the demonstration, Alex then ran through various tests, distinguishing colors, shapes, sizes, and materials (wool versus wood versus metal). He did some simple arithmetic, such as counting the yellow toy blocks among a pile of mixed colored blocks. And then, as if to offer final proof of the mind inside his bird's brain, Alex spoke up. "Talk clearly!" he commanded, when one of the younger birds Pepperberg was also teaching mispronounced the word "green." "Talk clearly!"

Alex knew all the answers himself and was getting bored. "He's moody," said Pepperberg, "so he interrupts the others, or he gives the wrong answer just to be difficult." Pepperberg was certainly learning more about the mind of a parrot, but like the parent of a troublesome teenager, she was learning the hard way.

11d Keep learning

Real life getting clarification

1 Look at the list of short courses offered by an adult education college. Use a dictionary if you need to. Which of the courses interest you and why?

2 46 Listen and answer the questions.

1 What kind of course is Ahmad interested in taking?
2 What course does Liz suggest for him instead? Why?
3 What does Ahmad decide to do?

3 Look at the expressions used by Ahmad. Which are used for repetition (R) and which are used for explanation (E)?

▶ GETTING CLARIFICATION

What do you mean by… ?
Can you speak up a little?
Can you explain what…?
I'm not really with you.
Are you saying that… ?
Could you give me an example of… ?
What was… again?
Hang on a second. That's too much to take in all at once.
I didn't catch…
Did you say… ?

4 46 Listen again. Complete the unfinished sentences in the box.

5 Pronunciation **linking in question forms**

a 47 In certain commonly used combinations (*did you, could you, what do you*) the words are strongly linked together. Listen to these examples.

Are you saying the course is full?
Can you speak up a little?
Could you give me an example?
Did you say Tuesday?
What do you mean?

b Work in pairs. Practice saying these sentences.

Can you explain what you mean?
Could you repeat that?
Did you mean September?
What are you trying to say?
What do you think?

6 Work in pairs. Act out a conversation, inquiring about the course. Then change roles.

Student A: You are a prospective student. Choose one of the courses in Exercise 1 or another course you would like to take. Ask Student B about your choice.

Student B: You are a college administrator. Prepare what you are going to say about Student A's chosen course.

ROUSHAM
ADULT EDUCATION CENTER

COURSE TITLE	FREQUENCY	EXAM COURSE
Basic car mechanics *Apr 5, 10 wks*	1 x 2hrs	✗
Psychology of human behavior *Jan 22, 18 wks*	1 x 2hrs	✓
Public speaking *Apr 11, 8 wks*	1 x 1.5hrs	✗
First aid *Apr 12, 4 wks*	2 x 1.5hrs	✓
Desert and jungle survival *Mar 1, 12 wks*	1 x 1.5hrs	✓
Ikebana: Japanese flower arranging *Jan 22, 18 wks*	1 x 2hrs	✗
Art appreciation *Apr 5, 10 wks*	1 x 2hrs	✗
Screenwriting *Jan 21, 18 wks*	1 x 2hrs	✗
Surfing *Apr 12, 6 wks*	1 x 3hrs	✓
Investing in stocks and buying shares *Apr 11, 8 wks*	1 x 1.5hrs	✗

11e The wrong course

Writing an email about a misunderstanding

1 Work in pairs. Read the email from a student to an adult education college. Answer the questions.

1 What is the misunderstanding about the course?
a the timing b the level c the subject
2 How would you describe the student's feelings?
a angry b offended c frustrated
3 How would you describe the tone of the email?
a complaining b reasonable c apologetic

> Dear Sir or Madam:
>
> I enrolled in your course "car mechanics 1" in August and have attended three sessions. When I originally inquired about the course, I was told that it was suitable for people with no previous knowledge of car mechanics. But in fact, everyone else in the course seems to know a lot already. So despite the fact that the lessons generally start with a basic concept, they move very quickly onto more complicated ideas.
>
> I don't blame the teacher. On the contrary, he does his best to explain concepts to me. But I feel that I am just holding everyone else back. They know how an engine works already, whereas I have no background at all in mechanics.
>
> I was going to wait a couple of weeks more before saying anything, but in the last session I felt so out of my depth that I have decided to write now and ask for a refund. While I understand this isn't really anyone's fault, I hope you will appreciate how frustrating the situation is for me.
>
> I look forward to hearing from you.
> Karen Redman

2 If you were an administrator at the college, how would you react to this email?

3 Writing skill **linking contrasting ideas**

a Find the words or phrases in the email that link these contrasting ideas.

1 The course should be for beginners. No one else is a beginner.
2 Each lesson starts with a simple idea. It progresses quickly to difficult ideas.
3 The teacher is not at fault. He helps me as much as he can.
4 The other students know a lot. I know nothing.
5 No one is to blame for this. I still feel it is unfair.

4. Clause, whereas clause. (or) whereas clause, clause.
5. While clause, clause.
(or) Clause while clause.

b Match these words and phrases to the ones in the email that they could replace.

1 although whereas. while . so despite
2 in actual fact
3 but on the other hand
4 but in reality

c Complete these sentences with appropriate linking phrases.

1 .... the brochure says the start date is September 12, the first real class is a week later, on the 19th.
2 The course is advertised as "practical," .... you learn a lot of theory as well.
3 .... the course fee is quite high, it's a great investment in your future.
4 The course isn't much fun, ... , you would expect a course in lifesaving to be serious.
5 The French conversation class focuses on everyday French, ... in the advanced French class you cover literature.
6 Surfing is not an easy skill to learn. .... , you need to have a lot of perseverance.

4 Imagine you enrolled in one of the other courses on page 136. Think of a misunderstanding that occurred with the course. Write an email to the college explaining the misunderstanding and asking for a refund.

5 Exchange letters with your partner and check the following items:

- Does the email make clear what the misunderstanding was?
- Is the tone reasonable?
- Has the writer used linking words and phrases correctly?
- Do you think the email will get the desired response?

11f Paraguay shaman
Video

Paraguay's renowned healers, called "shamans," have a deep knowledge of local medicinal plants.

Before you watch

1 Work in groups. Look at the photo and discuss the questions.

1 What do you know about shamans?
2 What techniques do you think they use?

2 You are going to watch a video about medicinal plants. Answer these questions.

1 What problem do you think faces these plants?
2 What solution to the problem might the video suggest?
3 Write down three kinds of people you're going to see in the video.

While you watch

3 Watch the video and check your answers from Exercise 2.

4 Cross out the wrong information in these sentences. Then rewrite the sentences correctly.

1 When the scientists arrive, Gervasio, the local shaman, is collecting plants in the forest.

....

2 Gervasio and the team set off to look for an insect the scientists are interested in.

....

3 The local people eat the root raw.

....

4 Later, back in the village, Gervasio shows the team a book he has written.

....

5 Watch the video again and answer the questions.

1 What illnesses are mentioned in the video?

....

2 How do traditional folk healers in Paraguay help scientists?

....

3 Why is it important to record shamans' knowledge urgently?

....

4 Why does Gervasio use chants and prayers before going into the forest?

....

5 Why are the scientists interested in the suruvi root?

....

6 What does the scientists' book set out to do?

....

6 Number these in the order you hear them.

a Recording and analyzing Paraguayan plants for possible medical cures is urgent business.
b To reach Gervasio, a group of researchers set out on a long journey through the reserve.
c Somewhere in this forest, maybe in this plant or that herb, there might be a cure for an illness.
d When he feels ready, Gervasio and his wife lead the group on the search.
e The rain forests of Paraguay have long been a source of medicinal cures.

After you watch

7 Roleplay interviewing a scientist

Work in pairs.

Student A: Imagine you are a National Geographic reporter. You are going to interview the scientist who made the documentary about Gervasio. Use the information below to prepare questions.

Student B: Imagine you are the scientist who made the documentary about Gervasio. Look at the information below and think about what you are going to say to the reporter.

- the journey to the reserve
- the journey to Tekoha Ryapu
- what it feels like to work with Gervasio
- the importance of Gervasio's knowledge
- what they were able to achieve on this trip
- how the book might help

Act out the interview, then change roles.

8 Work in groups and discuss these questions.

1 Do you know of any modern medicines that originated from rain forest plants?
2 Do you think traditional medicines from plants are effective?
3 What do you think about other forms of traditional medicine, for example acupuncture, massage therapy, and homeopathy?

chant (n) /tʃænt/ a kind of rhythmic song that uses only one or two notes
deforestation (n) /dɪˌfɔrɪˈsteɪʃən/ cutting down trees
folk healer (n) /ˈfoʊk ˌhilər/ a person who uses traditional methods to cure illnesses
multiply (v) /ˈmʌltɪˌplaɪ/ reproduce quickly
renowned (adj) /rɪˈnaʊnd/ famous
reserve (n) /rɪˈzɜrv/ an area of land where plants or animals are officially protected

UNIT 11 REVIEW

Grammar

1 Work in pairs. What is the maximum number of languages someone can speak fluently? Does speaking one language help you to learn another?

2 Underline the correct option below.

When police in Brazil arrested an illegal immigrant speaking an unrecognizable language, they immediately called Ziad Fazah, the world's greatest linguist. Fazah realized quickly that the man was speaking a dialect used in Afghanistan. With Fazah's help, the man [1] *explain / was able to explain* that he had escaped Afghanistan and was seeking asylum in Brazil. At that time, Fazah, originally from the Lebanon, [2] *could speak / managed to speak* 54 languages. He also [3] *could get / succeeded in getting* his name into the Brazilian *Guinness World Book of Records* as the world's greatest living polyglot. Fazah had done a lot of interpreting for the police, but unfortunately they [4] *couldn't pay / didn't manage to pay* him.

When Fazah was 17, his talents were recognized by the Lebanese government, who [5] *were going to use / would use* him as an interpreter, but soon after, he moved to Brazil. Eventually he began giving private language lessons. Fazah [6] *would remain / would have remained* unknown, but in 2006 his language abilities were tested on a Spanish television show and he got international attention. Then people began to question his abilities. [7] *Was he really able / Did he really manage* to speak over 50 languages? The show [8] *was supposed to show / would have shown* that he could, but the evidence was not convincing.

3 Answer the questions.

1 What is a polyglot?
2 What is Fazah's regular job?
3 How many languages is he really fluent in?

I CAN	
describe past abilities with *could, was able to, managed to,* and *succeeded in*	☐
talk about past intentions and predictions with the future in the past	☐

Vocabulary

4 Work in pairs. Complete the paragraph. The first letter of each missing word is given.

There are many ways to [1] a________ knowledge: by [2] t________ and error, from an authority, by reasoning, and by [3] o________ (in other words, just by watching). Some things, like bringing up children, are more instinctive; you have a gut [4] f________ about the right way to do things. Some things, like playing a musical instrument, you can [5] p________ up as you go along. But other things need to be taught. For example, you might have a basic [6] g________ of mathematics, but still be completely [7] i________ of how calculus works. For this type of learning, you need an authority like a book or a teacher that can help you to [8] e________ with the subject and understand it.

5 Tell each other how you learned to do two things (like cook or play an instrument).

I CAN	
talk about learning and knowledge	☐

Real life

6 Work in pairs. Match 1–5 to a–e.

1 What do you mean by that?
2 Could you give me an example?
3 Can you speak up a little?
4 What was that again?
5 I'm not really with you.

a I didn't catch that.
b I don't really understand.
c For instance?
d Can you explain that?
e I can't hear you very clearly.

7 Think of something you can do, but your partner probably can't. Give your partner some instructions. As you receive the instructions ask for clarification and repetition.

I CAN	
get clarification by asking someone to repeat or explain	☐

Speaking

8 Work in small groups. Tell each other about a good or bad learning experience.

At school we had a great art teacher who could inspire anyone. He had really good ideas, such as…

Unit 12 The economy

A woman in a pink mink coat next to her pink Rolls Royce, Hong Kong
Photo by Jodi Cobb

FEATURES

1 Work in pairs. Look at the photo. What does a matching luxury car and fur coat say about a person? Do rich people in your country like to show off their wealth?

2 Match the word (1–7) with its synonym (a–g).

1	afford	a	poor
2	hard up	b	have enough money
3	income	c	expensive
4	loaded	d	a good price
5	pricey	e	very rich
6	reasonable	f	comfortable
7	well-off	g	earnings

3 Work in small groups. What is the definition of "poor" in your country? How would <u>you</u> define *rich* and *poor*? Can you be rich without having a lot of money?

12a Saving for a rainy day

Reading

1 Work in pairs. What do you know about Norway: its landscape, its people, its industry? Look at the photo for ideas.

2 Read the article. In what ways is Norway a "rich" country?

3 Complete these summaries of each paragraph. Then compare answers with another pair.

1 For a long time, Norway has had a better .... than other countries.
2 The three reasons for Norway's success are: big oil reserves, ..., and ....
3 For Norwegians, being rich means ....
4 Norway is saving money for ....

4 Do you think that the Norwegians are right to save their money? Why?

Grammar **focusing adverbs *only, just, even***

▶ FOCUSING ADVERBS *ONLY, JUST, EVEN*

only
Only Luxembourg and a couple of other countries are richer.

just
Just 80 years ago, Norwegians were emigrating to the US.

even
This isn't even a competition anymore.

For more information and practice, see page 172.

5 Work in pairs. Look at the grammar box. Which of these statements (a–c) is true of *only, just,* and *even*?

a they always come directly after the word they are emphasizing.
b they always come directly after the main verb.
c they always come directly before the word they are emphasizing.

6 Find other examples of these words in the article. Do they follow the same rule?

SAVING FOR A RAINY DAY

Come on, Norway; this isn't even a competition anymore! For the last eight years, Norway has registered the highest quality of life among the world's nations. It is one of the wealthiest countries in the world; only Luxembourg and a couple of others are richer. Norwegians can also expect to get a good education, find the job they want (unemployment is only 2.5 percent), enjoy good health, and live a long life. People say the prisons are quite comfortable too!

Norway has not always been a rich country. Just 80 years ago, Norwegians were emigrating to the US by the thousands, in search of a better life. The rise in oil prices in the 1970s changed all that. But Norway's success is not only the result of its huge reserves of oil. Other countries have had such riches and squandered them. It is also due to the Norwegians' thrift and their strong work ethic.

When you arrive in Oslo for the first time, don't expect to be met with Dubai-style skyscrapers, entrepreneurs in designer suits, and rows of Ferraris and Porsches. Norway may be rich, but it is modest in its wealth. Norwegians also work hard and are always near the top in surveys of global worker productivity rates. But in today's high-tech world, where work seems to follow us wherever we go, the people of Norway are redefining what wealth means. Laws just recently passed by the government emphasize the importance of family and time off, offering generous maternity and paternity leave, subsidized childcare, and long vacations as well.

Also, the country is saving for the future. Every dollar earned from oil is put straight into what is now the world's biggest pension fund, worth over $200 billion. Extraordinarily, none of this money is allowed to be spent on state infrastructure projects. It is not even invested in new schools and hospitals. But at a time when most other countries are wondering how they will finance the pensions of a growing retired population, Norway is sitting pretty.

leave (n) /liv/ time off from work
sitting pretty (v) /ˈsɪtɪŋ ˈprɪti/ in a good or comfortable situation
squander (v) /ˈskwɑndər/ waste
thrift (n) /θrɪft/ carefulness when spending money

7 Discuss the meaning of each sentence (1–8), then match it to what follows logically (a–h).

1 Only visitors think Norway is expensive.
2 Visitors only think Norway is expensive.
3 Visitors think only Norway is expensive.
4 Among the Scandinavian countries, I have visited Norway just once.
5 Among the Scandinavian countries, I have visited just Norway.
6 Even fathers are given time off to be with their new babies.
7 Fathers are even given time off to be with their new babies.
8 Fathers are given time off even to be with their new babies.

a Of course mothers are given a lot of time off too.
b I have visited the others several times.
c They are also given time off to move and to look after elderly parents.
d ...but all the Scandinavian countries are.
e ...but actually it's quite reasonable.
f I haven't visited the others at all.
g The residents themselves find it reasonable.
h ...in addition to extra money.

8 Complete these sentences by putting a focusing adverb in the right place. Then compare answers with your partner. Tell them whether these facts are true of your country.

1 Many people work long hours during the week, so they see their children on weekends.
2 People with college degrees are finding it difficult to get jobs these days.
3 For most people, a job is a way to make money, not something they particularly enjoy.
4 The rich represent about five percent of the population.
5 You don't see extreme poverty. Poor people usually have food and somewhere to live.
6 The state pension gives you enough to live on, but not to live very comfortably.

Grammar focusing adverbs *too, as well, also*

9 Work in pairs. Look at the position of *too* and *as well* in these sentences. Find the same sentences in the article, but with the word *also*. What do you notice about the position of *also*?

1 Norwegians can expect to get a good education too.
2 It is due to the Norwegians' thrift as well.
3 Norwegians work hard too.
4 The country is saving for the future too.

▶ FOCUSING ADVERBS *TOO, AS WELL, ALSO*

sentence + *too*	*also* + main verb
sentence + *as well*	*be* + *also*
Also, + sentence	auxiliary verb + *also* + main verb

For more information and practice, see page 172.

10 Look at the grammar box. Which patterns from the box can you find in the article? Underline them. Then compare your answers with your partner.

11 Rewrite the sentences using the focusing adverbs given. Compare your answers with another pair.

1 Norwegians like their secure pensions, but they would like to see the government increase spending on healthcare. (*as well / also*)
2 Most countries have high public borrowing and a lot of debt. Norway has neither. (*too / also*)
3 Teachers in Norway receive a good salary and if they teach "heavy" subjects, they get extra payments. (*also / too*)
4 Artists can get a grant—not a loan—from the government of around $20,000 a year and support with childcare. (*also / as well*)
5 Food prices seem very high to outsiders and fuel is expensive. However, house prices are relatively low and so property is a good investment. (*too / also*)
6 Nurses in Norway get 42 weeks' maternity leave at full pay. They can use the hospital's day care when they return to work. (*as well / also*)

Vocabulary money

12 Look at the verbs below and find the right noun in Exercise 11 to make phrases with the same meaning.

1 pay money = make a ....
2 invest money = make an ....
3 borrow more money = increase your ....
4 spend less money = reduce your ....
5 be lent money = take out a ....
6 owe money = have a ....
7 earn money = receive a ....
8 be given money (by the government) = receive a ....

Speaking

13 Work in pairs. Prepare questions to ask each other about the economy in your country or countries (the cost of living, work-life balance, government spending, government grants for certain professions). Use the items in Exercise 11 to help you get ideas.

14 Now change partners with another pair and ask and answer your questions.

12b Don't do it yourself

Vocabulary domestic help

1 Work in pairs. Which of the domestic workers listed below is the person in the photo? What do the other jobs involve?

au pair	babysitter
cleaner	cook
dog walker	gardener
handyman	maid
nanny	personal shopper

2 Discuss these questions about the jobs in Exercise 1.

1 Have you done any yourself?
2 Have you (or your family) employed anyone in these roles?
3 Which jobs involve the greatest skill?
4 Would you like to do any of them? Why?

Listening

3 48 Listen to the interview with the author of a book called *The Servant Economy*. Answer the questions.

1 How many domestic workers are there in the US today? Who are they?
2 Does the author think the growth of the servant economy is good or bad?

4 48 Listen again and identify:

1 which jobs from Exercise 1 the speakers mention.
2 what other jobs are mentioned.
3 whether many people or only the rich employ such workers.

> **WORDBUILDING *the* + adjective**
> We can refer to a group of people using *the* + adjective.
> *the rich, the poor*

5 Work in pairs. What did the interviewer find strange about hiring someone to install a Christmas tree? Do you agree?

6 Complete Hilaire Belloc's quotation. Do you agree with it? Why?

"It is the duty of the .... man to give .... to the artisan." *Hilaire Belloc*

Grammar causative *have* and *get*

7 Look at the forms in bold (a–d). Answer the questions (1 and 2). Then look at the transcript on page 181 and find one more example of each type of phrase.

a Thirty years ago, the idea of **getting a worker to hand wash** your car was unthinkable.
b Nowadays, you can **have it washed** for $6.
c You don't have to be rich **to have a cleaner come** once a week.
d Another example would be **getting your windows cleaned** every few months.

1 Which phrases mean someone does a job for you?
2 Which phrases tell you who actually does the job?

(don't know who) so. get(s) sth done.
have
has

who does it so. get(s) so. +inf
have so. +base

> **CAUSATIVE *HAVE* and *GET***
>
> ***have/get*** **+ something + past participle**
> *I had/got the fence fixed yesterday.*
>
> ***have*** **+ someone + base form**
> *I had the gardener fix the fence.*
>
> ***get*** **+ someone + infinitive**
> *I got the gardener to fix the fence.*
>
> For more information and practice, see page 173.

8 Look at the grammar box. Then complete the paragraph.

> Nearly half of all homes in Britain get outside staff [1] ______ (do) their domestic chores for an average of six hours per week. The most common reasons that people gave for having someone [2] ______ (help) around the house were their own long working hours and to avoid arguments with their partner. A third of people said if they didn't have help, nothing would get [3] ______ (do). The most popular domestic jobs are having the house [4] ______ (clean) regularly, getting someone [5] ______ (do) the gardening and having a handyman [6] ______ (fix) things when they are broken. Some of these services do not come cheap either. People pay up to $800 per week to have a personal assistant [7] ______ (organize) their appointments or have their young baby [8] ______ (care) for.

9 Look at these things that a rich couple gets other people to do for them. Complete the sentences with causative forms. Note that you can complete the sentences in two different ways.

1. When they had a party last month, someone organized everything for them.
   They ______ everything for them. (get)
2. A personal trainer takes their children to the park to play.
   They ______ to the park to play. (have)
3. A driver picks their children up from school.
   They ______ from school. (have)
4. A travel agent plans their vacations for them.
   They ______ for them. (have)
5. A nanny looks after their children.
   They ______. (get)
6. Someone even packs their bags for them.
   They even ______ for them. (get)

10 Write down one thing that you would never consider getting someone else to do and one thing you would always get someone else to do. Compare lists with your partner.

11 Pronunciation the sounds /ʃ/, /ʧ/, /ʒ/, and /ʤ/

a **49** Listen carefully to how the underlined letters are pronounced in the following words. Then practice saying them with your partner.

/ʃ/	/ʧ/	/ʒ/	/ʤ/
carwash	chores	decision	change
shelves	richer	garage	college
shopper	watch	pleasure	fridge

b **50** Listen to these words. Discuss which of the four sounds above each one contains. Then practice saying them.

agent	arrange	champagne	cheese
choice	fashion	general	January
sugar	television	usual	

Vocabulary and speaking

12 Work in pairs. How many DIY (do-it-yourself) jobs can you make by matching verbs in A with nouns in B?

A

assemble	clean
decorate	fix
hang	plaster
put up	tile

B

a bed	the bathroom
a carpet	some curtains
a picture	the roof
a tap	some shelves
a wall	

13 Look at the room in the photo. First make a list of all the things that need to be done before you can live in it. Then decide what you will do yourself and what you will get professional help to do. Explain your plans to another pair.

12c The gift economy

Reading

1 How do you think a gift economy works?

2 Read the article and see if you were right. Then find three examples of the gift economy.

3 Choose the correct option (a–c).

1 The false understanding of human nature mentioned is that we are all trying to:
  a compete to get as much as we can.
  b be individuals.
  c keep from being hungry.

2 Hunter-gatherers:
  a had plenty and needed plenty.
  b had little and needed little.
  c had plenty and needed little.

3 American companies found it difficult to recruit Japanese employees because they:
  a couldn't offer good conditions.
  b couldn't offer job security.
  c didn't understand Japanese culture.

4 The message of the 4th paragraph is that Japanese employers are involved in:
  a organizing employees' vacations.
  b their employees' lives.
  c the quality of employees' work.

5 According to the author, the Internet has made it easier for people to:
  a get to know each other.
  b discuss problems.
  c give and receive help.

6 The message of the last paragraph is that big organizations need to:
  a be made smaller.
  b think about the common good.
  c give more of their profits back.

4 Look at these pairs of words from the article. Which definition (a or b) matches each word?

1 gain / reward
  a profit — b compensation
2 strive / thrive
  a do well — b do your best
3 common / mutual
  a shared by two — b shared by many
4 abundance / excess
  a too much — b plenty
5 prospects / aspects
  a future possibilities — b characteristics
6 accuracy / promptness
  a being precise — b being on time

5 Work in small groups. Tell each other what kind of relationship exists between employer and employees in your country. Is it more like the American system or the Japanese relationship?

Critical thinking **signposts to key information**

6 There are certain phrases that act as signposts to key information (just given or about to follow). Find the following phrases in the article and then draw out the key information they refer to.

at the heart of…	not only…	rather…
the main…	the real…	

7 Work in pairs. Compare your answers. Did you agree on what the key information was?

Word focus ***hard***

8 Work in pairs. Find three expressions in the article containing the word *hard*. Discuss their meaning.

9 With a partner, try to guess the meaning of each expression with *hard* from its context. Then compare your answers with another pair.

1 I'm sorry the boss didn't like your idea and preferred mine. **No hard feelings**, I hope.
2 Fran and Chris are pretty **hard up** these days. They've been unemployed for a year.
3 Did you hear that **hard-luck** story about the people who lost all their savings?
4 Don't **be hard on** Jake. It's not his fault he was late. His car broke down.
5 I tried to get him to sympathize with our situation because we're newly established, but he's a pretty **hard-headed** businessman.

Speaking

10 Work in groups of three. Discuss the customs of gift giving and exchange that you are familiar with. Think about:

- specific occasions (like weddings, dinner parties)
- visiting people
- help and favors
- business gifts
- returning home after a trip abroad

The Gift Economy

The banking crisis of 2008 again raised concerns that our economy is based too much on individual greed. Such an economic model, critics say, comes from a false understanding of human nature. Human society is not made up of individuals pursuing private gain through competition with each other. The real essence of human nature lies in the social bonds that we make through family, friendships, professional associations, and local communities. These bonds produce a sense of common purpose and shared values, in which groups of people strive for the common good: a sound education, a pleasant environment to live in, a healthy population. It is this idea of shared social interests that is at the heart of the gift economy.

Gift economies thrived in earlier times when people lived in a world of greater abundance and when their wants were fewer. Stone Age hunter-gatherers had shelter and enough food, and did not need many possessions, just a few weapons for hunting and clothing for warmth. They shared food and tools without any expectation of payment or immediate reward. But this is not only an idea that applies to a more primitive way of life. There are also many recent examples of the gift economy at work.

In the past, American companies operating in Japan found it difficult to attract Japanese recruits, even though, compared with Japanese employers, they offered more generous wages, shorter work hours, and better promotion prospects. But these factors were traditionally not so important to Japanese employees, who did not think of their services as being "bought." Rather, they felt they were entering into a long-term "gift exchange" relationship with their employer, which was of mutual benefit.

This relationship had many aspects. At its most basic it involves the simple exchange of physical gifts. For example, if an employee gets married, the company sends a gift and even a departmental manager to represent it at the wedding. Or the company gives its employees a yearly company vacation. On these organized weekends, coworkers share dormitories, eat together, and visit the same attractions, largely at the company's expense. For their part, the main gift employees give their company is their hard work, and this is why each Japanese employee pays such great attention to accuracy, quality in their work, and promptness in its delivery. Even the simplest tasks are carried out with extraordinary care.

Elsewhere, the Internet is facilitating the re-emergence of the gift economy. Neighborhood groups use online networks to share tools and skills. If you need a long ladder to repair your roof, you don't have to go out and buy one; simply put a message on the neighborhood discussion board and soon a neighbor will offer one. You probably will even get help with the repair, because helping and giving is part of human nature. On the Internet, knowledge and advice about almost everything are shared, from how a nuclear reactor works to building your own canoe.

"Fine," I hear you say, "but these are hard times. Helping our neighbor with his roof isn't going to pay the bills." But in an indirect way it is. The point is that by stressing the cooperative side of human nature, the gift economy helps us all. It keeps in check the excesses of big commercial organizations that seek to exploit situations for their own gain. So the big supermarket chains must understand that it is in the common interest not to force small shopkeepers out of business. Big industrial farms must realize that they cannot go on intensively farming the land until there is nothing left in it. Large companies should not always seek to drive the hardest bargain possible with their suppliers, but just pay them fairly. That is the real lesson of the gift economy.

12d The bottom line

Real life negotiating

1 Read this advice about negotiating. Do you agree with it? How does it relate to your own experience?

> "A famous negotiator's advice was to "Care, really care… but not that much." In other words, don't let the other person see how much you want the thing or you will be at a disadvantage."

2 51 Listen, and answer the questions.

1. How much does each person seem to care about agreeing on the lease?
2. On what point do they have trouble agreeing?
3. What does the woman suggest to get around this problem?
4. How does the negotiation end?

3 51 Work in pairs. Listen again and complete the expressions in the box.

NEGOTIATING

To be honest, it's absolutely 1 ______ .
A key thing for us is how long we'd be 2 ______ the lease.
I was hoping we could 3 ______ .
If you look at it from our point of view, we're a 4 ______ .
Let's face it, fifteen years is 5 ______ .

If your client could 6 ______ on that…
I think what you have to appreciate is that our client's main concern is...
At the end of the day, it gives them some security.
To tell you the truth, that's why the rent 7 ______ .
That's somewhat of a sticking point.
Is there no way around that?
Maybe if we signed… , then we could pay…
If I were in your shoes, I think I'd just 8 ______ .
When all's said and done, it has to 9 ______ .

4 Work in pairs. Look at the expressions in the box and discuss which are used to:

- say what the important thing is
- be direct
- talk about an obstacle to the agreement
- ask the other person to see your side

5 How do you think each person could have done better in the negotiation? Tell your partner.

6 Pronunciation **sentence stress in idiomatic phrases**

a 52 Listen to these phrases and underline the one or two words that are most stressed in each phrase.

1. To be honest…
2. A key thing for us is…
3. Let's face it…
4. At the end of the day,…
5. To tell you the truth…

b 53 Work in pairs. Look at these other phrases. Mark the words where you think the stress falls. Then listen and check.

1. The bottom line for us is…
2. The long and the short of it is…
3. The fact of the matter is…
4. One thing that's bothering me is…
5. To be frank,…
6. Am I right in thinking that… ?

7 You are spending eight months in a foreign country and want to get a car to use while you are there. You see a second-hand one advertised in the newspaper. It seems to be exactly what you are looking for. Work in pairs and negotiate the sale of the car. Student A look at page 153; Student B look at page 155.

12e This is what I propose

Writing a report

1 Work in pairs. Look at this quotation by the French mathematician Blaise Pascal. Discuss what he was saying about the art of writing.

"I'm sorry I wrote you such a long letter; I didn't have time to write a short one."

2 Look at these elements of a good report. Which is the one referred to by Blaise Pascal?

clear aims | clear recommendation | conciseness | good organization

3 Read the report below. What is the aim of the report? What is the recommendation? Tell your partner.

Summary

I visited our potential new offices at 1 Paradise Square yesterday, May 4, and was very impressed. They seem ideal for our needs, but the lease is for fifteen years, much longer than the six or seven we agreed on at our last meeting. These are the details:

Advantages

- Space — 2,000 ft^2 of flexible office space
- Low rent: only $67,000 per year
- Central location: close to stores and train station
- Maintained: cleaning, repairs are included

Disadvantages

- Long lease: fifteen years
- Maintenance fee is high: $17,000 annually

Recommendation

I propose taking these offices. We have been looking for five months and these are the best offices I have seen at a reasonable rent. If we have to leave before the end of the lease, I am confident that the remaining part of the lease can be sold to a new tenant.

---

4 Writing skill subheadings and bullet points

a The writer of the report has organized it into sections using subheadings and bullet points. What do you notice about the language after each bullet point?

b Read this first paragraph of a report on a language training course. Rewrite the report, dividing it into two sections with subheadings. Then break the points in the second section into bullet points.

> Last month the company sent me to a two-week "professional English" course at Falcon Business Language Training in Chicago. I stayed with a host family. Although the course did not focus on my particular job as an engineer very much, it was well organized. On the positive side, I was made to speak English all the time, both in the school and with my host family. The teachers were very professional and had a good knowledge of the business world. We were put in small groups of three to four students, which meant that we got a lot of individual attention.

c Work in pairs. Compare your answers. Did you organize your reports in the same way?

5 Now write the second half of the report including any negative comments and a recommendation. When you have finished, exchange your report with your partner.

6 Read your partner's report. Check the following:

- Is the report concise and clear?
- Has it been broken down into clear sections using subheadings and bullet points?
- Does it end with a clear recommendation?

12f Japan
Video

It is a land of dual identities.

Before you watch

1 Work in groups. Discuss the questions.

1 What do the photos show? Describe each one.
2 What two identities do you think the caption refers to?

2 Work in pairs. Write down things you associate with Japan.

While you watch

3 Watch the video and check your ideas from Exercise 2. Which of the things that you wrote down appeared in the video?

4 Watch the first part of the video (to 02:04). What do these numbers and dates refer to?

1 127 million ....
2 4 ....
3 35 million ....
4 1868 ....
5 1941 ....
6 1945 ....

5 Watch the second part of the video (02:05 to the end). Answer the questions.

1 What gave Japan political stability after the war?
....
2 What has helped it become a world leader in technology, manufacturing, and finance?
....
3 What does the tea ceremony emphasize?
a ....
b ....
c ....
4 Who did painters like Hiroshige influence?
....

6 Match the sentence beginnings (1–5) with the endings (a–e).

1 Japan is a country that harmonizes the forces of what is Western and modern
2 The bustling urban area of greater Tokyo is
3 It looked to the West for a new, more modern
4 Although it is a land of few natural resources, Japan has become
5 Beyond the bullet trains and neon of Tokyo,

a with those that are traditional Japanese.
b political and industrial model.
c there lies a rich cultural tradition.
d the largest metropolitan area on Earth.
e one of the most industrialized countries in the world.

7 Work in pairs. Describe the snow scene painting by Hiroshige.

....
....

After you watch

8 Roleplay a conversation between two different generations

Work in pairs.

Student A: Imagine you grew up in a small village in pre-war Japan. Look at the information below and think about what you are going to say to your grandchild.

- what life was like (the work you did, how you got around, the food you ate)
- the differences between life then and now
- the war years

Student B: Imagine you are a young Japanese business person talking to one of your grandparents. Look at the information below and think about what you are going to say to him/her.

- what life is like in the city (the work you do, how you travel to work, the food you eat)
- how you combine modern and traditional life in the city

Act out the conversation. Compare life in Japan pre- and post-war. Then change roles.

9 Work in groups and discuss the questions.

1 How has your country changed culturally and economically in the last 100 years?
2 Do cultural traditions always support economic innovation?
3 Are economic advances always beneficial? Why?

bustling (adj) /ˈbʌslɪŋ/ busy
feudal (adj) /ˈfjud(ə)l/ relating to a social system where most people work and fight for more powerful people who own the land
forge (v) /fɔrʤ/ make something under difficult conditions
glitz (n) /glɪts/ the quality of being shiny and superficially attractive
neon (n) /ˈniɑn/ a kind of brightly colored artificial light
raid (n) /reɪd/ an unexpected attack
shrine (n) /ʃraɪn/ a place where people go to meditate or pray
ubiquitous (adj) /juˈbɪkwɪtəs/ present everywhere
wrestling (n) /ˈreslɪŋ/ a sport where the contestants try to throw each other on the ground

UNIT 12 REVIEW

Grammar

1 Read the article and say why Japan has had a problem of relative poverty in recent years.

2 Insert the focus adverb into the right place in each sentence.

When we picture poverty we often think of people in under-developed countries without food or shelter. [1] But the so-called advanced economies of the world have their share of poverty (even). [2] Japan, for example, a few decades ago was enjoying an economic boom (just). [3] Yet by 2000, it had one of the highest rates of relative poverty among developed countries, with the US having a higher rate (only). [4] One reason was that Japan had one of the highest rates of non-regular workers (also). This means people who are working without proper social protection. [5] An increasingly elderly population—people who were not actively working—contributed to the problem (as well). [6] Making savings last when you live to be over 90 is a problem that people in developed countries will face in the coming years (even).

3 Put the verbs in the right form to complete this advice to people who are long-term unemployed.

1. The first thing to do is rewrite your resume and then get it ______ (check) by an expert.
2. Practice your interview technique. Have a friend ______ (play) the part of the interviewer and get them ______ (ask) you tricky questions.
3. Try to look professional when you go for an interview. Get your hair ______ (cut) and make sure your clothes are suitable. Again, get a friend ______ (help) you with this.
4. Call employers and go to see them in person. Show enthusiasm and get them ______ (see) that you are eager to work.

I CAN	
use focus adverbs to add emphasis	☐
talk about things that others do for me with *have* and *get*	☐

Vocabulary

4 Find a synonym or close synonym in B for each word/expression in A.

A	B
hard up	paint
hang	au pair
decorate	earnings
borrow from the bank	reasonable
cheap	take out a loan
income	put up
nanny	poor
owe money	be in debt

5 Work in pairs. Make a list of domestic help that you think most people can afford now and again.

I CAN	
talk about money and the economy	☐
talk about getting domestic jobs done	☐

Real life

6 Work in pairs. Put this conversation between a travel agent (TA) and customer (C) in order.

TA: To tell you the truth, they're not the kind of hotels you can negotiate with.
TA: So we're suggesting one week in the north of the island and one week in the south. Is this the kind of vacation you were looking for?
TA: OK, I'll give them a call and see what I can do.
TA: I understand that, and if I were in your shoes, I think I'd just go for it. At the end of the day, you only get one honeymoon.
TA: What you have to appreciate is that you've chosen two top hotels which aren't cheap.
C: I was hoping we could negotiate the price.
C: I know they aren't, but the key thing for us is to have nice accommodations.
C: Perhaps if we stayed at just one of them for the full two weeks we could get a better deal.
C: Yes it is, but to be honest, it's much more expensive than we expected.

7 Take the roles of travel agent and customer and finish the negotiation.

I CAN	
state my position and negotiate from it	☐

Speaking

8 Work in small groups. Do you think the idea below for a domestic service would work? Think of another idea. Then tell it to others in the class.

What about offering a cooking service where busy couples can have a meal prepared for them at home rather than eating out or getting takeout?

UNIT 3c, Exercise 11, page 38

Instructions

- Form a group of three or four people and ask the teacher which product you are going to present.
- Read the product description on page 154 or 155.
- Together prepare a brief presentation of the product: what it is, how it works, what it is appropriate for, and why it is special.
- Choose one person to give the presentation (the others will have to answer questions). Think about the questions you may be asked.
- Give and listen to the presentations, asking and answering questions as you go.
- Have a class vote for best product.

UNIT 4a, Exercise 10, page 47

Participation by art form

Art form	Creative participation %	Receptive participation %	Total participation %
Visual Arts & Crafts	22	38	49
Theater & Dance	7	40	42
Reading/ Creative Writing	16	84	84
Music	15	57	62

Participation in music

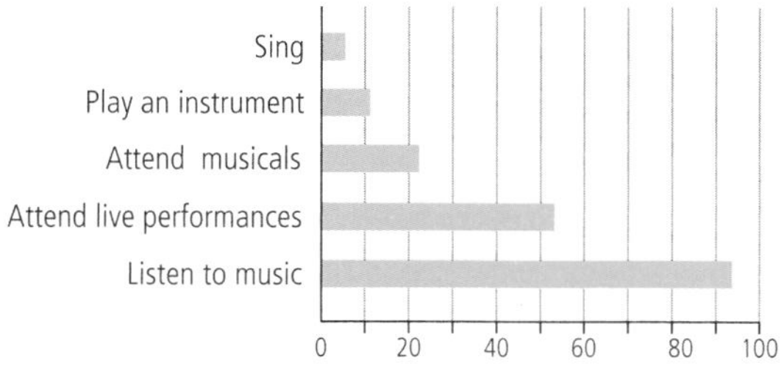

Reasons for non-participation

Reason	Non-participants %
difficult to find the time	54
not really interested	43
costs too much	41
not enough opportunities nearby	28

UNIT 8e, Exercise 4, page 101

- write to the university and ask them to speak to students about being considerate neighbors
- threaten to call the police if the students make noise after midnight
- have a friendly meeting with the students
- complain to town hall and ask them to put pressure on the university to find another solution

UNIT 5d, Exercise 5, page 64

Aston Homes for the Elderly

The bank gave the Aston Housing Association (AHA) a loan of $9 million in September 2009 to convert eight residential houses into groups of self-contained apartments for elderly people in the community who did not want to go into nursing homes.

Work started in December 2009, and so far five of the houses have already been converted, creating 40 self-contained apartments. The AHA has sold 30 of these, raising $4.5 million. It has also made repayments to the bank correctly and on time.

However, there have been complaints from local residents that AHA has sold some of the apartments to people who are not so elderly (one lady was in her late fifties), and that they have allowed people from outside the area to buy them. It seems that the price of the apartments is too high for many local people.

The AHA now intends to convert two more houses in the same area and is asking for an additional loan of $2.2 million.

UNIT 12d, Exercise 7, page 148

Student A

You want to buy this car. It is a seven-year-old VW Golf and the advertised price is $8,000. It is in good condition but has a lot of miles on it (100,000). Obviously you would like to get it for less, if you can. The problem is you have been looking for a long time and want to get a car quickly so that you can drive to work each day.

UNIT 3c, Exercise 11, page 38

Description 1

Portable Clay Cooler
Building on an ancient food-storage technique, the pot-in-pot system uses evaporation from a layer of wet sand between two pots to help keep produce fresh. Tomatoes can last weeks instead of days, meaning more income for farmers.

Developed by: Mohammed Bah Abba
Website: none available
Launch country: Nigeria

UNIT 9c, Exercise 10, page 110

* numbers in tens of thousands

UNIT 11c, Exercise 10, page 134

Quiz

Answer the questions then look at page 155 to see what type of learner you are. Do you agree?

1 WHEN I STUDY GRAMMAR, I LEARN BEST BY:
A reading clear rules. B writing down examples.
C putting it into practice in conversation.

2 IN CLASS, I PREFER:
A discussing. B looking at pictures, maps, diagrams, or videos.
C doing something practical.

3 I REMEMBER NEW VOCABULARY BEST WHEN IT IS ACCOMPANIED BY:
A a clear definition. B an image. C a demonstration.

4 IF I AM DISTRACTED IN CLASS, I USUALLY:
A hum or sing to myself. B doodle (draw) in my notebook.
C play with a pen or pencil.

5 WHEN LEARNING A NEW SKILL, I PREFER THAT:
A someone explain it to me. B someone demonstrate it.
C I just be allowed to get on with it myself.

6 WHEN I'M NOT SURE HOW TO SPELL A WORD, I:
A say the word aloud to myself. B try to visualize it in my mind.
C write down different versions.

7 I PREFER TO READ STORIES WITH LOTS OF:
A dialogue and conversation. B descriptive passages.
C action or adventure.

8 I PROBABLY LEARN THE MOST ENGLISH BY:
A listening to others. B watching movies.
C trying to use it.

UNIT 3c, Exercise 11, page 38

Description 2

Sugarcane Charcoal
Burning wood and dung, the main fuel sources for many in the developing world, has contributed to deforestation and breathing problems among inhabitants. These briquettes made from crushed sugarcane stalks not only make use of a local resource, they also burn more cleanly and allow residents to start a charcoal business for less than $50.

Developed by: MIT D-Lab
Website: http://d-lab.mit.edu/resources
Launch country: Haiti

UNIT 3c, Exercise 11, page 38

Description 3

Water Container
In poor rural areas, clean water is often miles away, leaving people vulnerable to diseases in unclean water. The strong Q Drum holds thirteen gallons in a rolling container that makes it easy to transport safe drinking water, a task that is usually done by women and children.

Developed by: P. J. and J. P. S. Hendrikse
Website: http://www.qdrum.co.za
Launch country: South Africa

UNIT 12d, Exercise 7, page 148

Student B

You want to sell this car. It is a seven-year-old VW Golf and the advertised price is $8,000. It is in good condition but has a lot of miles on it (100,000). You would like to get as close to the asking price as you can. However, it has been advertised for two months and you would like to sell it soon.

UNIT 11c, Exercise 10, page 134

Answers to quiz

Mostly As: you have an auditory learning style; you remember best when you hear things.

Mostly Bs: you have a visual learning style; you remember best when you see things.

Mostly Cs: you have a kinesthetic learning style; you remember best when you do things or when things are acted out.

UNIT 3c, Exercise 11, page 38

Description 4

Solar Wi-Fi Streetlight
The StarSight system consists of a series of pylons that use solar panels to power streetlamps, a Wi-Fi box for wireless Internet access, and if needed, closed-circuit TVs for security surveillance. The result is an integrated system of electricity and communication, plus better street lighting, which has been shown to help reduce crime.

Developed by: Kolam Partnership Ltd.
Website: http://www.starsightproject.com
Launch countries: Nigeria, South Africa, Turkey

UNIT 5b, Exercise 10, page 61

Questionnaire

1 HOW SATISFIED DO PEOPLE SEEM WITH THE AMOUNT OF MONEY THEY HAVE?

2 DO PEOPLE HAVE A GOOD BALANCE BETWEEN WORK AND FREE TIME?

3 HOW HAPPY ARE PEOPLE WITH THE EDUCATION THEY RECEIVE?

4 HOW CONFIDENT ARE PEOPLE IN YOUR COUNTRY'S HEALTH SYSTEM?

5 DO PEOPLE EAT HEALTHY FOOD?

6 HOW ENGAGED ARE PEOPLE POLITICALLY?

7 HOW OFTEN DO PEOPLE PARTICIPATE IN CULTURAL ACTIVITIES?

8 ARE PEOPLE TOLERANT OF OTHERS?

UNIT 8b, Exercise 8, page 97

1 false
2 true
3 half-true; it does increase life expectancy but no one can say how much
4 true
5 false; the zebrafish can heal its own heart, but not humans—yet!
6 true

UNIT 1

Present tenses review

Form

Simple present

Affirmative	Negative
I/you/we/they **live**	I/you/we/they **don't live** (don't = do not)
he/she/it **lives**	he/she/it **doesn't live** (doesn't = does not)

Interrogative	Short answer
do I/you/we/they **live**?	Yes, I/you/we/they **do**. No, I/you/we/they **don't**.
does he/she/it **live**?	Yes, he/she/it **does**. No, he/she/it **doesn't**.

Present continuous

Affirmative	Negative
I**'m living** ('m = am)	I**'m not** living ('m not = am not)
you**'re**/we**'re**/they**'re** **living** ('re = are)	you/we/they **aren't living** (aren't = are not)
he**'s**/she**'s**/it**'s** **living** ('s = is)	he/she/it **isn't living** (isn't = is not)

Interrogative	Short answer
am I **living**?	Yes, I **am**. No, I**'m not**.
are you/we/they **living**?	Yes, you/we/they **are**. No, you/we/they **aren't**.
is he/she/it **living**?	Yes, he/she/it **is**. No, he/she/it **isn't**.

Present perfect

Affirmative	Negative
I**'ve**/you**'ve**/we**'ve**/ they**'ve lived** ('ve = have)	I/you/we/they **haven't lived** (haven't = have not)
he**'s**/she**'s**/it**'s lived** ('s = has)	he/she/it **hasn't lived** (hasn't = has not)

Interrogative	Short answer
have I/you/we/they **lived**?	Yes, I/you/we/they **have**. No, I/you/we/they **haven't**.
has he/she/it **lived**?	Yes, he/she/it **has**. No, he/she/it **hasn't**.

Note the spelling rules for *-ed* endings:
*work → work**ed**; play → play**ed**; die → die**d**; lie → lie**d**;*
*try → tr**ied**; study → stud**ied**; stop → sto**pped***
Some verbs have irregular past participles, for example:
do → done; find → found; have → had; make → made

Present perfect continuous

Affirmative	Negative
I**'ve**/you**'ve**/we**'ve**/ they**'ve been living** ('ve = have)	I/you/we/they **haven't been living** (haven't = have not)
he**'s**/she**'s**/it**'s been living** ('s = has)	he/she/it **hasn't been living** (hasn't = has not)

Interrogative	Short answer
have I/you/we/they **been living**?	Yes, I/you/we/they **have**. No, I/you/we/they **haven't**.
has he/she/it **been living**?	Yes, he/she/it **has**. No, he/she/it **hasn't**.

Note the spelling rules for *-ing* endings:
work → working; play → playing; live → living;
have → having; stop → stopping; run → running;
die → dying; lie → lying

Use

Simple present

We use the simple present to talk about:

- facts or things which are generally true. *Orangutans **eat** fruit and leaves. The Earth **doesn't move** around the Moon. Where **do** polar bears **live**?*
- daily routines and habits. *I **work** in that factory every day. I always **take** a shower in the morning.*
- a permanent state or situation. *She **doesn't play** the piano. **Do** you **live** in Bahia?*

We often use adverbs of frequency (*always, usually, often, sometimes, rarely, never*) and expressions of frequency (*once a week, on Fridays, on the weekend, in the summer, every Saturday*) with the simple present to talk about how often we do something.
*We **always** play football on Saturday morning.*
*She **never** talks to strangers.*

Present continuous

We use the present continuous to talk about a situation in progress or things which are happening now or around now. With the present continuous, we often use these time expressions: *at the moment, (right) now, this week, this summer.*
*The boys **are playing** tennis in the park.*
*Paul **isn't living** in San Miguel this summer.*
***Are** you **doing** your report, Vikram?*

Present perfect

We use the present perfect to talk about a recent action or situation which started in the past. The situation may also continue into the present or have a result in the present.
*Michael can't come with us because he **hasn't renewed** his passport.*
***Have** you **visited** your grandparents lately?*

Present perfect continuous

We use the present perfect continuous to talk about an action or situation that was in progress in the recent past. The situation may also continue into the present or have a result in the present. We use the present perfect continuous, not the present perfect, to emphasize the duration of an action.

*I've **been working** here for months.* (And I still am.)
*They've **been behaving** like this since they arrived.*
*What **have you been doing** since I last saw you?*
*She **hasn't been working** hard enough lately!*

We often use the present perfect and present perfect continuous with *since* and *for* to talk about how long a situation has continued. We use *since* with the point of time when the activity started, for example *since Monday, since I was a boy*. We use *for* to talk about a period of time up to now, for example *for an hour, for a long time*.

*We've been friends **since** we were twelve years old.*
*We've been playing at the club **since** 2010.*
*I've lived in this house **for** six months.*

Practice

1 Choose the correct option.

Can you believe these other amazing and unlikely friendships between animals?

- A baby hippo [1] *has been living* with a giant tortoise since a devastating tsunami in 2004. They [2] ______ and [3] ______ together.
- One intrepid explorer says that his Eskimo dogs [4] ______ an extraordinary relationship with some polar bears. They [5] ______ together each year since 2008, when the dogs first traveled through the Arctic lands of Canada.
- Ellie, a dog, and Hattie, an elephant, [6] ______ the best of friends since they met in 2009.
- At a reserve in South Africa, a leopard cub and a dog often [7] ______ together, and at the moment, they [8] ______ in the same kennel.

People are amazed by these friendships. "It's true to say that there has been an evolution in the animal kingdom recently," says one animal expert.

1 a has been living b has lived c is living
2 a are eating b have eaten c eat
3 a are sleeping b have slept c sleep
4 a have been b have been getting c have got
5 a are playing b have played c have been playing
6 a become b are becoming c have become
7 a play b are playing c have played
8 a sleep b are sleeping c have slept

The passive voice

Form

We form the passive voice with the correct tense? of the verb *to be* + past participle.

Tense	Active	Passive
Simple present	makes/make	**is/are** made
Present continuous	is/are making	**is/are being** made
Present perfect	has/have made	**has/have been** made

Use

We use the passive voice when we want to focus on an action or the object of the action, rather than the person doing the action. The object of the active sentence becomes the subject of the passive one.

Active: Parents (subject) are questioning the new values (object).

Passive: The new values (subject) are being questioned by parents (object).

In a passive sentence, we can say who did the action (the agent) using *by*. We use *by* + agent when it is important to know who did the action. It isn't always necessary to use *by* + agent. We don't usually use the agent when it is obvious who has done the action, when we don't know, or when it isn't important.

*The best products are selected **by the product manager**.*
Guests are asked ~~by the hotel~~ to sign the visitors' book.

We also use the passive when we don't want to identify the agent.

I'm sorry, but the window has been broken ~~by my son~~.

Practice

2 Rewrite the sentences in the passive voice. Use *by* + agent where appropriate.

1 They are changing people's lives every day.
People's lives are being changed every day.
2 We make new plans all the time.
______
3 The government is making some new laws.
______
4 They have changed the whole system since I was a student.
______
5 Young people are forgetting the old way of life.
______
6 We haven't seen good manners for a long time.
______
7 We are still respecting a lot of the old customs.
______
8 Are they respecting the way that people used to live?
______

UNIT 2

Simple past and present perfect

Form

Simple past

We add *-ed* to regular verbs to form the simple past.

Affirmative	Negative
I/you/he/she/it/we/they **worked**	I/you/he/she/it/we/they **didn't work** (didn't = did not)

Interrogative	Short answer
did I/you/he/she/it/we/they **work**?	Yes, I/you/he/she/it/we/they **did**. No, I/you/he/she/it/we/they **didn't**.

Note the spelling rules for other regular verbs:

- for verbs ending in *-e*, we add *-d*: *realize* → ***realized***
- for verbs ending in *-y*, we change the *-y* to *i* and add *-ed*: *carry* → *carr**ied***
- for verbs ending in vowel + consonant (not *-w*, *-x*, or *-y*), we double the consonant: *plan* → *pla**nned***

Some verbs have an irregular affirmative form in the simple past:
be → *was/were; do* → *did; go* → *went; see* → *saw; write* → *wrote*

Present perfect

We form the present perfect with the simple present of the verb *to have* + past participle.

See page 156: Present perfect

Use

Simple past

We use the simple past to talk about finished actions in the past when there is a clear link to a specific time in the past. We often use a time phrase (*yesterday, last week, five years ago*) with the simple past.
*He **finished** the movie script two hours ago.*
*They **didn't go** to the movies last night.*
***Did** you **meet** Alex earlier?*

We use the simple past to talk about someone's life when they are dead.
*He **fought** as a soldier in the Civil War.*

Present perfect

We use the present perfect to talk about a recent action or situation which started at some time in the past. The situation may also continue into the present or have a result in the present. We use the present perfect when the experience is more important than the time, and the time is not stated.
I've seen a lot of different movies in the last five years.
He hasn't seen the new Lord of the Rings *movie yet.*

We also use the present perfect to talk about life experiences (when the people are still living).
I've never been to Peru. Have you ever gone?

When we talk about a period of time that is not finished, we use the present perfect, even if the action itself is finished.
Have you talked to him today? (It is still today.)

When the period of time is finished, we use the simple past.
Did you talk to him earlier? (It is now later.)

Practice

1 Choose the correct option.

1 I *(saw)* / *have seen* a very interesting movie yesterday.
2 *Did you ever read / Have you ever read* poetry?
3 I *didn't like / haven't liked* the end of the movie.
4 They *enjoyed / have enjoyed* watching the play last night.
5 Elena *didn't study / hasn't studied* literature for a long time.
6 The students *wrote / have written* some very original short stories in last year's class.
7 Lately his parents *told / have told* him a lot of funny anecdotes from when he was a child.
8 When *did you find out / have you found out* about the stories of Borges?

Past tenses review

Form

See page 158: Simple past

Past continuous

Interrogative	Short answer
was I/he/she/it **working** there?	Yes, I/he/she/it **was**. No, I/he/she/it **wasn't**.
were you/we/they **working** there?	Yes, you/we/they **were**. No, you/we/they **weren't**.

Past perfect

Affirmative	Negative
I'**d**/you'**d**/he'**d**/she'**d**/ it'**d**/we'**d**/they'**d worked** ('d = had)	I/you/he/she/it/we/they **hadn't worked** (hadn't = had not)

Interrogative	Short answer
had I/you/he/she/it/we/ they **worked**?	Yes, I/you/he/she/it/we/they **had**. No, I/you/he/she/it/we/they **hadn't**.

Past perfect continuous

Affirmative	Negative
I'**d**/you'**d**/he'**d**/she'**d**/ it'**d**/we'**d**/they'**d been working** ('d = had)	I/you/he/she/it/we/they **hadn't been working** (hadn't = had not)

Interrogative	Short answer
had I/you/he/she/it/we/they **been working**?	Yes, I/you/he/she/it/they **had been working.** No, I/you/he/she/it/they **hadn't been working.** (hadn't = had not)

Use

Simple past

We use the simple past to talk about the sequence of the main events of a story.
*Giles **got up** at six o'clock and **left** the location early.*

Past continuous

We use the past continuous to describe a background event which was in progress around the time of the main event. We often use the past continuous with the simple past.
*The sun **was coming up** as Paul arrived at the park.*

Past perfect

We use the past perfect to talk about what happened earlier, before the main event.
*When Julieta saw the animals, she remembered what the trainer **had said** the day before.*

Past perfect continuous

We use the past perfect continuous to describe an action that was in progress before or up to the main event in the past.
*When Salma arrived, the other actors **had** already **been rehearsing** for two hours.*

We don't usually use stative verbs in either the past continuous or the past perfect continuous.
*I **knew** the route well.* (Not *I ~~was knowing~~ the route well.*)
*I **had known** him for ten years.* (Not *I ~~had been knowing~~ him for ten years.*)

Practice

2 Complete the text with the correct past tense form of the verbs.

Elena [1] .... (walk) in the park near her home. It [2] .... (be) a beautiful evening. The sun [3] .... (shine) all day and now it [4] .... (set) behind some tall trees by the river. Suddenly she [5] .... (hear) a scream. She thought that it [6] .... (come) from the direction of the river so she [7] .... (run) there as fast as she could. When she [8] .... (reach) the river, she [9] .... (see) a young boy in the water. He [10] .... (slip) on the muddy bank and [11] .... (fall) head first into the water. Now he [12] .... (struggle) and unable to swim. Elena quickly [13] .... (take) off her shoes and [14] .... (jump) in. She [15] .... (catch) the boy by the arm and [16] .... (drag) him out.

UNIT 3

Future forms review

Form

will

Affirmative	Negative
I/you/he/she/it/we/they**'ll** go ('ll = will)	I/you/he/she/it/we/they **won't** go (won't = will not)

Interrogative	Short answer
will I/you/he/she/it/we/they go?	Yes, I/you/he/she/it/we/they **will.** No, I/you/he/she/it/we/they **won't.**

going to

Affirmative	Negative
I'm going to visit	**I'm not going to** visit
you**'re**/we**'re**/they**'re going to** visit	you/we/they **aren't going to** visit
he**'s**/she**'s** /it**'s going to** visit	he/she/it **isn't going to** visit

Interrogative	Short answer
am I **going to** visit?	Yes, I **am.**/No, **I'm not.**
are you/we/they **going to** visit?	Yes, you/we/they **are.** No, you/we/they **aren't.**
is he/she/it **going to** visit?	Yes, he/she/it **is.** No, he/she/it **isn't.**

about to

Affirmative	Negative
I'm about to start	**I'm not about to start**
you**'re**/we**'re**/they**'re about to** start	you/we/they **aren't about to** start
he**'s**/she**'s**/it**'s about to** start	he/she/it **isn't about to** start

Interrogative	Short answer
am I **about to** start?	Yes, I **am.**/No, **I'm not.**
are you/we/they **about to** start?	Yes, you/we/they **are.** No, you/we/they **aren't.**
is he/she/it **about to** start?	Yes, he/she/it **is.** No, he/she/it **isn't.**

See page 156: Simple present, Present continuous

Use

will

We use *will* to talk about:

- a prediction. *I expect he'**ll** be here in a minute.*
- a decision we have made at the time of speaking. *"I can't start my car." "Don't worry. I'**ll give** you a ride."*
- a future event in an *if* or *when* clause. ***If** the population increases, there **won't be** enough food.*

going to

We use *be* + *going to* + base form

- to talk about a plan or intention for the future. This has been decided before the moment of speaking. *When I'm in Chile, I'm **going to travel** to Arica.*
- to make a prediction about the future based on present information. *My team is playing very badly. They're **going to lose** this game.*

about to

We use *be* + *about to* to talk about an event in the immediate future.
*I can't talk to you now—I'm **about to go** into a meeting.*

We often use *just* in front of *about to.*
*Tell me the details later—I'm **just about to go** into town.*

Present continuous

We use the present continuous to talk about:

- an intention or previously made decision or arrangement. *They **aren't coming** to the theater.*
- a formal arrangement. *They're **coming** at noon.*

We often use the present continuous with a specific (or understood) time in the future.
*I'm traveling to New York **on Thursday evening**.*

Simple present

We use the simple present to talk about:

- a scheduled event. *The concert **starts** at eight o'clock. What time **does** the train **leave**?*
- a simple statement of fact. *Water **boils** at 212°F.*

Practice

1 Complete the conversation with the correct future tense of the verbs.

A: The first talk 1 .... (start) at five.
B: 2 .... you .... (go) to it?
A: No, I think I 3 .... (pass). It's not really a subject that interests me.
B: Really? I think it 4 .... (be) really interesting.
A: Well, I 5 .... (meet) a colleague in half an hour anyway to discuss the presentation we 6 .... (give) later.
B: Oh. When does that 7 .... (start)?
A: It 8 .... (be) at 2:00 p.m.
B: Oh good. I 9 .... (try) to come to that.
A: Great! Anyway, you'd better go. Your talk 10 .... (be) to start.

Future continuous and future perfect

Form

Future continuous

We form the future continuous with *will be* + *-ing*.

Affirmative	Negative
I/you/he/she/it/we/they **will be doing**	I/you/he/she/it/we/they **won't be doing**

Interrogative	Short answer
will I/you/he/she/it/we/they **be doing**?	Yes, I/you/he/she/it/we/they **will**. No, I/you/he/she/it/we/they **won't**.

Future perfect

We form the future perfect with *will have* + past participle.

Affirmative	Negative
I/you/he/she/it/we/they **will have done**	I/you/he/she/it/we/they **won't have done**

Interrogative	Short answer
will I/you/he/she/it/we/they **have done**?	Yes, I/you/he/she/it/we/they **will**. No, I/you/he/she/it/we/they **won't**.

Use

Future continuous

We use the future continuous to talk about an action which you know or think will be in progress at or during a certain period of time in the future.
*In five years' time, everyone **will be using** HD phones.*
*This time tomorrow I **won't be sitting** in this office.*
*What **will** scientists **be researching** ten years from now?*

Future perfect

We use the future perfect to talk about an action which is going to be completed at or before a certain point of time in the future.
*In 50 years' time, people **will have stopped** using cash.*
*He **won't have finished** the work by the weekend.*
***Will** you **have sent** that email by five o'clock?*

Practice

2 Choose the correct option.

1 Next year people *will be using* / *will have used* wind power for their electricity.
2 By next January the company *will be designing* / *will have designed* a smaller computer chip.
3 Scientists *will be making* / *will have made* some important breakthroughs by 2020.
4 It is predicted that *we will be living* / *will have lived* on Mars in the next 50 years.
5 I expect that I *will be working* / *will have worked* in a laboratory next month.
6 I'm sure he *will be studying* / *will have studied* biology all his life.

UNIT 4

Expressions of quantity

Form

(not) many, (a) few, a (small/large) number of, several **+ plural count noun**

There were ***not many people*** *at the concert.*
Eda has only been to ***a few*** *classical* ***concerts****.*

(not) much, (a) little (of) a (large/small) amount of **+ noncount noun**

There isn't ***much live music*** *at the festival.*

a lot of, lots of, plenty of, loads of, (a) lack of, (almost) no, (not/hardly) any, some, enough **+ plural count or noncount noun**

You can buy ***plenty of food and drink*** *at the show.*
There were ***hardly any cars*** *in town today.*

Use

We use quantifiers with count or noncount nouns to talk about quantity (how much or how many of something).

Large quantities

To express large quantities, we use:

- *a large number of, a huge number of* with plural count nouns
- *a large amount of, a huge amount of* with noncount nouns
- *some, a lot of, lots of, loads of, plenty of* with plural count or noncount nouns

An enormous number of *people are involved.*
Some *visitors return three or four times a year.*
There were ***a lot of/loads of*** *great bands at the festival.*
Note that *loads of* is less formal than *a lot of/lots of*.

Small quantities

To express small quantities, we use:

- *(not) many, (a) few, a (small) number of, several* with plural count nouns.
- *(not) much, (a) little (of), a small amount of* with noncount nouns.
- *some, a lack of, (almost) no, (not/hardly) any* with plural count or noncount nouns.

In most towns, there are ***a few*** *interesting places to visit.*
Hardly any *artists become rich in their lifetime.*

We use *little/a little* and *few/a few* to talk about small quantities in affirmative statements. *A little* and *a few* have a positive meaning (= some, but not many). *Little* and *few* have a negative meaning (= only a small number of).
A few *people watched his latest play.* (= at least some, if not many)
Few *people watched his latest play.* (= almost none)
They arrived very late so they only saw ***a little*** *of the show.* (= some, but not much)
He ate ***little*** *of his dinner in the restaurant because he didn't like seafood.* (= almost none)

We don't usually use *much* in affirmative statements. We normally use *a lot of/lots of*.
They don't have much knowledge of the local area.
We have a lot of brochures about the area.

Several usually means three or more things or people.
There were ***several*** *people in the audience.*

enough

We use *enough* to say we have the correct or sufficient quantity. We use *not enough* to say we have less than we want or need.
There are ***enough*** *members of the orchestra now.*
There ***aren't enough*** *artists signed up for the festival yet.*

We can use *a large amount, enough, plenty, several, not much, not many* without nouns when the meaning is clear.
Do you have many theaters in your town? Yes, we have ***several****. / No, there are****n't many****.*

Practice

1 Choose the correct option.

1 There aren't *much / many / a little* movies playing this week.
2 There is *a few / several / lots of* gas in the car.
3 Is there *many / much / a few* interest in art?
4 *Few / Not much / A little* people were there.
5 *Much / Many / Some* art books are on the shelf.
6 There is only *a little / lots of / plenty of* talent among these new actors.
7 The exhibition had *a little / not much / almost no* good paintings.
8 Are there *a bit of / enough / not much* bands playing at the festival?

Determiners

Form

each, every, either, the whole **+ singular noun**

Each visitor *to the gallery receives a plan of the exhibition.*
Every exhibit *in the museum is catalogued.*
People can buy ***either*** *a one-day or a season ticket.*

all, both **+ plural noun**

All *the shortlisted artists gained a lot of publicity.*
Both *artists exhibited three pictures.*

any, no **+ singular or plural noun**

Have you seen ***any*** *good movies this month?*
They received ***no*** *complaints.*

all, any, no + noncount noun
All *literature has value.*
Can we use ***any*** *material we like?*
No *culture is superior to another.*

Use

every, each, all

We use *every, each,* and *all* to talk generally about people or things.
Every *musician played well.*
Each *artist had some interesting work on display.*
All *the paintings were very good.*
We use *each* and *every* to refer to the individuals or individual parts of a group. We use *all* to refer to the whole group.

We use *every* (+ singular noun) and *all, all the, all of the* (+ plural noun/noncount noun) when the plural noun refers to **three** or more people or things.
Every *person had the opportunity to be an artist for a day.* (There were three or more people.)
All of the *participants wrote a poem about nature.* (There were three or more participants.)
We use *each* (+ singular noun) to talk about **two** or more people or things.
Each *member of the group made some form of contribution.* (There were two or more people.)

both, either

We use *both* and *either* to talk about **two** things or people. We use *both/both of the* (+ plural noun) to say the same thing about two people or things. We use *either* (+ singular noun) to say there are two possible options.
Both (of the) *sculptors made three works of art.*
They could choose to use ***either*** *stone or clay.*

We use *neither* to express the opposite of *both.*
Neither *contestant made it to the final.*

(not) any, no

We use *(not) any* or *no* to talk about a negative idea.
They ***didn't*** *allow* ***any*** *graffiti on the walls at all.*
There are ***no*** *original ideas left in art.*

We can use *(not) any* without a noun when the meaning is clear.
Did you get the tickets? No, there ***aren't any left****.*

Practice

2 Complete the sentences with a suitable determiner. More than one answer is possible.

1 There were ten pianists in the competition, and they were <u>*all*</u> very good.
2 .... member of the band is talented.
3 Gilberto and Jorge work as a pair, but .... men are artists in their own right.
4 They were both good players, so .... of them could have won.
5 .... performer was better than the others.
6 .... student was asked to bring a sketch.

UNIT 5

Verb + infinitive or *-ing*

Form

Verb + infinitive	
verb + infinitive	*They* ***wanted to create*** *a luxury resort.*
verb + *someone* + infinitive	*He* ***asked his father to lend*** *him the money for the deposit.*
verb + *someone* + base form	*She* ***helped her friend establish*** *a new theme park.*

Verb + *-ing*	
verb + *-ing*	*I* ***enjoy going*** *to shopping malls.*

Use

verb + infinitive

After certain verbs we use infinitive. This is often to talk about hopes, intentions and decisions.
He offered ***to draw*** *the plans for the redevelopment.*
They didn't want ***to work*** *on the project any more.*
Common verbs which are followed by infinitive include: *agree, appear, arrange, choose, decide, expect, hope, intend, manage, need, offer, plan, prepare, pretend, promise, refuse, seem, want, wish, would like.*

verb + *someone* + infinitive

Some verbs are followed by an object and infinitive.
He reminded ***his employees to arrive*** *early.*
They'd like ***the contractors to submit*** *their proposal.*
Common verbs which are followed by *someone* + infinitive include: *allow, ask, expect, force, help, invite, like, need, remind, teach, tell, want, would like.*

verb + *someone* + base form

Some verbs are followed by an object and the base form.
She ***helped her daughter expand*** *her business.*
Common verbs which use this form are: *feel, hear, help, notice, see, watch.*

verb + *-ing*

We use verb + *-ing* after certain verbs.
The architect ***suggested adding*** *some green space.*
Common verbs which are followed by *-ing* are: *avoid, can't help, like, love, enjoy, prefer don't like, hate, can't stand, (not) mind, keep, miss, practice, risk, suggest.*

Practice

1 Choose the correct option.

1 I always enjoy (*going*) / *to go* to work.
2 Dubai *growing* / *grows* richer every day.
3 Ana asked them *sending* / *to send* help.
4 We decided *to invest* / *investing* in property.
5 The ministers suggested *to start* / *starting* an investment bank.
6 The government refused *giving* / *to give* them planning permission.

Verb + *-ing* or infinitive

Form

verb + *-ing* and verb + infinitive (two different meanings)

He ***remembered listening*** *to the program.*
They ***remembered to record*** *the program.*

verb + *-ing* and verb + infinitive (no change in meaning)

He ***continued traveling*** *around Asia.*
He ***continued to travel*** *around Asia.*

Use

Some verbs can be followed by either *-ing* or infinitive but the meaning changes.
Jan ***stopped talking*** *to journalists.* = action has ended (Jan used to talk to journalists but then he stopped.)
Jan ***stopped to talk*** *to a local resident.* = the reason for stopping (Jan stopped so that he could talk to a local resident.)
Common verbs which can be followed by *-ing* or infinitive with a change in meaning are: *forget, go on, mean, regret, remember, stop, try.*

Some verbs can be followed by either *-ing* or infinitive with very little or no change in meaning.
Lizze ***likes reading*** *business economics books.*
Lizzie ***likes to read*** *business economics books.*
Common verbs which can be followed by *-ing* or infinitive with little or no change in meaning are: *begin, continue, hate, love, prefer, start.*

Practice

2 Complete the sentences with the correct form of these verbs.

ask bring borrow ~~buy~~ change inform

1 I forgot *to buy* some milk.
2 I don't remember .... any money from Mike but he says I did.
3 We regret .... you that your bank account has been closed.
4 I meant .... them if the water was safe to drink or not.
5 Did you remember .... the plans with you?
6 If we want the company to be profitable, it means .... our prices.

UNIT 6

not

Form

Negative infinitive

We form the negative infinitive by putting *not* in front of the infinitive. Note that *not* goes before *to*.
We decided ***not to go*** *abroad on vacation this year.*

want, would like

To make a sentence negative with *want* or *would like*, we make the main verb negative.
She ***didn't want*** *to visit India.*
They ***wouldn't like*** *to work there.*

must not **and *don't have to***

The negative form of *must* is *must not* and the negative form of *have* to is *don't/doesn't have* to. (Note that in British English, the contracted form *mustn't* is commonly used in place of *must not*.)
You ***must not*** *travel without your passport.*
You ***don't have to*** *go.*

hope **and *think***

The negative forms of *hope* and *think* are different. When we form a negative sentence with *hope*, we make the verb that follows negative. When we form a negative sentence with *think*, we use *don't/doesn't think*.
I ***hope he isn't*** *late.*
He ***doesn't think*** *she should travel alone.*

let's

To form the negative of *let's*, we use *let's not*.
Let's not *go on vacation this year.*

Use

Negative infinitive

We often use the negative infinitive to give advice or orders about what **not** to do.
It would be better for you ***not to meet*** *him tomorrow.*

want, would like

We use *don't/doesn't want* and *wouldn't like* to talk about a wish not to do something in the future.
I ***don't want*** *to go.* (Not *I ~~want not~~ to go.*)
I ***wouldn't like*** *to read that book again.*

must not and *don't have to*

We use ***must not*** to say that it is important not to do something.
*You **must not** forget to apply for your visa.* (= It's important that you not forget.)

We use *don't/doesn't have to* to show that something is not important or essential.
*He **doesn't have to** get a new passport before he goes.*

hope and *think*

*I **hope** my vacation **won't be** a disappointment.* (not *I ~~don't hope~~…*)
*I **don't think** her hotel **will be** cheap.* (not *I think her hotel ~~won't be~~ cheap.*)

let's

We use *let's not* + base form when we want to make a negative suggestion: ***Let's not** go out.*

Practice

1 Complete the sentences using *not* and the correct form of the verb. Use contractions where possible.

1 He told me ......*not to spend*...... (spend) too much.
2 Bo .... (want) to go to the museum.
3 Let's .... (tell) Ping about it—it will upset him.
4 Orel asked me .... (book) the flights.
5 We .... (think) the airplane will take off on time.
6 We decided .... (stop) off in Managua on the way.

Negative and tag questions

Form

Open questions (no confirmation of opinion demanded)

We form open questions using an auxiliary verb (like *do, have*) and inverting the subject and verb.
***Do you enjoy** traveling by train?*
***Has he played** tennis before?*

Negative questions

We form negative questions using the negative form of the verb. We usually use the contracted form.
***Don't you enjoy** traveling by train?*
***Hasn't he played** tennis before?*

Tag questions

To form tag questions, we use the auxiliary of the verb in the main sentence. When the main verb in the sentence is affirmative, the tag question is negative:
***They were** at the party, **weren't they**?*
When the main verb in the sentence is negative, the tag question is affirmative:
***He didn't** stay late, **did he**?*

When you write tag questions, put a comma between the main sentence and the tag.

Note that when the subject is a pronoun, we repeat it in the tag question. When the subject is a noun, we use an appropriate pronoun in the tag question.
***It**'s very interesting, isn't **it**?*
***Mike** travels to South Africa every year, doesn't **he**?*

Tense	Positive-negative	Negative-positive
to be (*am, is, are, was, were*)	***It's** a long way, **isn't it**?* ***I was** bad, **wasn't I**?*	***It isn't** a long way, **is it**?* ***I wasn't** bad, **was I**?*
Simple present (*do/does*)	***She works** there, **doesn't she**?*	***She doesn't work** there, **does she**?*
Present continuous (*am, is, are*)	***They're arriving** soon, **aren't they**?*	***They aren't arriving** soon, **are they**?*
Simple past (*did*)	***She went** there, **didn't she**?*	***She didn't go** there, **did she**?*
Past continuous (*was, were*)	***They were eating, weren't they**?*	***They weren't eating, were they**?*
Present perfect and present perfect continuous (*has, have*)	***You've been here** before, **haven't you**?* ***They've been studying** late, **haven't they**?*	***You haven't been** here before, **have you**?* ***They haven't been studying** late, **have they**?*
Past perfect (*had*)	***They'd gone, hadn't they**?*	***They hadn't gone, had they**?*
will	***You'll do** it, **won't you**?*	***You won't do** it, **will you**?*
Modals (*must, should, can, would*)	***I can** go, **can't I**?* ***He should** know, **shouldn't he**?*	***I can't** go, **can I**?* ***He shouldn't** know, **should he**?*

Use

Open questions

We use open questions when we don't know what the answer will be or when we don't expect a particular answer.
Are you going on vacation this year? (Possible answers: *Yes, I am. No, I'm not. Well, maybe. I don't think so.*)
Did he tell you where he was going? (Possible answers: *Yes, he did. No, he didn't. I can't remember.*)

Negative questions

We use negative questions to check information that is probably true. We answer with *yes* or *no*.
***Don't** you always visit your parents on Sunday? Yes, I do.*
***Wouldn't** you prefer to stay in a hotel? No, I wouldn't.*

We also use negative questions.

- to show surprise. *Don't you enjoy eating out?*
- to make a suggestion. *Don't you need to go now?*
- to request something, especially when we expect a negative answer. *Can't I have a different room?*

Tag questions

We use tag questions to ask for information, or to check and confirm information.
*We're meeting at two o'clock, **aren't we**?*

Practice

2 Complete the negative and tag questions.

1 ___Don't___ you want to stay here? It's nice.
2 India is a very diverse country, ___isn't it___ ?
3 Ana didn't go out, ________ ?
4 ________ you booked the flights yet? I thought I asked you to last week.
5 The group won't be taking a train to Cuzco, ________ ?
6 They wouldn't be much use, ________ ?
7 ________ he pay for his hotel before he arrived?
8 ________ she like to go somewhere else for a change?

UNIT 7

Mixed conditional sentences

Form

	If-clause	Main clause
First conditional	*If* + simple present	*will* + base form
	***If** it **rains**, the drought **will end**.*	
Second conditional	*If* + simple past	*would/could/might* + base form
	***If** we **recycled**, we **could reduce** our trash.*	
Third conditional	*If* + past perfect	*would/could/might have* + past participle
	***If** they **had saved** more water, there **wouldn't have been** a drought.*	
Mixed second and third conditional	*If* + simple past	*would have* + past participle
	***If** the policy **worked**, the government **wouldn't have needed** extra food.*	
Mixed third and second conditionals	*If* + past perfect	*would/could/might* + base form
	***If** the water **hadn't been stored**, there **wouldn't be** a harvest this year.*	

Remember, we can use *if* in two positions:

- *If*-clause first: *If we use less water, we should be able to provide enough for the whole population.*
- Main clause first: *We should be able to provide enough water for the whole population if we use less water.*

When the *if*-clause is at the beginning of the sentence, we use a comma to separate it from the main clause.

Use

First conditional

We use the first conditional to talk about a possible future action or situation. We can also use it to talk about things that are generally true.
*If they **pollute** the water, we **won't be able** to drink it.* (It's possible that they will pollute the water in the future. Then we won't be able to drink the water.)

Second conditional

We use the second conditional to talk about hypothetical situations in the present or future.
*If they **changed** their environmental views, perhaps they **would get** the contract.* (This is a possible situation in the future.)
Note that when we use the simple past with *if*, it refers to the present or future. It <u>does not</u> refer to the past.
We can also use *could* and *might* instead of *would* in the main clause.
*If they **changed** their environmental views, they **might/could get** the contract.*
*Fossil fuels **might not** run out if people conserved more.*

Third conditional

We use the third conditional to talk about imagined past situations or events that did not happen and their hypothetical consequences.
*If they **had built** the dam, those villages **wouldn't have flooded**.* (But they didn't build the dam and the villages were flooded.)

We can use *could/might (not) have* to speculate on a possible consequence of the imagined past situation.
*If they had built the dam, those villages **might not** have flooded.* (They did not build the dam; it's possible that the villages wouldn't have been flooded but we are not certain.)

Mixed conditionals

We use mixed conditionals to talk about unreal situations when the *if* clause and the main clause don't refer to the same time.

We use mixed second and third conditionals to talk about an imagined situation in the present or future with the hypothetical past result or consequence.
*If the pro-forest organization **didn't exist**, more of the Amazon forests **would have disappeared**.* (But the organization does exist, and so more of the Amazon forests didn't disappear.)

We use mixed third and second conditionals to talk about an imagined situation or action in the past, with the imagined consequence in the present or future.
*If the activists **hadn't intervened**, the Amazon **would be** much smaller now.* (But the activists did intervene, so the Amazon is bigger than it would have been without their help.)

Practice

1 Complete the sentences. Use mixed conditionals.

1 Rafa didn't say anything at the summit meeting because he didn't know anything.
If Rafa *had known* (know) anything, he *would have said* (say) something.
2 They didn't dam the river because people protested about it.
If people ______ (not protest) about it, the river ______ (be) dammed today.
3 The job required environmental knowledge. Katrin doesn't know about the environment, so she didn't apply.
Katrin ______ (apply) for the job if she ______ (know) about the environment.
4 They need people with experience in conservation, but I don't have any.
If I ______ (have), I ______ (join).
5 I worked hard on the mining project, so I felt I needed a rest that weekend.
If I ______ (not work) so hard on the project, I ______ (be) tired that weekend.
6 You were writing reports last week. You're feeling very tired today.
If you ______ (not write) so many reports, you ______ (not feel) so tired today.

wish, would rather, and *if only*

Form

wish / if only **+ noun/pronoun + simple past**
*I **wish** / **If only I knew** more about the plan.*

wish / if only **+ noun/pronoun + past perfect**
*I **wish** / **If only he hadn't signed** the contract.*

wish / if only **+ noun/pronoun +** ***would*** **+ base form**
*I **wish** / **If only they would approve** the plan.*

would rather **+ base form**
*They **would rather save** the rain forest than mine for oil.*

would rather **+ object + simple past**
*The company **would rather you proposed** a more energy efficient solution.*

Note that when we use the verb *to be*, we use *was* in everyday speech; we use *were* in formal speech and writing, for example:
- Informal spoken: *I wish I was on vacation.*
- Formal spoken/written: *I wish I were on vacation.*

Use

We use *wish* and *if only* to talk about regrets and to describe an imaginary situation which is the opposite of the real situation.
- To express a wish about a present situation, we use *wish / if only* + simple past.
I wish I knew the answer. (But I don't.)
- To express a wish about a past situation, we use *wish / if only* + past perfect.
I wish I'd bought a smaller car. (But I didn't.)
- To express a wish for someone to do something differently in the present or future, we use *wish / if only* + noun/pronoun + *would* + base form.
I wish you would be more environmentally friendly. (You won't be more environmentally friendly, but I want you to be.)
Notice that you can't use the same subject in both clauses with *would*. You can't say: *I wish I would be more environmentally friendly.*

We use *would rather* + base form to talk about preferences.
*I **would rather use** my car less.*

When we use *would rather*, we can also include *than* + an alternative.
*I'd rather use my car less **than** spend more on gas.*

We use *would rather* + object + simple past to state what we would prefer someone else to do.
***I'd rather you used** energy-saving lightbulbs.*

Practice

2 Complete the sentence using the correct conditional form of the verbs.

1 If only there *were* (be) a way to stop people from using fossil fuels, but there isn't.
2 I wish they ______ (stop) using pesticides on crops, but they won't.
3 If only the river ______ (not flood) their village, things would be OK now.
4 I wish they ______ (understand) how to protect their environment, but they don't.
5 If only people ______ (consider) the consequences before cutting down the forest, but they didn't.
6 I wish there ______ (not be) a nuclear power station here, but there is.
7 I wish they ______ (leave) the downtown area alone, but they didn't.

UNIT 8

Reporting verbs

Form

Reporting verbs use different patterns.

verb + base form
*She **promised to investigate** the story.*
Reporting verbs with this pattern include: *agree, offer, promise, refuse, threaten.*

verb + someone + base form
*He **asked the photographer to send** the files.*
Reporting verbs with this pattern include: *advise, ask, convince, encourage, invite, persuade, remind, tell, urge, warn.*

verb + *-ing*
*He **admitted faking** the document.*
Reporting verbs with this pattern include: *advise, admit, deny, mention, propose, recommend, suggest.*

verb + preposition + *-ing*
*He **complained about working** long hours.*
Reporting verbs with this pattern include: *apologize (for), complain (about), insist (on), object (to).*

verb + someone + preposition + *-ing*
*The editor **blamed him for not checking** his facts.*
Reporting verbs with this pattern include: *accuse* (+ *of*), *blame* (+ *for*), *compliment* (+ *on*), *congratulate* (+ *on*), *criticize* (+ *for*), *forgive* (+ *for*), *thank* (+ *for*), *warn* (+ *about*).

Other common verb patterns are:
verb + someone + *that*
*He **warned us that** the journey would be difficult.*
Reporting verbs with this pattern include: *advise, persuade, tell, warn.*

verb + *that*
*We **agreed that** she was the best candidate.*
Reporting verbs with this pattern include: *admit, agree, explain, deny, know, realize, say, think, warn.*

Use

Say, tell, think, and *ask* are the most common reporting verbs, but we often use others to report what people said. When we decide what reporting verb to use, we think about the function or the purpose of the speaker's words.
"Remember to download your photos." = **remind** (*He reminded me to download my photos.*)
"I'll sign up later." = **promise** (*She promised to sign up later.*)

Practice

1 Report the statements using these verbs. You may need to use a preposition after the verb.

admit apologize complain invite offer tell thank ~~urge~~

1 I really think you should go to the meeting.
Ki *urged me to go to the meeting.*
2 It was me that informed the press.
Rebecca ....
3 I'm really grateful that you read my article.
Fatima ....
4 I really dislike having to write business reports.
Leo ....
5 I'm sorry, but I made a mistake.
Clara ....
6 Please come to my house tomorrow.
Ji-hu ....
7 I'll give you a ride to the press conference.
Jaime ....
8 Don't send that email.
Aisha ....

Passive reporting verbs

Form

Passive reporting verbs are formed with *It* + *be* + past participle of reporting verb + *that* + clause.

When we report ideas in the present, we use the verb *be* in the simple present.
*It **is** believed that…*

For a present report of a present event, we use the simple present in the *that*-clause.
*It is said that people **are** less happy nowadays.*

For a present report of a past event, we use the simple past in the *that*-clause.
*It is believed that they **lived** unknown to the outside world for over 200 years.*

For a present report of a future event, we use *will* + base form in the *that*-clause.
*It is understood that reporters **will leave** them alone.*

When we report ideas in the past, we use the verb *be* in the simple past.
*It **was** believed that…*
*It **was** reported that…*

For a report and event at the same time in the past, we use the simple past in the *that*-clause.
*It was claimed that the break-in **happened** that morning.*

For a report in the past of an event that happened before the report, we use the past perfect in the *that*-clause.
It was believed that the break-in ***had happened*** *earlier.*

For a past report of a future event, we use *would* + base form in the *that*-clause.
It was understood that the survivors ***would go*** *straight to the hospital when they returned.*

Use

We use passive reporting structures to talk about events when the speaker is unknown or unimportant, or when someone wishes to remain anonymous. We can report ideas in the present or in the past.
It ***is*** *said that people consume on average 50 times more sugar than they did ten years ago.*
It ***is*** *believed that tickets will be available soon.*
It ***was*** *reported that there had been violence.*
It ***was*** *thought that there wouldn't be enough money.*

For passive reporting, we use verbs such as *believed, claimed, considered, estimated, expected, known, reported, said, suggested , thought,* and *understood.*

Practice

2 Write sentences using the prompts.

1 Present report about a present event: report / story / not be / true
It is reported that the story is not true.

2 Present report about a past event: understand / those people / live / there / for twenty years
....

3 Present report about a future event: suggest / people / travel / to Mars / next year
....

4 Past report about a past event: think / women / be / less intelligent
....

5 Past report about a distant past event: said / men / not see / the Arctic ice / then
....

6 Past report of a future event: not believe / newspapers / become / so powerful
....

UNIT 9

Articles: *the* or no article?

Form

Definite article *the*:
Armstrong walked on ***the*** *Moon.*

No article:
He was a hero to ***millions****.*

Use

We use *the* + singular count noun, plural count noun or noncount noun:

- to refer back to the same thing or person. *I applied for a job. It was* ***the*** *perfect job for me.*
- when there is only one. *He was the youngest person to cross* ***the*** *Atlantic Ocean by boat.*
- before a superlative adjective: *That was* ***the*** *most terrifying experience I've ever had!*
- to talk about a specific thing or things, person or people.
Did you see ***the*** *space shuttle landing earlier?*
I have a lot of admiration for ***the*** *relief workers there.*
- to talk about professional groups. *He worked in* ***the*** *navy for many years.*
- with certain countries, place names, geographical regions, oceans and seas, deserts, mountain ranges and rivers, for example: *the USA, the UK, the Republic of China, the Philippines, the United Arab Emirates, the Great Wall, the White House, the Middle East, the Antarctic, the Pacific, the Indian Ocean, the Atacama Desert, the Andes, the Himalayas, the Amazon.*

We use no article + plural count and noncount nouns:

- to talk in general about things or people. *Do you use computers in your job? I don't like potatoes.*
- before certain familiar places (*work, home, college, school*). *What time do you go to work?*
- before most cities, countries, continents, lakes, mountains, languages, and names of people. *Have you ever been to* ***Beijing****? She lives in* ***Bolivia****. He worked in* ***India*** *for many years.* Other examples are: *New York, Lima, Argentina, China, Asia, South America, Lake Titicaca, Mount Everest, Mandarin, Spanish, Japanese, Christopher Columbus.*
- before certain time expressions. *I'll meet you* ***next week****. He was born in* ***1953****.*

Notice that there are exceptions, for example:
time expressions: *in* ***the*** *sixties, on* ***the*** *weekend, in* ***the*** *summer, in* ***the*** *18th century*

Practice

1 Complete the text with *the* or no article (–).

I was listening to [1] *the* news at ten o'clock [2] .... last night, when it was reported that [3] .... President of [4] .... United States was on [5] .... vacation for [6] .... two weeks. They said that he was visiting [7] .... town where he was born. Apparently he doesn't like going to [8] .... places where there are lots of people, preferring [9] .... peace and quiet. [10] .... reasons why someone in his position does this are obvious!

Relative clauses

Form

Relative pronouns introduce defining relative clauses. To give information about:

- people, we use *who* or *that*. *He's the man **who** got the job.*
- things, we use *which* or *that*. *That's the network **which** is used for public access.*
- places or times, we use *where or when*. *This is the place **where** the information is stored. It was a time **when** space was unknown.*
- possession, we use *whose*. *She's the person **whose** job was advertised.*

Reduced relative clauses

We can sometimes shorten relative clauses by omitting the relative pronoun and using a present or past participle.
If the verb in the relative clause is in the active, we use the present participle.
*People **who visit** the area have admired its lakes.*
*People **visiting** the area have admired its lakes.*

If the verb in the relative clause is in the passive, we use the past participle:
*It is a subject **which is studied** by many people.*
*It is a subject **studied** by many people.*

We can't use a reduced relative clause when the relative pronoun is the object of the relative clause.
The expedition, which I am leading, is in June.
Not: ~~The expedition leading is in June.~~

Use

We use a relative clause to give more information about a noun in the main clause of the sentence.
We use a **defining** relative clause when the extra information in the relative clause is essential for identification. The meaning in the main clause is unclear without it.
*This is the forest **where the new species was discovered**.*

We use a **non-defining** relative clause when the extra information is not essential. The meaning of the main clause is still clear. The non-defining relative clause is separated from the main clause by commas.
*Stefano Calabrio, **who is eighty-five,** still works as a mountain guide.*
The ship Arctic Krestrel, ***which was built in Glasgow,*** *is registered in Russia.*

The relative pronoun in a relative clause can be:

- the subject of the clause. *Explorers are people who make discoveries.*
- the object of the clause (with a noun or pronoun following it). *He's the explorer who I met in Laos.*

We can omit the relative pronoun when it is the **object** of a **defining** relative clause.
That's the explorer (who) I met in Laos.
We cannot omit the relative pronoun when it is the subject of a defining relative clause or in a non-defining relative clause.

We often use reduced relative clauses in announcements and reports.
Passengers ~~who are~~ traveling to Mumbai, please proceed to gate 25.
Due to the bomb scare, all bags ~~which were~~ left unattended were removed and destroyed.

Practice

2 Write sentences using relative clauses. Use reduced relative clauses where possible.

1 He is an explorer. He likes traveling to remote places.
He's an explorer who likes traveling to remote places.

2 This is the lake. The fish was discovered here.
....

3 Equipment is often left on Mount Everest. It is regularly removed.
....

4 That is the biologist. Her papers were lost in the storm.
....

5 Lake Titicaca is very large. It is on the border of Bolivia and Peru.
....

6 GreenSpace created the prototype. The prototype was copied by a rival company.
....

UNIT 10

Simple present, present continuous, and *will* for repeated actions

Form

Simple present

Adverbs of frequency come before the main verb with the simple present, but after the verb *be*.
*We **always have** a family celebration at Thanksgiving.*
*He'**s usually** on time for his extra class.*

Present continuous with *always*

Always comes between the verb *be* and the *-ing* form of the verb.
*They're **always** criticizing their children.*

will

*Children **will** naturally choose to play rather than study.*

Use

We use the simple present for repeated actions (often with adverbs of frequency) or to talk about a simple fact or general truth.
*He **listens** to the radio news every morning.*
*Water **freezes** at 32° Fahrenheit.*

We use the present continuous with *always* to talk about a habit which we find annoying or which we wish to criticize.
*I try to avoid Zhang at work. He **is always talking** about his children's achievements.*
*She**'s always complaining** about work.*

We use *will* to talk about typical behavior.
*Westerners **will** often avoid unfamiliar food.*

Practice

1 Write sentences using the prompts. Use the simple present (SP), present continuous (PC) with *always*, and *will* (W).

1 (SP) Mary / read / detective novels
Mary always reads detective novels.

2 (W) Cats don't like swimming. They / do / anything to avoid getting wet

3 (SP) James / ride/ his bike everywhere

4 (PC) Ria / talk / with / her mouth full

5 (SP) Kumar / stay / at work until 7:00 or 8:00 at night

6 (W) Cats / sleep / all day / rather than go out

7 (PC) My mom / complain / about my messes

8 (SP) Li Wei / get / to work early most days

used to, usually, be used to, and *get used to*

Form

Affirmative	Negative	Interrogative
used to + base form I/you/he/she/it/we/they **used to** live	I/you/he/she/it/we/they **didn't use to** live	**did** I/you/he/she/it/we/they **use to** live?

usually + simple present I/you/we/they **usually play**	I/you/we/they **don't usually play**	***do*** I/you/we/they ***usually*** **play**?
he/she/it **usually plays**	he/she/it **doesn't usually play**	**does** he/she/it ***usually*** **play**?

be used to + noun or *-ing* **I'm used to** playing	**I'm not used to** playing	**am** I **used to** playing?
you**'re**/we**'re**/they**'re used to** playing	you/we/they **aren't used to** playing	**are** you/we/they **used to** playing?
he**'s**/she**'s**/it**'s used to** playing	he/she/it **isn't used to** playing	**is** he/she/it **used to** playing?

be getting used to + noun or *-ing* **I'm getting used to** playing	**I'*m not getting used to*** playing	**am** I **getting used to** playing?
you**'re**/we**'re**/they**'re getting used to** playing	you/we/they **aren't getting used to** playing	**are** you/we/they **getting used to** playing?
he**'s**/she**'s**/it**'s getting used to** playing	he/she/it **isn't getting used to** playing	**is** he/she/it **getting used to** playing?

Use

We use *used to* (+ base form) to talk about past habits, situations, and states.
*I **used to go** out to eat a lot when I lived in Paris.*
*She **didn't use to enjoy** opera when she was younger.*

We use *usually* + simple present to talk about present habits.
*We **usually have** dinner with my parents on Sundays.*
***Do** you **usually go** shopping on Friday nights?*

We use *be used to* to talk about familiar (and unfamiliar) habits and situations.
***Is** he **used to using** his new laptop yet?*
*He **isn't used to** his new laptop yet.*

We use *get used to* to talk about habits that are becoming familiar.
*Sara **is getting used to working** in the store now.*
*Sara **is getting used to** the store now.*

Practice

2 Choose the correct option.

1 Since his illness, he .... very healthy food.
a (usually eats)
b used to eat
c is getting used to eat

2 Paul has worked for a multinational company for years, so he .... now.
a usually travels
b used to travel
c is used to traveling

3 They both .... golf when they were boys.
a usually play
b used to play
c are used to playing

4 Li .... at her new college.
a usually studies
b used to study
c is getting used to studying

5 Didn't Jana .... to her co-director every day?
a usually speaks
b usually speak
c is getting used to speaking

6 Jorge .... different food since he went to Thailand last week.
a used to
b is used to trying
c didn't use to try

7 Petra's worked here for years, so she ....
a used to get up early
b is used to getting up early
c is getting used to getting up early

8 My brother .... very late on Saturday nights.
a usually stays out
b is used to staying out
c is getting used to staying out

UNIT 11

could, was able to, manage to, and *succeed in*

Form

Affirmative	Negative	Interrogative
could + infinitive base form I/you/he/she/it/we/they **could do**	I/you/he/she/it/we/they **couldn't do**	**could** I/you/he/she/it/we/they **do**?
was/were able + infinitive I/he/she/it **was able to do** you/we/they **were able to do**	I/he/she/it **wasn't able to do** you/we/they **weren't able to do**	**was** I/he/she/it **able to do**? **were** you/we/they **able to do**?
manage + infinitive I/you/he/she/it/we/they **managed to finish**	I/you/he/she/it/we/they **didn't manage to finish**	**did** I/you/he/she/it/we/they **manage to finish**?
succeed in + *-ing* I/you/he/she/it/we/they **succeeded in making**	I/you/he/she/it/we/they **didn't succeed in making**	**did** I/you/he/she/it/we/they **succeed in making**?

Use

To talk about a general ability in the past, use *could*.
*He **could swim** when he was three years old.*
*He **couldn't find** the herbal medicine he was looking for.*

We use *was / were able to, manage to* + base form and *succeed in* + *-ing* to talk about the ability (or lack of ability) to successfully complete a particular task or activity, but not to talk about general ability.
*She **was able to find** the quickest route immediately.*
*They **weren't able to finish** the journey.*
*He finally **managed to publish** his book.*
*Did she **manage to get** that scholarship in the end?*
*We **succeeded in raising** enough money for our trip.*
*Unfortunately, she **didn't succeed in getting** the job.*
We use *manage to* + base form only with people or living things.
The plant managed to grow without light.
Not: ~~*The car didn't manage to accelerate.*~~
We often use expressions such as *finally* and *in the end* with *manage to* and *succeed in* to emphasize that the activity was an effort.
*I **finally** managed to pass my exams.*
***In the end**, I succeeded in becoming a doctor.*

Practice

1 Look at the sentences (a and b) and choose the best option.

(1a) Did you manage to find out about the Mexican cure for blisters?
1b Could you find out about the Mexican cure for blisters?
2a In the past, people didn't succeed in accessing as much information about plants as they can today.
2b In the past, people weren't able to access as much information about plants as they can today.
3a A recent survey found that most people in the US weren't able to identify common plants.
3b A recent survey found that most people in the US didn't manage to identify common plants.
4a The medicine didn't always succeed in treating the illness.
4b The medicine didn't manage to treat the illness.
5a Sally didn't manage to publish her latest article. She submitted it too late.
5b Sally couldn't publish her latest article. She submitted it too late.

Future in the past

Form

***going to*: See page 159**

***about to* + base form: See page 159**

Affirmative	Negative	Interrogative
would + base form I said (that) I/you/he/she/it/we/they **would do**	I said (that) I/you/he/she/it/we/they **wouldn't do**	they asked if I/you/he/she/it/we/they **would do**
would have + past participle I/you/he/she/it/we/they **would have made**	I/you/he/she/it/we/they **wouldn't have made**	**would** I/you/he/she/it/we/they **have made?**
be supposed to + base form I/he/she/it **was supposed to finish** you/we/they **were supposed to finish**	I/he/she/it **wasn't supposed to finish** you/we/they **weren't supposed to finish**	**was** I/he/she/it **supposed to finish?** **were** you/we/they **supposed to finish?**

Use

We use *was / were going to* to talk about:

- an intention which may or may not have been fulfilled. *I **was going to call** you, but I got too busy.*
- a plan or arrangement which changed. *We **were going to meet** at 2:00 but came late.*

We use *be about to* to say that we were very close to doing something, but were prevented at the last moment.
*I **was about to leave** the house when the telephone rang.*

We use *would* to report what somebody said they would do.
*Jane said that she **would work** that evening.*
*He promised he **would send** me the report.*

We use *would have* to refer to a future action in the past which didn't happen.
*I **would have bought** it, but I didn't have enough money.*

We use *supposed to* to talk about actions which people should have done, but didn't.
*They **were supposed to get** here at eight o'clock! Where are they?*

Practice

2 Complete the second sentence so it has the same meaning as the first. Use the words in bold.

1 He planned to tell you, but he didn't see you.
going He *was going to tell* you, but he didn't see you.

2 "I'll work harder next week."
would John said that he ________ harder next week.

3 She intended to tell you, but she forgot.
would She ________ you, but she forgot.

4 Maria was going to bring enough food for everyone! Where is it?
supposed Maria ________ enough food for everyone! Where is it?

5 They intended to start studying tomorrow, but they went out instead.
going They ________ studying tomorrow, but they went out instead.

6 He wanted to say something, but decided not to.
about He ________ something, but decided not to.

7 Why didn't you ask? She wanted to tell you.
would She ________ you if you had asked.

8 "I'll remember."
would Lin said that she ________.

UNIT 12

Focusing adverbs: *only, just, even, too, also, as well*

Form

only, just, even

Only, just, and *even* always come directly before the word they are emphasizing.
Only*/*Just *Dave knows how hard they worked.*
*It is **only*/*just** two days since I saw him.*
*A lot of people don't **even** have any savings.*

too, also, as well

- sentence + *too*:
  *We can invest in that company **too**.*
- sentence + *as well*:
  *We bought a new iPad **as well**.*
- *Also* + sentence:
  ***Also**, she runs a successful accounting business.*
- *also* + main verb:
  *Most people **also** want to plan for their future.*
- be + *also*:
  *He's good at tennis. He's **also** a good badminton player.*
- auxiliary verb + *also* + main verb:
  *They are **also** going to the game.*

Use

We use focusing adverbs to emphasize a particular piece of information. Sentences which include focusing adverbs can exist without them.
Only and *just* focus on one particular thing to the exclusion of all others.
***Only/Just** she and I know her secret.*
*It's **only/just** banks that accept travelers checks.*

We use *even* to show that we think something is unusual or surprising.
*The question was so easy that **even** Bill knew the answer.*
***Even** football doesn't interest him any more.*

We use *also, as well,* and *too* to emphasize an additional piece of information in a sentence. *Also* comes before most verbs, but after the verb *to be*, or at the beginning of a sentence. *As well* and *too* come after the verb (and the object if there is one).
*He likes sports, but **also** enjoys playing chess.*
*He likes sports, but enjoys playing chess, **as well/too**.*

Practice

1 Choose the correct option.

1 I *only* (circled) / *too* heard about his financial situation yesterday.
2 Did you want to go to the bank *even / too*?
3 He *even / too* asked the accountant about it!
4 He usually works late on Thursdays *even / as well*.
5 They *only / as well* have a few thousand dollars left.
6 The money has *just / as well* been deposited in your account.
7 The boys *also / too* wanted some of the money.
8 The recession is a big problem for us *too / only*.

Causative *have* and *get*

Form

have/get + something + past participle
*I **had/got my car repaired** last week.*

have + someone + base form
*I **had a gardener help** me with the garden.*

get + someone + infinitive
*I **got a gardener to help** me with the garden.*

Use

We use *have/get something done* to explain that we asked someone to do something for us but we don't say who. We often pay for the work.
*She **has her house cleaned** by a cleaning company.*
*We **get our car serviced** every six months at the local auto shop.*

We use *have someone do / get someone to do* to explain that you have asked someone to do something for you. With these expressions, we say who does the job. Notice that with *get* we use infinitive. With *have* we use the base form.
*I **have a gardener mow** the lawn.*
*I **get a window cleaner to clean** the windows.*

Practice

2 Write sentences using the prompts. Use causative forms.

1 I / get / hair cut / yesterday
I got my hair cut yesterday.
2 I / have / accountant / go over / my accounts / on Saturday
....
3 We / get / mortgage rate / fix / last week
....
4 She / get / neighbor / pay for / new fence / this afternoon
....
5 He / get / friend / open / an account / last summer
....
6 She / have / new credit card / send out / this morning
....

Unit 1

1

It's known that animals often cooperate in their own social groups, helping each other to hunt or raise their young. Some highly intelligent animals, like elephants, go even further than this, and help other animals who are not in their own family group. But cooperation between animals of different species is unusual, so that's why the story of Suriya, the orangutan, has attracted a lot of interest.

Suriya lives with his keepers at the Institute of Greatly Endangered and Rare Species in Myrtle Beach, South Carolina, which is a kind of sanctuary for rare animals. Recently this orangutan has made an unlikely friend in a local hound dog. Now most dogs avoid apes because they are scared of them basically, but these two have formed a strong bond.

Each day the dog comes into the compound and searches out Suriya. When he finds him, they carry on like long-lost friends, wrestling and hugging and playing together. They've been doing this every day since they first met, and their friendship has attracted the curiosity of millions of viewers on the National Geographic Channel. The founder of the institute, Dr. Antle explains: "It's clear they are having the time of their life. What is more striking is that Suriya has also understood that the hound dog is very hungry, so he regularly shares his monkey biscuits with him. Orangutans are very generous creatures. If you give one a piece of candy, often they will break it in half and hand one piece back to you."

So how does he explain the fact that their relationship has a lot of the characteristics of what we call friendship? Antle says that the two animals are fulfilling a basic social need in each other that perhaps we don't normally associate with animals. "It's a relationship with attributes of fun and interaction that they are not getting from anyone else."

2

G = Greta; T = Tan

G: Tan, hello! Imagine bumping into you here! How are you?

T: Greta! Wow, what a surprise! Hi!

G: It's been a long time. What have you been up to?

T: I know. It's been way too long. Umm, I've been working abroad for the last eighteen months.

G: Anywhere exciting?

T: Yes, in India, actually. I had a contract with the consulate to do teacher training.

G: Well, it obviously suits you: you're looking very tanned and relaxed.

T: Oh, thanks, it's been a lot of fun. And you? You're looking well too. How are things?

G: Oh, you know, busy as ever. I've been completely swamped with work the last few months, trying to get my online shoe store off the ground.

T: Is it going OK?

G: Well, you know. It has its ups and downs. But we're getting there.

T: And what about Amanda? Do you see much of her?

G: Yeah, we still get together now and then. She was asking about you the other day, actually.

T: Oh. Well, I probably won't have time to look her up this time. I'm only back for a week. But do tell her I said hi.

G: I will.

T: And the next time I'm back, maybe we can all meet and catch up.

G: Yeah, that'd be great. How long will you be gone for?

T: I've just got to do another two months over there. Then I'll be back in the US for a while, I hope.

G: OK. Well, give me a call when you're back. You've got my number, don't you?

T: Yes, if it's still the same one.

G: Yeah, it is. I'll look forward to that. Is Shan going out there with you?

T: She has been with me, but uh, she's not coming this time.

G: Oh. Well, say hello to her from me. Look, I don't mean to be rude, but I need to get back to work—but it was really nice seeing you. Hope the trip goes well.

T: Thanks. Yeah, I've got to run too. Anyway, great to see you too, Greta. Take care… and see you soon. Good luck with the business.

3

1 Imagine bumping into you here.
2 I had a contract with the consulate.
3 Is it going OK?
4 Do you see much of her?
5 We still get together now and then.
6 I'm only back for a week.

Unit 2

4

P = Presenter; M = Mark Mowlam

P: Take a best-selling book, a great storyline and a great cast, add an experienced director and a large budget and what do you get? A box office success, you would think. Think again. There's no guarantee that a book that has enjoyed great success will make a good movie. Some movie adaptations have worked, others have flopped. So what's the secret? That was the question I put earlier to film critic Mark Mowlam, who's followed the progress of many book-to-film adaptations in his time and has recently reported on the making of Tolkien's *The Hobbit*.

M: Well, the goal is really to make a good movie that remains true to the spirit of the book. There are many examples of adaptations which have failed because they tried to remain too faithful to the plot and the characters of the book. Probably because at the time, the producers worried that they'd alienate loyal readers if they departed too much from the original text. But in fact, that's a mistake: what works well on the page doesn't necessarily work well on the screen; you have to give the screenwriter freedom to create a script that flows, even if that means changing the original. So what we find is a lot of good films—*Sense and Sensibility*, *The Shining*, for example—that are completely unlike the original book. And readers are generally OK about this because they think of books and movies as two separate works of art. But there are movies that have managed to stay true to the book and still be good. What they've done—a little like in cooking, I suppose—is to put in all the book's good ingredients and then boil them down to a concentrated mixture that's packed with the flavor of the original work. Probably the best example of this is *The Lord of the Rings* trilogy by Peter Jackson. The central theme of the book—which is a struggle between the forces of good and evil—perhaps wasn't so difficult to portray, but J.R.R. Tolkien created a very original other world and reproducing that was a much more difficult task, because each reader has his or her own very distinct idea of what this world was like. I think Jackson did a fantastic job, using the spectacular scenery of New Zealand for the film's location. The other thing about the *The Lord of the Rings* is that it's a very substantial work—three books, each containing over twenty long chapters—so Jackson had to leave some elements of the story out. To compensate for this, he took the most important scenes and then put all the emotional force behind them. The result is that it has become one of the most successful movies of all time, a blockbuster that has grossed almost $3 billion.

5

1 I haven't been to India.
2 It isn't far.
3 You aren't allowed.
4 It doesn't matter.
5 I hadn't noticed.
6 They weren't late.
7 She hasn't called.
8 We didn't care.

6

Conversation 1

A: The bus broke down on the highway, so we were all left stranded until help could arrive.
B: What did you do?
A: Luckily another bus came within about 15 minutes and we all transferred to that one.
B: That must have been a relief.

Conversation 2

A: My pants got caught on the door handle and as I walked away, they tore.
B: Oh, that's awful.
A: Yes, I had to walk right across the restaurant back to our table with my hands over the hole.
B: How embarrassing!

Conversation 3

A: I bent the key trying to force it into the lock and when I tried to straighten it, it snapped.
B: How did you get in?
A: I went to the neighbors', but they weren't at home, so I just had to wait 'til someone came home.
B: Yeah, something like that happened to me once.

Conversation 4

A: The elevator got stuck between floors twenty-five stories up, and two of the occupants were completely panic-stricken.
B: What a nightmare!
A: It was. Then the lights went off and one of them started screaming.
B: Yeah, I think I would have done the same thing.

Conversation 5

A: The tires on my bicycle were badly worn and when I hit a bump in the road, one of them burst.
B: Poor you!
A: Well, I fell off and cut my hand. Thank goodness there were no cars behind me.
B: That was lucky.

Conversation 6

A: My computer froze while I was working.
B: Really? How strange!
A: Yeah, I thought I'd lost about four hours' work, but I when I rebooted the computer, I searched for some of the key words in my document and found a temporary file which had most of the document in it.
B: That was good thinking.

7

That must have been a relief.

So what did you do?

8

1 What a nightmare!
2 Oh, that's awful.
3 How embarrassing!
4 Really? That's odd.
5 That was good thinking.
6 Something like that happened to me.

Unit 3

9

Hello everyone… one moment, I'll just adjust my microphone… OK, that's better. I can see a lot of hopeful-looking faces out there. I'm speaking to a government committee tomorrow and I hope they look as bright-eyed as you do… Let me just say that I'm afraid that those of you who have come looking for immediate answers to overpopulation are going to be disappointed, but I hope I can at least give you some cause for optimism. I'm not going to speak for too long because I'd like to hear what you have to say too, but let me tell you first how I see the situation…

In 1798, an English economist, Thomas Malthus, claimed that the population always grows faster than the food supply until war, disease, or famine arrive to reduce the number of people. A century and a half later in 1968, Paul Ehrlich wrote in his book *The Population Bomb* that medical science was keeping too many people alive and that we had failed to control the birth rate. He predicted that as a result hundreds of millions of people would soon starve to death.

But his bomb was a dud. Yes, medical science has extended life expectancy and the population carries on growing: around 7 billion today and it will probably peak at around 9 billion by 2050. But mass starvation? It hasn't happened. Why? Because science stepped in with better seeds and better pesticides to boost food production, and it's about to step in again with nanotechnology, which will help us to engineer safer and cheaper foods.

So what about overpopulation? Let me give you a fact: if in 2045 there are 9 billion people in the world, the population density will still be only half that of France today. And no one complains about overcrowding there: France is the world's favorite vacation destination! Some of the new megacities of Asia might not be such pleasant places to live… But the problem is not just the number of people. The problem is how people consume resources.

By 2030, more than a billion people in the developing world will belong to the "global middle class." That's a good thing, but it will be a bad thing for the planet if those people start eating meat and driving big cars every day. Some ultracautious people say we should bring in wartime emergency measures to conserve resources. I don't think that's the answer, but then I'm a scientist at heart even if I'm semi-retired now. For me the answer lies in innovations like biofuels and other alternative energy sources.

I'll talk about these specific solutions in the second part of my talk, but let's just go back to Malthus for a moment. People, he argued, are basically lazy. They won't do anything unless they are forced to by necessity. But what he didn't take into account is that faced with disaster, people are not lazy. Mankind and science will rise to the challenge—that is my sincere belief.

10

B = Ben; S = Sophie

B: Can you give me a hand? I'm having trouble printing this map.
S: Hang on, I'm just finishing a letter. I'll be with you in a second… OK. What do you want to do exactly?
B: I'm just giving directions to some friends who are staying in our house next week. I'm trying to paste this map into a Word document.
S: Are you going to email it to them? Because if so, you could just email them the link to the map.
B: No, I'm going to print it out and give it to them when they get here, because we're going away… The trouble is, it won't allow me to copy it.
S: Let me take a look. Oh, I see… It's a Google map; you can't select and copy them, I'm afraid.
B: Oh… what should I do then?
S: Well, there are two possibilities. You can either take a screen shot or…
B: What does that involve?
S: Here I'll show you. Just press alt print screen like this, then open a new Word document and paste it in. That should do the trick.
B: Oh, I see, but it came out very small. That's going to be too hard for them to read. What else do you suggest?
S: Have you tried looking for a different map? If you do a search, you might find one that you can copy.
B: OK. I'll give that a try. Thanks.
S: Feel free to ask me again if that doesn't work.

11

What do you suggest?

What does that involve?

It won't allow me to copy it.

First select the picture,…

What are you trying to achieve?

What solution do you propose?

Did you attach the document?

Unit 4

12

"Nature has done everything for Sydney, man nothing; man has done everything for Melbourne, nature nothing," a visitor to Australia once noted. Herein lies the essential difference between Australia's two largest cities. Melbourne is Australia's second city, but it has plenty of first-class qualities, from a buzzing art scene to an enormous range of restaurants. It may have a few gray days, and a muddy river instead of a beautiful harbor, but don't let that worry you. The lack of natural attractions has meant that Melbourne has had to create its own man-made pleasures, and in doing so it has become Australia's cultural capital. Theater, music, street sculpture, fashion—in fact, there are hardly any forms of artistic expression which you can't find here. All thrive, alongside a cosmopolitan mix of cafés, restaurants, and bars.

What's great about Melbourne for the visitor is how accessible all these arts are. In addition to traditional museums and galleries like the National Gallery of Victoria and concert halls like Hamer Hall, there is an enormous number of smaller art spaces and venues which cater to every kind of taste. Art is not something for a small minority. In fact, for most inhabitants of Melbourne a weekly visit to the movie theater or an art exhibition is a routine event. Several festivals take place during the winter months, including the International Film Festival in July and the Fringe Festival in September, which has loads of interesting (even if not always good!) comedy, dance, and theater acts.

If the locals appreciate their art, they absolutely love their sport. Lots of people around the world will know the Australian Formula One Grand Prix and the Australian Open Tennis, which attracts over half a million spectators to Melbourne in a carnival atmosphere, but few people will be familiar with the sports Melburnians themselves follow. Australian Rules football and cricket enjoy a huge amount of support and, if you have enough time, a visit to see either is well worth it just for the atmosphere. If you're looking to participate rather than just watch, why not try some surfing or swimming? Biking, jogging, or a visit to one of Melbourne's many gyms are other possibilities. All this information is on our website…

13

a huge amount of support

a huge number of galleries

a lack of natural attractions

a lot of information

lots of people

14

I = Interviewer; W = Walid

I: OK, Walid, I'm going to fire some statements at you about what various people say art should be, and I want to know which of these you agree with. OK?

W: Uh, OK, but I'm already a little suspicious, because I don't really think that "should" has a lot to do with it. People have a very fixed idea about what art "should" be—a certain kind of portrait or landscape, very often—but, anyway, anyway, I'll play the game, so… let's hear what they say…

I: Good, here's the first one then: *Art should be pleasing for the viewer.*

W: Mmm, no, not necessarily—the artist's intention might be to make you feel uncomfortable, not to give you a warm feeling.

I: OK. What about this, then? *Art should involve effort on the part of the artist.*

W: Well, that's more interesting, but still the answer is "not necessarily." Monet did some of his paintings in five minutes.

I: Did he? I didn't know that. That's amazing! Well, that ties in with the next one, perhaps. *Art should involve technical skill.*

W: Um, I can think of quite a lot of examples of successful art that wasn't technically difficult, but was just based on a clever idea.

I: OK, *Art should have a social message or make a political point.*

W: No, certainly not. Is the Mona Lisa political? I don't think so. Look, an artist's role is simply to present an idea in a visual form. The viewer's role is to give that effort their time and attention and then say either "Yes, I really like that," or "That moves me," or "No, I'm afraid that doesn't do anything for me."

15

J = Jae; T = Tomas

J: Hey, Tomas, how was *The Lion King*?

T: I loved it, even though I'm not generally a fan of musicals.

J: No, me neither. I never feel particularly inspired by the music in them, which should really be the whole point of them, with a few exceptions maybe—like *West Side Story* or *Grease*, which have terrific music. So what was so good about it?

T: Well, visually it's absolutely stunning, the opening scene in particular. All the animals—giraffes, wildebeest, zebra, antelope—congregate on the stage to set the scene, which is the plains of the Serengeti where the story takes place. And they're in these fabulous costumes. They're difficult to describe, but the effect is that they actually seem to move like real animals. Everyone in the audience was spellbound.

J: But is the story the same as in the Disney movie? I remember there were a couple of pretty annoying characters in the movie, like that bird who's supposed to be there for comic effect—well at least I think it is—but after a while, really begins to annoy you.

T: You mean Zazu. Yeah, I know what you mean about that kind of Disney character. They can get on your nerves, but this production's different. It actually seems much more adult than the movie. It's very well done. I found the story really moving.

J: What about the music?

T: It's essentially the same score as the film—I think Elton John wrote most of it, but it's all based on African rhythms and vocals.

J: Doesn't really sound like my kind of thing.

T: Oh, well, I'm really into Elton John. I think he catches the mood of this really well. Have you heard *Circle of Life*?

J: Uh, no, I don't think so.

T: Well, I'm not going to sing it. Anyway, I really recommend it. It's not cheap to go, but if you get a chance you should. I can't stand the high prices they charge for musicals these days, but actually I didn't mind for this one. It was worth it.

Unit 5

16

I = Interviewer; J = Journalist

I: I know you like exotic places. Have you tried visiting India?

J: I was just there actually, in Kerala, in the southwest. I was meaning to go on to tour other parts of India, but Kerala was so fascinating I stayed longer.

I: Were you on vacation?

J: No. Well, it was meant to be a vacation, but it actually turned into more than that.

I: Oh dear…

J: Oh, no! I don't regret changing my plans! I became so interested in the place that I started to write an article about it for the newspaper I work for.

I: Really? Is it a travel article?

J: Not really. It's more sociological, I guess. I'm trying to show what a remarkable place Kerala is in the developing world. You see, it's a small state with a big population, and the average income is only about $300 a year. Usually that would mean people having a fairly poor quality of life, but that's not the case. In fact, Kerala stands out as a kind of model of social development. The population is highly literate and well-educated and they seem very well-off, compared to other parts of India. They're healthy and live almost as long as Americans or Europeans. It seems that infant mortality is also very low. Also, women, who've, uh, traditionally been the head of the household, continue to be very active (and equal) participants in society.

I: Huh, that's really interesting. I remember going there with my wife in the 1990s. But we were just tourists and my memories of it are as a very tranquil and beautiful place, with gorgeous beaches and lagoons.

J: Well, of course that's the part of it that tourists like to spend time visiting. But tranquil is not necessarily the adjective I would use. Trivandrum, the main city where we stopped to visit an Indian journalist I know—a highly cultured man, by the way—is absolutely hectic. The people there are very politically engaged: they never stop debating. There are often strikes on the buses or parades of demonstrators. Some medical students started protesting when we were there and went on protesting for four days.

I: So why do you think it's such a successful society?

J: Well, there are essentially two reasons, I think. The first is that the Keralites are naturally tolerant people: you find Hindus, Muslims, and Christians all living peacefully beside each other, and foreigners are treated no differently than anyone else. And second, the government has invested a lot in health and education and goes on investing a lot. The land is incredibly fertile and well managed. Small farmers cultivate every inch of it so none is wasted, which I regret to say is not always the case in some developing countries.

I: Sounds fascinating. Please remember to send me a copy of the article when it's published.

J: Of course I will.

17

1	state weight	5	main plane
2	low though	6	stopped opt
3	head said	7	none fun
4	course force	8	waste faced

18

P = Patricio; A = Ana; I = Isabel

P: OK, Ana, I believe you've prepared a brief summary of the Howard Park project. [**Ana:** Yup]. Could you just take us through the main points?

A: Yes, sure. Well, the Howard Park project began two years ago. We agreed to lend the local government $750,000 to redevelop a green space in the Howard's Hill area of the city. The aim was to give the local residents a nicer park, first of all, but also some new recreation facilities: a mini-golf course, two tennis courts, a small café, and a new children's play area. The play area was in terrible condition—full of trash—so it was actually pretty dangerous. So here we are two years later, and what progress have they made? Well, they've done a good job of cleaning the area up: they've planted trees and laid new grass, so it looks much, much better. They've also built the café and the children's play area. However, they've also done some things that weren't part of the original plan. For example, they've built a fountain near the café, and six months ago they also bought a sculpture, at a cost of $80,000, to place near the fountain. Now they've run out of money and are asking for a new loan of $250,000 to complete the tennis courts and mini-golf course. What do you think?

I: If you ask me, that's completely wrong. They've been spending money on things they had no right to. I don't think we should give them another cent.

P: Well, hang on a minute. Let's not be too hasty. I agree that they should have told us about these other changes, but we need to consider whether they are in the spirit of the original aims of the project.

A: That really depends on the opinion of the local residents. The way I see it, it's probably a good thing if residents like it and it means they'll use the park more.

I: Well, I just find it arrogant of them.

P: OK, so what should we do? Personally, I don't think we should lend them any more until we know what local people think of the work they've already done.

A: Yes, I'd go along with that. We need to ask them to conduct a survey of local opinion and then show us the results.

P: Exactly. Are we all in agreement, then?

I: Yes, I guess so. Yes, that seems fair to me.

Unit 6

19

P = Presenter; K = Katie Samuel

P: Now, have you ever thought of doing a little building work during your vacation? Or helping to look after animals on a wildlife preserve? You probably thought that kind of vacation was for eighteen-year-olds in their gap year, didn't you? But it seems more and more working adults are opting for volunteer vacations. With us today is Katie Samuel, author of *Good Travel*, a guide to alternative vacations. Katie, I can see that this might attract a few people, but wouldn't most people who only get a few weeks off a year prefer a more relaxing option?

K: Well, that depends very much on how your volunteer vacation is organized. The good companies in this field are certainly conscious of the fact that this should be a rewarding travel experience, not just a work trip.

P: But isn't the whole point to go and lend a hand to people in need of help? It's not really a vacation as we know it, is it?

K: Well, no, perhaps it isn't, but it is more like what real travel should be about: a cultural experience where each side gives something and takes something. A good example is a program next to Kenya's Tsavo National Park, where volunteers help local people to find ways of making a living that don't involve poaching or killing local wildlife. So they help them to plant crops, build fences, develop ideas for tourist businesses, and so on. In return, the locals take them for bush walks, which are like mini-safaris, teach them about local wildlife, talk about the history of their community.

P: But the volunteers pay for the trip, don't they?

K: Yes, of course, they have to pay for their flight, their living expenses, and something to cover the organization's costs.

P: And do you need to be qualified to volunteer? I imagine organizations don't want people turning up to teach or build or whatever who have no idea of what they're doing, do they?

K: Again, it depends. There are a few projects which are only open to people with professional experience, uh, like people with a medical background, but for the most part, volunteers can be trained to do the work. The Cultural Restoration Tourism Project (CRTP), which helps to restore cultural heritage sites around the world, gives volunteers the chance to work with local architects and artists. They have a project restoring a 300-year-old monastery in Nepal where you can get training in doing wall paintings from a world-famous painter.

P: So, you could actually come back with a skill you didn't have when you left?

K: Absolutely. It might not be a skill you'll ever use again: helping to bottle-feed milk to orphaned lion cubs—that's a project in Zambia—is unlikely to be of direct use to you back at the office, but we all benefit from new and different experiences, wouldn't you agree?

P: Yeah, I'm sure that's true. So could you tell us a bit more about…

20

Do you like visiting new places? Yes, now and then.

Don't you like visiting new places? No, not at all.

You like visiting new places, don't you? Yes, I love it.

You don't like visiting new places, do you? No, you're right. I don't.

21

1 You like the idea of volunteer vacations, don't you?
2 Don't you think it's an interesting idea?
3 You've been on a volunteer vacation, haven't you?
4 Didn't it seem strange to pay money in order to work?
5 You won't be going again this year, will you?

22

M = Manuel; P = Paul

M: Hi Paul, this is Manuel, your host. You emailed me about staying next Thursday for a couple of nights.

P: Oh hi, hi Manuel. Thanks for getting back to me. Is that still OK?

M: No, that's all fine. I just thought I'd give you a call to explain how to get here, because it's a little complicated. How are you getting to Hamilton, first of all?

P: I'm coming in by train sometime in the afternoon.

M: OK. I wanted to pick you up, but my car's in the garage that day.

P: Hey, that's nice of you, but I can find my own way.

M: OK. Well, I'm at work 'til about five thirty, so feel free to come over any time after six.

P: That sounds perfect. And how do I get to you from downtown?

M: Well, you could just catch a taxi, but it's about eleven miles from downtown, so it won't be cheap. Alternatively, you can hop on a bus to Stoney Creek. Look out for the Stoney Creek Arena on your right and get off there. It's only a twenty-minute ride. From there, Cherry Heights is another fifteen minutes on foot, straight up King St. Once you reach the crossroads at Gray Road, the easiest thing is to give me a call and I'll come out and meet you.

P: So: bus to Stoney Creek, walk up King St. to Cherry Heights and call from there?

M: Yup. Call when you get to the crossroads at Gray Road.

P: OK, got it. That sounds great. If I get held up in any way I'll let you know, but otherwise expect a call around six thirty.

M: Great. See you next Thursday then. Bye.

P: Bye.

23

I wanted to pick you up, but my car's in the garage that day.

You could just catch a taxi, but it's about eleven miles from downtown.

Unit 7

24

Speaker 1: Liam from the United Kingdom

I live in Manchester, which is probably one of the wettest places in the UK. If I had been brought up somewhere like Saharan Africa, where I had to walk miles each day just to fetch water, I'd obviously be a lot more conscious of water conservation. But I'm afraid I don't set a very good example. I probably waste a lot—leaving the tap running when I brush my teeth and so on. Clearly we're not going to run out of water in the UK, but I know water conservation is important. If we all used less water, the water companies wouldn't have to use so much energy treating water to make it clean. And of course that would be more environmentally-friendly.

Speaker 2: Gemal from the United Arab Emirates

I'm not saying the idea of desalination plants is wrong. If desalination methods didn't exist, this country would not have been able to develop in the way it has. Nowadays we use water in our homes more or less as we want to. But I don't think we can continue like this. You see, the waste from the desalination process is a kind of brine with a dangerously high salt content which will eventually destroy life in the sea. I am interested in discovering farming techniques that use salt water. There are grasses and other types of plant that can grow with sea water. If we were to use more of these, it would give our natural fresh water springs a chance to recharge.

Speaker 3: Daniel from the United States

Americans (and I'm as guilty as the rest) use water like there is no tomorrow. I think it's well-known that the Colorado River doesn't reach the sea anymore. If you had visited the area around the old delta in Mexico 100 years ago—rich wetlands, full of wildlife—you'd be shocked to see it now. It's all dried up, a kind of salt flat. The reason is agriculture. The river has been dammed and diverted in various places along its route to irrigate fields and provide enough water for people living in the desert areas of Nevada and California. Unless we change the way we think about water and stop wasting so much, the river will keep on getting smaller.

Speaker 4: Carmen from Mexico

My water needs are the same as most people's, I think: I have a small vegetable garden; I have to wash myself and my clothes. I don't have to save water, but I want to, you know. I collect rainwater for the garden, I fill a basin to wash in rather than running the tap, I wash my dishes every other day. But now governments are discussing big projects for transporting water from one part of the world to another using huge pipes and tankers. I think if more people thought and acted like me, things would not have come to this point, you know.

25

E = Elena; A = Anne; J = Jim; R = Rick

A: Elena, what do you think about all these people who say that there's no proof that climate change is man-made?

E: My position is that I don't know if climate change is man-made and I'm not sure anyone can say for sure. Let me give you an example, an analogy. Imagine you were losing your hair and I told you that some people had found that if they ate a banana every day it prevented hair loss. Even though you had no proof it worked, you would probably try eating a banana every day, wouldn't you? Well, it's the same with global warming. We don't know that we're causing it, but some people say we might be, with all the fossil fuels we burn. And I, for one, am happy to be a little more careful in how I pollute in case they're right.

A: Mmm, well, I don't accept that. I used to believe in climate change, but the last few winters here in the US have been much colder than normal. To be honest with you, I'd believe it more if I wasn't getting up in the morning and scraping ice off the inside of my windows rather than the outside.

E: Yeah, but that's not the point, Anne, is it? You know, regional temperatures may be lower, but average global temperatures keep on rising.

J: Well, look, there's no doubt that the weather's changing, but I don't believe it's a man-made problem. It's just part of a natural weather cycle. Yeah, I know you'll say "Oh, that's just your excuse to drive a big car and fly to exotic places for your vacations," but actually that's not the reason. I don't believe it simply because no scientist has successfully proved it yet.

R: We're approaching this debate all wrong by saying "it's a big environmental problem that we need to address." Because it's not just an environmental problem. It's an economic problem, a social problem, even an ethical problem. We all need to do what we can to prevent climate change.

26

I don't know and I'm not sure anyone knows for sure.

27

1 We don't know that we're causing it, but some people say we might be.
2 …scraping ice off the inside of my windows rather than the outside.
3 Regional temperatures may be lower, but average global temperatures keep on rising.
4 Because it's not just an environmental problem. It's an economic problem, a social problem, even an ethical problem.

Unit 8

28

And finally… it was thought that the Large Blue butterfly was extinct in Britain, but it seems to have made a remarkable comeback. The Large Blue, which disappeared 30 years ago, is only found in certain fields. What these fields have in common is that their grass is very short because rabbits, sheep and cows graze there. Originally it was believed that greedy butterfly hunters had killed off the Large Blue, but it is now agreed that changes in farming techniques were responsible for its decline. As a result of recent efforts to protect its natural habitat, it is estimated that around 20,000 of these beautiful creatures will be seen in the British countryside this summer.

And finally, researchers believe they may have found a cure—or at least some relief—for the common cold. In tests, it was reported that people who started taking zinc at the first signs of a common cold got well sooner. There have been many previous studies into the effectiveness of zinc but they were inconclusive. The new study, involving over 1,000 people of various ages, found that, on average, people who took zinc supplements recovered from their colds one day earlier than those who took nothing. The effectiveness of zinc in preventing a cold in the first place was less certain, although it was said that those who took it regularly suffered less serious symptoms than those who didn't.

And finally, believe it or not, eating chocolate might be good for you after all. In the past it was thought that eating candy would result in tooth decay and weight gain. But now it is claimed that a new chocolate bar, invented by the world's largest chocolate maker, can actually slow the aging process of your skin. The special chocolate contains antioxidants, which help hydrate the skin and fight wrinkles. The market for healthy foods has grown by over five percent a year in recent years and it seems now that even the sellers of traditionally unhealthy snacks are trying to get in on the act. However, doctors have warned against rushing out to buy extra chocolate—good skin and chocolate are not generally natural partners, they say.

And finally, Costa Rica today has the honor of being named the world's happiest nation. According to the latest Happy Planet Index, it is said that Costa Rica has the best balance of human well-being—that is to say, good health, a long life, low levels of poverty—and a low ecological footprint, in other words the amount of natural resources it uses. In fact, Latin American countries took nine of the top ten places, while richer, so-called developed countries, like the US at number 74, were much further down in the list.

29

J = Jess (female); P = Phil

J: Hey, Phil. Did all that noise in the street wake you up last night?
P: No, it didn't, but then I'm a deep sleeper. What happened?
J: Well, I didn't see it myself but I heard that it was an argument between two drivers and supposedly it got pretty nasty.
P: Really? Who told you about it?
J: Tara at number 42. It seems that both drivers got out of their cars and started shouting at each other. She says they almost started fighting.
P: Well, I'd take what Tara says with a grain of salt, if I were you. She tends to blow things out of proportion.
J: No, I believe her actually—people do get very frustrated not being able to pass each other in this street. Anyway, the police were called…
P: The police? It wasn't that serious, was it?
J: Well, no. The cars didn't crash or anything. But Tara says that they got out of their cars and started arguing. She figures that if the police hadn't arrived, there would have been a fight.
P: Did the cars make contact?
J: No, they were just coming in opposite directions and they met where the street gets narrow and neither one would back up to let the other pass. So they just stayed there, in the middle of the road, with neither one giving way.
P: How childish.
J: Yeah, right? Someone said they'd seen one of the drivers before. Apparently he's a local politician.
P: It wasn't Tara getting her facts mixed up again, was it?
J: No, it was Chris. I think I'd take his word for it; he's not the type to spread gossip.
P: So what did the police do about it?
J: Well, according to Chris, they took them both away for questioning.

30

apparently	generally
supposedly	happened

Unit 9

31

Q: Can you tell us something about the Emerging Explorers program?
A: It's an awards program set up by the National Geographic Society to encourage young adventurers, scientists, photographers, and storytellers to continue their work and to realize their potential. Each year, between eight and fifteen explorers whose work is really outstanding are selected and given money to help them continue their research and exploration.
Q: So Emerging Explorers are generally young people?
A: Not necessarily. Emerging Explorers are generally people who are at an early stage of their careers. What they have in common is that they are all people who are pushing the boundaries of their field, whether that's exploring undiscovered deep-water caves or watching the stars through a telescope.
Q: And how does National Geographic encourage them?
A: Well, first of all National Geographic awards each one of them $10,000, which is intended to go towards further research and exploration. Of course their profiles are also raised by the articles and news that appear in *National Geographic*. In other words, the magazine is a place where other interested people can read about their work.
Q: And what kind of fields do the winners come from?
A: We have so many different types of explorer, chosen from fields as diverse as anthropology, space exploration, mountaineering, and music.
Q: You mentioned storytellers earlier. What did you mean by that, exactly?
A: Well, there are all these people doing important work out there in the various fields that I've described. And that's great, but it's also very important that everyone hears about this work. That's the skill of the storytellers: communicating with pictures and words important facts about the planet and life on the planet in a way that grabs everyone's attention. A really good example is Alexandra Cousteau, whose father Philippe Cousteau was well-known for his documentaries about marine life. She works as a conservationist, trying to persuade people to protect scarce resources like water. Alexandra, inspired by her father's success as a storyteller, is researching ways in which the environmental community can use new media—social networks, video games—to communicate its message.

32

S = Sarah; P = Panit

S: So, you're 24 years old, you graduated a year ago, and you're looking for work with a charity. What attracted you to Shelterbox?
P: Well, I'm familiar with your work because I have a friend who volunteered for you last year packing boxes, and I think it's a fantastic concept. But, umm, mainly I'm really interested in working abroad in foreign countries.
S: Mm, I see. And what makes you think you'd be suited for that? I see you studied economics at Stanford. Don't you think that's a pretty different world?
P: Yes, it's true that I specialized in economics but, actually, I'm good at coping with difficult environments. I spent three months helping to build a school in Chennai in India last

summer. And the year before that, I trekked across the Mojave Desert. So I think I'd be well-suited for the work.

S: OK, well, they're certainly not easy places to adapt to, although in fact you'd also be spending a good part of the time here in the office doing paperwork.

P: Yeah, that's also fine. I was expecting that. I have quite a lot of experience sitting at a desk for my studies. What sort of paperwork is it?

S: Well, each trip involves a lot of preparation and a certain amount of follow-up, too. Keeping spreadsheets, writing reports. Are you OK doing that sort of thing?

P: Yeah, I'm pretty good with computers. I'm comfortable with all the usual programs—Excel, Word, some financial software…

S: OK. There's just one thing that's worrying me though. You're clearly a bright person and you have a good degree. How do I know that you won't just do this job for a few months and then go and get a better-paid job with a bank or a consulting company?

P: That's a good question. It's actually what a lot of my friends from college have done, but I'll tell you why that's not for me. First, I'm really serious about wanting to help people in need. Second, I think I need to become more knowledgeable about the world, before I use my economics degree to do something else. If you put your faith in me, I will be absolutely committed to doing the best job that I can for two or three years at least.

33

although	comfortable
environments	foreign
knowledgeable	months
specialized	suited
world	

34

clothes	February	folk	island
lengths	receipt	surface	thorough

Unit 10

35

Different people's diets rarely surprise me these days. We didn't use to think so much about what we ate. But today, well, we live in an age when people are just very conscious of their diets. A day hardly ever passes without a story in the news about a particular food that's good for your health or bad for you if you eat too much of it.

So I was very interested to read a story the other day about the diet of the Nochmani tribe of the Nicobar Islands in the Indian Ocean. People used to think that these tiny islands—which are about 600 miles from the coast of India—that they were uninhabited by humans. But in 2004, aid workers in helicopters spotted some tribespeople on a mountainside. Scientists were particularly surprised that there were inhabitants there, because people usually need mammals—you know, cows, goats and so on—and their produce—meat, milk, et cetera—in order to live. But the Nicobar Islands have almost no mammals. So what were the Nochmani surviving on? Fish, perhaps? No. Amazingly, their diet consisted largely of insects, in particular beetles, of which there were over 1,700 varieties on the islands, but also other insects including spiders.

This presented a problem for the aid workers, who'd brought with them standard survival meals, including chicken, beef, and pork. The Nochmani, who weren't used to eating meat at all, were disgusted by these offerings. All they'd take from the aid workers were sweets and cakes. It wasn't just a matter of taste, either. If you're used to a certain type of food—even insects—other types may be completely indigestible.

Insects are, in fact, very nutritious: high in protein and fat and low in carbohydrates, making them an ideal food source for humans. But what was even more amazing was that just as we usually help our animals to live by providing food for them, so the Nochmani cultivate certain fungi and mosses to attract and feed the insects they eat. Perhaps we can learn from this tribe. If more of us could get used to eating unconventional foods such as insects, it might help the world's food problems.

36

M = Marie; E = Esther

M: I know of henna painting as a custom from Indian weddings, but you came across it in Turkey, didn't you?

E: Yes, in eastern Turkey when I was traveling there. It takes place a few nights before the wedding.

M: Was it a little like a bachelorette party?

E: Well, in the sense that it marks the last evening that a bride spends with female family and friends, I suppose it is a little like that. What happens, typically, is that women from both families get together with the bride, to celebrate with music, song, and dance. But it's not just a party. It's an occasion for sadness too, because it symbolizes the end of life as a single person and the start of another stage.

37

M = Marie; E = Esther

M: So what happens exactly?

E: Well, the ceremony begins with preparation of the henna. It's traditional for this to be done by the daughter of a couple who have had a successful marriage themselves. Then, after the bride's head has been covered in a red veil, her hands and feet are decorated with henna. After that, a gold coin is put into the remaining henna. While this is happening, the guests sing, umm, separation songs—these are rather sad, as you can imagine. The party continues well into the night. Then, on the morning of the wedding, a child presents the hennaed coin to the groom as a symbol of future prosperity and good fortune.

38

M: I know of henna painting as a custom from Indian weddings, but you came across it in Turkey, didn't you?

E: Yes, in eastern Turkey when I was traveling there. It takes place a few nights before the wedding.

M: Was it a little like a bachelorette party?

E: Well, in the sense that it marks the last evening that a bride spends with female family and friends, I suppose it is a little like that. What happens, typically, is that women from both families get together with the bride, to celebrate with music, song and dance. But it's not just a party. It's an occasion for sadness too, because it symbolizes the end of life as a single person and the start of another stage.

M: So what happens exactly?

E: Well, the ceremony begins with preparation of the henna. It's traditional for this to be done by the daughter of a couple who've had a successful marriage themselves. Then, after the bride's head has been covered in a red veil, her hands and feet are decorated with henna. After that, a gold coin is put into the remaining henna. While this is happening, the guests sing, umm, separation songs—these are rather sad, as you can imagine. The party continues well into the night. Then, on the morning of the wedding, a child presents the hennaed coin to the groom as a symbol of future prosperity and good fortune.

39

custom	dress	friends
music	suppose	weddings

40

across	eastern	lose	place
rings	single	spends	surprise

Unit 11

41

Have any of these things happened to you? You were about to give a speech or make a comment at a meeting, and then your mind went blank. You were supposed to send a friend a card for his birthday, but then you forgot. You recognized someone in the street and would have spoken to her, but you didn't because you couldn't remember her name. You promised you would mail a letter for someone and two days later you found it still in your pocket. You were going to write down a great idea you had, but when you found a pen and paper, the idea had gone. I could go on, but I won't because I'm sure everyone recognizes these common failures of memory.

42

We all would like to remember more but would it actually make us any happier?

I want to tell you the story of a 41-year-old woman from California known in medical literature as AJ, who remembers almost every day of her life since the age of 11. She remembers that at 12:34 p.m. on Sunday, August 3, 1986, a young man she was attracted to called her on the telephone. She remembers that on March 28, 1992, she had lunch with her father at the Beverly Hills Hotel. It's a bit like certain smells that evoke strong memories: AJ's memory is stimulated in the most intense way by dates.

You'd think that being able to retrieve facts and knowledge in this way would make us more confident and wiser. But in fact for AJ, an incredible memory is as much a burden as it is a benefit. That's because most memories are selective: they provide us mostly important things, and mostly good things too. AJ remembers every detail, good or bad, important or not.

So when we curse our poor memories for forgetting to send a birthday card, actually we should be grateful also for all the things that our memories hide away because they don't need to be remembered or thought about. Umm, technology, of course helps us with this. We don't need to remember the precise content of a report or the exact time of a meeting, because it's stored on our computer or in our smart phone.

But interestingly, the growth of this technology—what psychologists call our external memory—is having an effect on what and how much we remember. Even our memories of happy events—like parties or vacations—get stored in photograph albums on our computers. So our internal memories are probably worse than those of people 100 years ago. Medical science is trying to address the problem of poor memory and this is what I want to talk about next.

43

Have any of these things happened to you? You were about to give a speech or make a comment at a meeting, and then your mind went blank. You were supposed to send a friend a card for his birthday, but then you forgot. You recognized someone in the street and would have spoken to her, but you didn't because you couldn't remember her name. You promised you would mail a letter for someone and two days later you found it still in your pocket. You were going to write down a great idea you had, but when you found a pen and paper, the idea had gone. I could go on, but I won't because I'm sure everyone recognizes these common failures of memory.

We all would like to remember more but would it actually make us any happier?

I want to tell you the story of a 41-year-old woman from California known in medical literature as AJ, who remembers almost every day of her life since the age of 11. She remembers that at 12:34 p.m. on Sunday, August 3, 1986, a young man she was attracted to called her on the telephone. She remembers that on March 28, 1992, she had lunch with her father at the Beverly Hills Hotel. It's a bit like certain smells that evoke strong memories: AJ's memory is stimulated in the most intense way by dates.

You'd think that being able to retrieve facts and knowledge in this way would make us more confident and wiser. But in fact for AJ, an incredible memory is as much a burden as it is a benefit. That's because most memories are selective: they provide us mostly important things, and mostly good things too. AJ remembers every detail, good or bad, important or not.

So when we curse our poor memories for forgetting to send a birthday card, actually we should be grateful also for all the things that our memories hide away because they don't need to be remembered or thought about. Umm, technology, of course, helps us with this. We don't need to remember the precise content of a report or the exact time of a meeting, because it's stored on our computer or in our smart phone.

But interestingly, the growth of this technology—what psychologists call our external memory—is having an effect on what and how much we remember. Even our memories of happy events—like parties or vacations—get stored in photograph albums on our computers. So our internal memories are probably worse than those of people 100 years ago. Medical science is trying to address the problem of poor memory and this is what I want to talk about next.

44

Have any of these things happened to you? You were about to give a speech or make a comment at a meeting, and then your mind went blank. You were supposed to send a friend a card for his birthday, but then you forgot. You recognized someone in the street and would have spoken to her, but you didn't because you couldn't remember her name. You promised you would mail a letter for someone and two days later you found it still in your pocket. You were going to write down a great idea you had, but when you found a pen and paper, the idea had gone. I could go on, but I won't because I'm sure everyone recognizes these common failures of memory.

45

1 I was going to ask Sanjip to come, but I asked Kumar instead.
2 She was supposed to be in Cairo this week, but she's sick.
3 He promised he would send me the original, but he sent me a copy.
4 We would have been there by ten o'clock, but the train didn't get in until eleven fifteen.
5 He was about to announce that he would retire, but now he thinks he'll stay another year.
6 The city planners were going to build a new shopping mall downtown, but residents opposed it.

46

A = Ahmad; L = Liz

A: Hi there, I'm interested in taking a class at your college—umm, the history of art course.
L: Is that the two-year advanced course?
A: Excuse me, what do you mean by advanced?
L: The advanced art history course is a two-year college-level course with exams at the end of each year.
A: Oh no, no, no! I don't want to take any exams. It's just for interest.
L: OK. In that case, we have a one-year art appreciation course.
A: Sorry. Can you speak up a little? I can't hear you very well.
L: Yes, we have a one-year art appreciation course.
A: Umm, can you explain what the course involves?
L: Yeah, it's a two-hour class once a week and, basically, it teaches you how to look at art so that you get the most from the experience.
A: No, sorry, I'm not really with you. Are you saying that it doesn't really deal with the history of art?
L: No, there's some history of art in it, of course, but it's mainly learning about composition, techniques, references and so on.
A: Hmm… Could you give me an example of the kind of thing students do in the class?
L: Sure. Typically, students look at works of art and then comment on them. Then they're told more about the artist, what he or she was trying to achieve, and then they look at their work again, with fresh eyes, so to speak.
A: Mmm, OK. It sounds pretty interesting. What was the course called again?
L: Art appreciation.
A: And when is it?
L: Every Tuesday from 7 p.m. til 9 p.m., starting on… one minute… yeah, starting on September 29th. The cost is $298 for the year, unless you're a registered student.
A: Hang on a second. That's too much to take in all at once. I'm trying to write

it down. I didn't catch the start date. Did you say November 29th?

L: No, September 29th.

A: OK. Well, thanks. I'll think about it, but it sounds good.

L: OK, bye.

47

Are you saying the course is full?

Can you speak up a little?

Could you give me an example?

Did you say Tuesday?

What do you mean?

Unit 12

48

I = Interviewer; D = David Stiles

I: Thirty years ago, the idea of getting a worker to hand-wash your car would have been unthinkable—except to the very rich. Either you washed it yourself at home on a Sunday morning, or you took it the carwash. Nowadays, you can have it washed inside and out by a team of willing and capable workers for as little as $6. So, what's changed? I have here with me David Stiles, author of *The Servant Economy*. David, are we just getting too lazy to do our own domestic chores. or is this part of some new economic phenomenon?

D: Well, first of all hi and thanks for having me on your show. In answer to your question, yes, it's said that in the US today there are more workers doing domestic jobs than there were in the 19th century—perhaps as many as two million: gardeners, nannies, maids. And this is a direct consequence of globalization and the freeing up of the labor market. You see, many of these workers are migrants—in the case of the US, mostly Latin Americans. Umm, and I think that in capitalist economies, anyway, the richer classes will always provide employment for the poorer classes. As the Victorian satirist Hilaire Belloc famously said, "It is the duty of the wealthy man to give employment to the artisan."

I: Yes, but that's the point, isn't it? A 19th-century-style servant economy actually emphasizes the inequalities between rich and poor in a society.

D: Well, yes, it can, but it also creates employment. You don't have to be especially rich to have a house cleaner come once a week. Quite a lot of working people do that. A lot of so-called ordinary people get their windows cleaned every few months. But there are some—uh, rich—people who get it into their heads that they're too busy or important to do any domestic chores. So they'll hire a personal shopper, and have someone walk their dog every day. If they're having a party at home, they'll get an outside catering company to prepare the food. I know some people who even have their Christmas tree installed in their living room and then decorated for them. That really *is* a statement of wealth.

I: Hmm… It seems more a statement of confused priorities to me. Walking the dog and decorating the Christmas tree are supposed to be a pleasure, aren't they?

D: Well, of course they are. But look at it another way: these are all things that create employment. As long as the staff are treated well—you know, as employees, not as servants—and are fairly paid and their skills are valued, just as you would show respect to your hairdresser when you get your hair cut, then I don't see a problem.

49

carwash	shelves
shopper	chores
richer	watch
decision	garage
pleasure	change
college	fridge

50

agent	arrange
champagne	cheese
choice	fashion
general	January
sugar	television
usual	

51

LA = Leasing agent; W = Woman

LA: So, you've had a look at the offices. What do you think?

W: Well, yeah, I really like the building. To be honest, it's absolutely perfect for our needs.

LA: That's wonderful! So you'd like to take it?

W: Well, yes, ideally I would but, umm, a key thing for us is how long we'd be tied into the lease.

LA: Well, it's a fifteen-year lease. I think that was in the details I sent you.

W: Yes, it was, but I was hoping we could negotiate that down. Because if you look at it from our point of view, we're a young business and we don't really know how things are going to go for the next few years. Who does? And let's face it, fifteen years is a big commitment. So if your client could give a little on that…

LA: Hmm… I think what you have to appreciate is that our client's main concern is securing a rental for a reasonable length of time. You know, at the end of the day, it gives them some security. To tell you the truth, that's why the rent is so low. The fifteen-year period is a kind of compensation for that. So I'm not at all sure we're going to get anywhere there.

W: Oh, that's somewhat of a sticking point then, isn't it? Is there no way around that?

LA: Uh, not that I can think of offhand. What did you have in mind?

W: Well, maybe if we signed a fifteen-year lease but with an exit clause after, say, six years, then we could pay some kind of penalty to get out of the contract.

LA: Umm, well, the normal penalty would be that you paid the remaining nine years' rent, so I don't really think that would work.

W: Oh, I see. Well, that's a shame because I really like it and we need a place pretty urgently.

LA: Look, we have other people interested in the premises, so someone will take it. If I were in your shoes, and found the terms of the lease difficult, I think I'd just leave it. When all's said and done, it has to feel right to you.

W: But that's just the problem, it does feel right to us. Give me a moment. I'm just going to call my business partner and see what he thinks.

LA: OK, no problem.

52

1 To be honest…
2 A key thing for us is…
3 Let's face it…
4 At the end of the day,…
5 To tell you the truth…

Inside Photo: 3 tl (Shivji Joshi), 3 tc (Dario Mitidieri/Hulton Archive/Getty Images), 3 tr (sellingpix/Shutterstock.com), 3 tl (EMANUELE PICCHIRALLO/National Geographic Creative), 3 tc (GEORGE STEINMETZ/National Geographic Creative), 3 tr (SUDRES Jean-Daniel / hemis.fr/Alamy), 3 cl (DAVID DOUBILET/National Geographic Creative), 3 c (CHINA OUT Reuters/Stringer/Reuters), 3 cr (Robert Harding Travel/Photolibrary Group/Getty Images), 3 bl (NIGEL SWINN/National Geographic Creative), 3 bc (GEORGE STEINMETZ/National Geographic Creative), 3 br (JODI COBB/National Geographic Creative), 8 tr (IS09908XU/Image Source / Alamy), 8 tc (Patrick Aventurier/Getty Images/News/Getty Images), 8 tl (Barry Bland/Barcroft Media/Getty Images), 8 bl (TIM LAMAN/National Geographic Creative), 8 bc (MICHAEL NICHOLS/National Geographic Creative), 8 br (David Ewing/INSADCO Photography/Alamy), 8 cr (Andrew Peacock/Aurora Open/Aurora Photos / Alamy), 9 t (© Regien Paassen/Shutterstock.com), 10 t (Stevi Calandra/National Geographic Channel/National Geographic Creative), 12-13 (RANDY OLSON/National Geographic Creative), 15 t (PAUL THOMPSON/National Geographic Creative), 16 br (Corbis), RF/Alamy), 17 b (© iStockphoto.com/hadynyah), 18 (Edwin Levick/ Hulton Archive/Getty Images), 20 cl (JOEL SARTORE/National Geographic Creative), 21 t (Dario Mitidieri/Hulton Archive/Getty Images), 22 b (Adam Woolfitt/Corbis), 24 b (STEVE WINTER/National Geographic Creative), 27 br (JOEL SARTORE/National Geographic Creative), 28 br (Oote Boe 2 / Alamy), 29 b (© Ralph Loesche/Shutterstock.com), 30 (John Springer Collection/Corbis), 32 tl (BEVERLY JOUBERT/National Geographic Creative), 33 t (© sellingpix/Shutterstock.com), 34 t (RANDY OLSON National Geographic Creative), 35 br (© Michael Rosskothen/Shutterstock.com), 36 b (OLIVER UBERTI /National Geographic Creative), 38 bl (RENEE COMET/National Geographic Creative), 38 bc (RENEE COMET/National Geographic Creative), 38 bc (Renee Comet/National Geographic Creative), 38 br (RENEE COMET/National Geographic Creative), 39 b (KENNETH GARRETT/National Geographic Creative), 44 bl (AMY WHITE & AL PETTEWAY/National Geographic Creative), 45 t (EMANUELE PICCHIRALLO/National Geographic Creative), 46 t (ANNIE GRIFFITHS/National Geographic Creative), 48 b (Alexandre Orion), 51 b (DAVID ALAN HARVEY/National Geographic Creative), 52 t (STEPHEN MORRISON/epa/Corbis), 53 tr (Justin Kase zfivez / Alamy), 54 (Patrick Aventurier/Getty Images), News/Getty Images), 56 cl (STEPHEN SHARNOFF/National Geographic Creative), 57 t (GEORGE STEINMETZ/National Geographic Creative), 58 b (Smar Jodha/National Geographic Creative), 60 tl (Frans Lanting/Frans Lanting Studio / Alamy), 60 tr (MICHAEL MELFORD/National Geographic Creative), 63 b (CHIEN-CHI CHANG/MAGNUM PHOTOS/National Geographic Creative), 64 b (© thebezz/Shutterstock.com), 66 (IS09908XU/Image Source / Alamy), 69 t (SUDRES Jean-Daniel / hemis.fr/Alamy), 70 br (CHRIS JOHNS/National Geographic Creative), 72 bkgd (©Pichugin Dmitry/Shutterstock.com), 73 tr (Ivo Roospold/Alamy), 75 tr (Ian Trower/Age Fotostock/Photolibrary Group/Getty Images), 75 tr (RICHARD NOWITZ/National Geographic Creative), 75 cr (Sextantio Press), 75 br (Juergen Henkelmann Photography / Alamy), 76 b (KEENPRESS/National Geographic Creative), 78 (David Ewing/INSADCO Photography/Alamy), 80 c (FARRELL GREHAN/National Geographic Creative), 81 t (DAVID DOUBILET/National Geographic Creative), 82 b (Liysa/Perspectives/Getty Images), 83 cr (GERD LUDWIG/National Geographic Creative), 84 t (PANORAMIC IMAGES/National Geographic Creative), 87 bkgd (©Nazzu/Shutterstock.com), 88 b (©Tinna/Shutterstock.com), 90 (TIM LAMAN/National Geographic Creative), 92 cl (XPACIFICA/National Geographic Creative), 93 t (CHINA OUT Reuters),/Stringer/Reuters), 94 cl (STEVE MCCURRY/National Geographic Creative), 94 bl (Steve McCurry/National Geographic Creative), 96 bl (IS098Q1KE/Image Source / Alamy), 96 inset (©Holger Wulschlaeger/Shutterstock.com), 96 bl (©withGod/Shutterstock.com), 96 bl (©Cheryl E. Davis/Shutterstock.com), 97 br (Corbis), Cusp/Alamy), 99 br (Cate Gillon/Getty Images News/Getty Images), 102 (Andrew Peacock/Aurora Open/Aurora Photos / Alamy), 104 tl (Wong Maye-E/Associated Press/Press Association Images), 106 b (courtesy of nasaimages.org/NASA), 109 t (Robert Harding Travel/Photolibrary Group/Getty Images), 109 t (Wes C. Skiles/National Geographic Creative), 109 bl (Kira Salak), 109 bc (Stephon Alexander/Diana Rogers), 109 br (Wes C. Skiles/National Geographic Creative),111 t (KENNETH GARRETT/National Geographic Creative), 111 b (Kenneth Garrett/National Geographic Creative), 112 tl (Shelterbox), 112 tl (Bjoern Bertheau/Synthesis International),113 tr (©wavebreakmedia/Shutterstock.com), 114 (Ben Ramos / Alamy), 117 t (NIGEL SWINN/National Geographic Creative), 118 br (Asiaselects/Alamy), 120 t (©jeep2499/Shutterstock.com), 123 t (STEFANO MASSAI/National Geographic Creative), 124 br (JAMES L. STANFIELD/National Geographic Creative), 125 (©zhu difeng/Shutterstock.com), 126 (Barry Bland/Barcroft Media/Getty Images), 128 cl (KRISTA ROSSOW/National Geographic Creative), 129 t (GEORGE STEINMETZ/National Geographic Creative), 130 cr (Renee Fadiman), 132 l (Maggie Steber/National Geographic Creative), 135 b (Vincent J. Musi/National Geographic Creative), 136 br (©Lisa F. Young/Shutterstock.com), 138 (MICHAEL NICHOLS/National Geographic Creative), 140 cl (©Michael Klenetsky/Shutterstock.com), 141 t (JODI COBB/National Geographic Creative), 142 br (LUKA TAMBACA/National Geographic Creative), 144 t (MARIA STENZEL/National Geographic Creative), 145 br (JOEL SARTORE/National Geographic Creative), 147 b (XPACIFICA/National Geographic Creative), 148 br (Sterba Martin/CTK / Alamy), 150 t (MATTIAS KLUM/National Geographic Creative), 150 bkgd (Sam Abell/National Geographic Creative), 152 tl (Justin Guariglia/National Geographic Creative), 153 c (Motoring Picture Library / Alamy), 154 tl (RENEE COMET/National Geographic Creative), 154 cr (RENEE COMET/National Geographic Creative), 155 tl (Renee Comet/National Geographic Creative), 155 tr (Renee Comet/National Geographic Creative), 155 c (Motoring Picture Library / Alamy).

Illustration: Bob Lea P 42, Celia Hart P 100, David Russell P 40, National Geographic Maps/National Geographic Creative P 8.